"*Energy Tapping* offers an instant way out of negative emotions and into the positive. You'll love it."

—Mark Victor Hansen, co-creator of the *New York Times* best-selling series *Chicken Soup for the Soul*®

"The understanding of how psychological programs can get locked into your energy systems is a major breakthrough. Fred Gallo and Harry Vincenzi are pioneers in this important energy discipline."

—Donna Eden, author of *Energy Medicine*

"*Energy Tapping* is an exciting, valuable breakthrough book in the field of self-help. Readers can easily apply the powerful techniques of energy tapping and enhance performance immediately. It is an excellent and useful guidebook for self-change and healing—a must-read. It might just change your life."

—Philip H. Friedman, Ph.D., author of *Creating Well-Being*

"A clear, concise manual of self-help energy tools to build the life you have always dreamed of."

—Barbara Stone, Ph.D., author of *Cancer as Initiation*

D1247469

ENERGY TAPPING

SECOND EDITION

How to Rapidly Eliminate Anxiety, Depression, Cravings, and More Using Energy Psychology

FRED P. GALLO, PH.D.
HARRY VINCENZI, ED.D.

New Harbinger Publications, Inc.

Publisher's Note

Distributed in Canada by Raincoast Books

Copyright © 2008 by Fred P. Gallo and Harry Vincenzi
New Harbinger Publications, Inc.
5674 Shattuck Avenue
Oakland, CA 94609

Acquired by Jess O'Brien; Cover design by Amy Shoup;
Edited by Kayla Sussell; Text design by Tracy Carlson

ISBN-13: 978-1-57224-555-6

To my sister, Kathy, and my brothers, Philip, David, and Michael.

—FPG

To my parents.

—HV

Contents

Preface to Second Edition

Since the release of *Energy Tapping* in 2000, the popularity of energy tapping (ET) has continued to grow worldwide. More therapists are including ET in their repertoire and these techniques are being taught by more and more educators every year. Research support is also growing as a National Institute of Health funded study found that energy psychology was an effective treatment for weight maintenance. This second edition is an update of the original material, with coverage on more topics including high blood pressure, allergies, immunity issues, eating disorders, and ways to sustain and enhance passion and romance. We believe that many people, including therapists and medical practitioners, will find these and the original chapters to be useful and even valuable.

It's important to understand that the protocols covered here are not sacrosanct. Surely there are other tapping protocols that can be used to treat the conditions covered. However, we have found these protocols effective to a large extent, and that is the important claim we are making. Also, because you are a single individual, it's possible that some protocols we've laid out will not work for you and other sequences may be needed. Please always keep this in mind and feel free to experiment to achieve what you are seeking. The important thing is to get results that enhance your health and happiness. Enjoy!

Acknowledgments

We are deeply indebted to the contributions of Huang Ti, who catalogued meridian theory approximately 4,500 years ago; George J. Goodheart, founder of applied kinesiology; and John Diamond and Roger J. Callahan, for their contributions to the application of meridian theory in the treatment of emotional problems.

We would like to thank our family, friends, colleagues, and readers of the first edition for their support and encouragement throughout the writing of this book. We would also like to acknowledge David and Justin Lee for helping us create the diagrams used in *Energy Tapping*.

Finally, thank you to all the talented people at New Harbinger Publications, including Matt McKay, editor-in-chief, and Kristin Beck, Jess O'Brien and Catharine Sutker, in acquisitions, for contacting us and supporting this project. Appreciation and acknowledgment go to Jueli Gastwirth, our editor of the first edition, for her patience, warmth, and energetic attention throughout the writing of *Energy Tapping*. And special appreciation and gratitude to Kayla Sussell, our editor of this second edition, for her patience, warmth, amazing attention to details, and willingness to tap along with us.

PART I

Understanding and Using
Energy Psychology

Introduction

Your body has the ability to heal itself.

—Andrew Weil, MD

Energy Tapping is a unique book that will help you to learn how to use your body's energy system to better manage your life. Although several different names can be used to identify this process, the term we use is *energy psychology*. This healing technique is based on the ancient Chinese art of acupuncture, although instead of using needles to stimulate a change in the way you think and feel, energy psychology uses a simple tapping method of two fingers on specific points of your body. Once you understand this process and the location of the meridian points (provided via the diagrams throughout this book), you will learn how you can cope with or eliminate problems that you have struggled with for years. As psychologists who have been trained in numerous techniques and strategies, we have found energy psychology to be the most effective and efficient process for creating rapid change and effectively treating emotional and/or psychological issues.

THE GENESIS OF ENERGY WORK

It is not clear when the development and use of energy work began, but legend has it that it was first discovered five thousand years ago in China. At that time, when wars were fought with knives and bows and arrows, a strange phenomenon occurred: Soldiers who received minor wounds in just the right places found that the physical pains and ailments that they had suffered with for years suddenly disappeared. It has been said that incidents such as these led the Chinese to discover the existence of an energy system that communicates energetic information throughout the human body. This energy system has been called chi (pronounced chee), and is also known as life force, ki, prana, and life energy.

Acupuncture

The discovery of the human energy system eventually led to the development of acupuncture, a procedure by which the body's energy is altered by stimulating, with needles, specific points along twelve major pathways that are known as *meridians*. Each of the meridians passes through a specific organ of the body, such as the lungs, heart, or stomach. The entire system is interconnected so that the chi, or life energy, travels from one meridian to the next, circulating throughout the body. These meridians interact with a number of more *concentrated energy fields* called "chakras."

In acupuncture treatments, needles are inserted into the body at selected *tonification* or stimulation points (to increase energy), or at selected sedation points (to decrease energy). Through trial and error, acupuncture has been developed and used by Chinese physicians to treat a wide variety of illnesses and to eliminate pain. Interestingly, several countries now use acupuncture as an alternative anesthesia during surgery.

Increasingly, more people in the United States are accepting acupuncture as a viable alternative health care treatment (although we think many people hesitate because they don't like needles). The World Health Organization cited 104 conditions that can be treated by acupuncture, including gastrointestinal disorders and sciatica problems (Burton Goldberg Group 1993).

Scientific Research

From a scientific viewpoint, one problem with energy psychology is the challenge of creating the concrete proof that it exists. Trying to prove that there is an energy system with meridian points, for example, is much like trying to prove that gravity or energy in general exists. You can't see it, but intuitively you know that it's there and you can create tests that will verify its existence.

Fortunately, modern technology has helped researchers provide some evidence of meridians and acupoints. Yang et al. (2007) used infrared technology to document the existence of infrared radiant tracks that matched human meridian maps. Langevin, Jason, and Yandow (2002) used ultrasound images to show that connective tissue is found at meridian points. Then they used a computer-controlled acupuncture instrument and compared acupoints to sham points. They found that needle grasp of the tissue, measured by the resistance in removing the needle, was greater at meridian points. The evidence of connective tissue in close proximity to meridians and nerve endings supports a *gate theory*, where the higher resistance stimulates sensory nerves, which then activate neuron signals. The researchers believe that this neural stimulation may produce changes in connective tissue that lead to increased biochemical and bio-electrical signals, which may explain the therapeutic effects demonstrated by stimulating the meridian points.

One of the early findings that support the belief that an energy field or *aura* surrounds each person was conducted in the 1970s. A researcher at Yale, Harold Saxon

Burr (1972), took measurements of the electromagnetic fields around trees, animals, and human beings. He called these energy fields *Life Fields* or *L-Fields*. His work suggests that the body grows into an already existent energy field that serves as a blueprint of its physical form. For example, even after a section of a leaf is severed, the energy form of the severed section continues to be detectable. Other studies (Burr 1972) have demonstrated that a baby animal has a detectable energy field that approximates its size as an adult.

Richard Gerber (1988), author of *Vibrational Medicine*, suggests that physical disease may begin at the energy level and then eventually migrate into or show up in the physical body. Therefore, if disturbances can be detected at the energy field level before physical problems develop, treatment methods in time will emerge that can alleviate the energy disturbance and thus prevent the physical disease from ever occurring. This is not so far-fetched when we consider the fact that human bodies regenerate completely approximately every four years. That is, not one single atom of your body today existed four years ago. And some parts of our bodies are recycled even more frequently. For example, we get a new liver every six weeks. This all points to the existence of energy fields as the basis of all physical form. The energy field is what holds the body together and provides the mold into which the body and its parts can be created anew.

Louis Langman (1972) conducted another study examining the relationship between energy and disease. He found that in a sample of 123 women with malignant cervical conditions, 5 had a positive energy charge in the cervix, and 118 had a negative electrical charge. The numbers were reversed in a sample of women with no cancerous conditions. This study does not prove that negative polarity causes cancer, because it is possible that the cancer itself leads to the negative charge. However, this research does demonstrate that an energy difference exists between those who are healthy and those with a disease.

There have been several attempts to document the existence of meridian points. Robert Becker is an orthopedic surgeon who wrote *Cross Currents* (1990) and co-authored *The Body Electric* (Becker and Selden 1985). He was encouraged to further explore acupuncture when it became of general interest in the 1970s after President Nixon's trip to China and journalist James Reston's remarkable acupuncture treatment for postoperative pain and healing. Much of the early research has disproved the theory that acupuncture works as a result of a placebo effect. That effect occurs when a person believes in a treatment to such an extent that it proves to be effective (Becker and Selden 1985).

Becker examined the concept that meridian *acupoints* are electrical conductors and that meridians are used to send messages back and forth between the brain and the injury site to promote healing and create the conscious perception of pain. He developed an interesting and pertinent research approach. He proposed that the meridians were the electrical conductors that relay information from the site of an injury to the central nervous system. He thought that perhaps acupuncture needles served to block the pain message from getting to the brain by short-circuiting the electromagnetic current in the meridian.

Becker theorized that the acupoints functioned similarly to booster amplifiers that are positioned along power lines. He noted that because the electric current of the meridians would have to be of a very low intensity, the booster amplifiers would have to be placed very close to each other (within inches). This is the case with the acupoints.

Maria Reichmanas, a biophysicist associate of Becker's, developed a pizza-cutter-like device that could be rolled along the meridians to detect differences in electrical skin resistance. They theorized that if an electrical charge really existed at the location of the acupoint, then there would be a difference in skin resistance at that point when compared to the surrounding skin. Their findings were consistent enough across subjects to strongly suggest that acupoints and meridians do exist. In fact, all of these studies imply that meridian pathways exist and that they are used to transmit information.

THE DEVELOPMENT OF ENERGY PSYCHOLOGY

The development of energy psychology began in the early 1960s, as George Goodheart, a chiropractor from Detroit, Michigan, experimented with tapping on various meridian acupoints to relieve pain while treating patients holistically. In the 1980s, psychiatrist John Diamond (1985) and psychologist Roger Callahan (1987) each experimented with the treatment of mental health problems. They found that tapping on acupoints helped to eliminate negative emotions, such as anxieties, phobias, and painful memories. Callahan, whose system is one of the "power' therapies known as Thought Field Therapy, provided the majority of the clinical work. In the 1990s, Fred Gallo (1998) and Gary Craig (Craig and Fowlie 1995) developed their own accessible approach to energy psychology and helped mental health clinicians throughout the world learn its procedures.

These studies show that the same concepts used in acupuncture can be used to treat psychological problems effectively. The discovery that psychological change can occur in such a simple way is a breakthrough in the treatment of mental health. It's a radical departure from talk therapy, which dominated psychology in the twentieth century.

Many people still believe that the most effective and healthy method of emotional change occurs through talk therapy, in which new knowledge is learned or new life skills are developed through verbal communication. Although it may not seem realistic that tapping on meridian points located on your face or hands can change how you think or feel, we have not found another treatment that is as fast or effective as energy psychology. Many people, however, remain skeptical until they use this method to eliminate one of their own problems.

Although the concepts of energy psychology will be explored further, the basis of the technique is that you eliminate psychological issues by simply thinking about a painful issue or memory while tapping on specific meridian points. Additionally, we will examine a related treatment that helps to eliminate self-sabotaging thoughts and beliefs that often occur after someone has been traumatized or is in the middle of a stressful situation.

> *Energy Psychology* provides you with the keys to unlock psychological issues by helping you understand and use the power of your own energy system.

A STEP-BY-STEP PROCESS FOR CHANGING YOUR LIFE

The book is divided into two parts: Part I addresses the basic concepts required to help you understand and utilize the methods of energy psychology. Part II provides specific treatment methods for a variety of psychological issues, including self-sabotaging behaviors, trauma, and negative emotional states (such as shame, fear, and depression). The book concludes by examining more complex issues, such as weight loss, addictive behavior, and relationships. A chapter on improving your sports performance is included. Chapters 14, 15, and 16 are completely new and cover lowering your blood pressure, allergies and your immune system, and eating disorders, respectively. Chapter 18 is also a new chapter that deals with the intricacies of sustaining love and passion.

It is important that you first learn how to treat common problems before attempting to heal the more complex ones. Often, complex issues consist of several smaller problems that must first be treated before complete healing can occur. Once you've learned the basics of energy psychology that are presented in this book you'll have a new set of skills that will help you to eliminate self-sabotaging behaviors and to better manage your life.

Many of the chapters guide you through specific treatment methods. Because an experienced energy psychology therapist will not be present to help you determine where your energy imbalances exist, we have developed treatment sequences (patterns of places to tap) for each of the problems we explore in this book. We also pose questions that may help you to determine which of your feelings and/or behaviors are disruptive and need to be treated. A brief outline of each chapter follows:

Chapter 1 further explores energy psychology and helps you to understand how different levels of energy affect your behavior.

Chapter 2 provides figures and diagrams of locations for each of the meridian points that you will be tapping for particular problems. These diagrams also appear in the chapters that deal with the specific psychological challenges we will be addressing. You will learn in chapter 2 which emotional areas are affected by each meridian, and how to do a simple treatment sequence.

Chapter 3 addresses how potential toxins, such as food, tobacco, or alcohol, can negatively affect your energy system. It has been found that these substances produce symptoms that weaken your energy. Various solutions, such as detoxification, are examined.

Chapter 4 explores the beliefs and habits that are negatively affecting your life. It also addresses several approaches that will help you to change habits that are no longer productive.

Chapter 5 provides a format that will help you develop a personal profile of the problems that you want to resolve.

Chapter 6 reveals ways to identify and treat psychological reversals. Reversals are the primary cause of self-sabotage in your life. Your energy can be disrupted in a way that causes you to act in opposition to something you may be consciously trying to attain. For example, you may tell yourself, "I'm tired of fighting with my spouse; tonight we are going to relax." Yet, for some reason, after your mate comes home and you begin to interact, a fight still takes place. It's not a lack of willpower; it is a reversal in your energy system.

Chapter 7 addresses your fears and phobias, which often can lower your self-confidence and limit your life experiences. Several specific fears and phobias are explored, including fears of heights, insects, animals, public speaking, elevators, test taking, flying, intimidating situations, and panic attacks.

Chapter 8 helps you learn to better manage the common but powerful feelings of anger, rage, embarrassment, guilt, jealousy, shame, loneliness, and rejection.

Chapter 9 offers a drug-free approach to effectively deal with depression, which is a widespread problem throughout the United States.

Chapter 10 focuses on trauma, which occurs in everyone's life at some time. Trauma includes everything from the loss of a job or a home to even more difficult experiences, such as losing a loved one, suffering child abuse, or being in a severe accident. Painful memories affect many people and prevent them from moving forward with their lives. The ability to learn how to cope with a past event and move on can be attained through energy psychology. This chapter focuses on these issues and discusses how to treat them. In many cases, a painful memory can be addressed with a single treatment.

Chapter 11 provides strategies to eliminate sports anxiety and other self-sabotaging beliefs that create mental errors during sporting activities.

Chapter 12 is the first chapter to deal with the more complex issues. This chapter addresses weight loss, which is a complex issue because many related issues often sabotage your efforts to lose weight. Although many people have trouble losing weight, there actually is a relatively simple solution: diet and exercise. It is an energy imbalance and, most likely, a psychological reversal that prevents the obese or overweight person from losing weight. In this chapter, you will identify the beliefs that sabotage your ability to stay on a diet. By learning to balance the energy in your meridians, you will be able to pick a diet of your choice, have the control to stick to it, and achieve the elusive goal of having a slimmer, healthier body.

Chapter 13 addresses addictive behavior, which by itself is a form of self-sabotage. This chapter also helps you to identify any possible avoidance behaviors you may have. The chapter has a very strong focus on exploring belief systems and psychological reversals. Because addictions are very hard to break and often exist for a reason, emphasis is placed on daily treatment methods as well as on identifying replacement activities or behaviors.

Chapter 14 explores the problem of high blood pressure (hypertension) and teaches you how to use energy tapping to relieve the stress that can be a major factor in perpetuating this life-threatening condition.

Chapter 15 deals with allergies and the immune system, offering some simple energy tapping strategies (integrated with other important information) for relieving allergic reactions and for improving immunity.

Chapter 16 covers anorexia, bulimia, and binge eating, providing a framework for understanding these problems and describes how to apply energy tapping for coping with and eventually eliminating these problems.

Chapter 17 focuses on relationships, complex issues that have no easy answers. Energy psychology provides an approach to help people understand how they may be sabotaging their relationships by the partners they choose or by their own behaviors. This information is used to determine which problems must be addressed and which energy psychology treatments will be most helpful.

Chapter 18 offers a variety of energy tapping and related strategies for accessing and sustaining passion and romance.

Chapter 19 addresses what we believe will be future directions in the use of energy psychology and concludes by summarizing the current uses of this unique tool. It is an approach that anyone can use to help eliminate old problems and cope with new ones. Energy psychology provides the tools that will allow you to create the balance and control that have been missing from your life.

Finally, this book ends with an appendix about case studies and clinical research in energy psychology that will be of interest to anyone seeking experimental and other research-based evidence on the effectiveness of energy psychology and energy tapping.

FREQUENTLY ASKED QUESTIONS

In this section, we hope to answer many of the questions that you may have about energy psychology.

Q: *What types of issues or problems does energy psychology address?*

A: Energy psychology addresses two types of problems: the events in your life that cause energy imbalances and psychological reversals. The first type often occurs when an event affects specific meridian points in your energy system. The result is an energy imbalance that creates consequences that you interpret as painful memories or feelings of inadequacy.

There are a number of ways to think about your energy system. When a term like *balance* is used, it means that your energy is flowing freely through your body and each meridian has the same amount of energy. When one of your meridians is impacted by a trauma, some of the energy in that meridian may become depleted, creating an imbalance. Tapping on the acupoints stimulates the meridian and increases the energy, which in turn creates balance. Although most of this book addresses specific problems, it also is possible to stimulate meridians to move to a higher energy level and thus increase your ability to deal with life issues in general.

The second type of problem energy psychology addresses is *psychological reversals*, that is, when your energy system is reversed. For example, once you have experienced a trauma, each time you encounter or think about that specific trauma or any similar situations, your energy responds as if it were reexperiencing it. Psychological reversals create negative or false beliefs, which is why people behave in ways that sabotage their lives. Although this may sound strange, it explains why people do things that they know will be bad for them. They can't stop themselves because their behavior seems like the right thing to do. Psychological reversals also prevent the energy balance in your meridians from being restored.

Q: *How is an energy system disrupted?*

A: The simplest explanation is that an energy disruption is caused by a traumatic situation, although your perception and heredity can also be involved. The resulting imbalance in your energy system leaves you unable to resolve that problem and vulnerable to similar problems. Every situation you encounter is embedded in your nervous system, and although your mind may forget particular events, your body remembers them. When you experience a trauma, for example, you respond in a normal manner, feeling the appropriate emotion. If you were set upon and beaten and robbed, for instance, fearfulness would be natural at the time and for some time afterward. The problems, however, arise when this trauma creates an energy imbalance that perpetuates the fearful experience indefinitely. The result can be that you develop a phobic reaction that limits your lifestyle and the manner in which you interact with other people.

> It takes an external experience to disrupt your energy system. Another external experience (energy treatment) is required to balance it.

There are numerous social reasons why energy imbalances occur in people. For example, for at least two generations there have been more than one million divorces each year in the United States. Divorce is one example of a type of trauma that can affect you, resulting in feelings of anger, sadness, or a loss of trust. Another is the changing dynamics of communities. As communities continue becoming more transitory and family members continue choosing to live far apart, the sense of belonging to and the safety of living in a caring community are undermined. If you feel that no one cares about you, this easily can lead to other problems.

It also is possible that energy imbalances can be passed on from one generation to another. Rupert Sheldrake's (1988) research examines how instinctual information is passed on to new generations. As there is no evidence that emotional feelings are passed through one's DNA, Sheldrake believes that emotional feelings and learned behaviors can be passed on from one generation to another via energy fields. Under this theory, a trauma suffered by your grandmother could be passed on to you in the form of an energy imbalance. This may explain why babies respond to situations with distinct patterns of behavior. For example, different babies' abilities to cope with frustrating situations are very observable within a few months of birth.

Of course, once children are born, their energy system is affected by their parents and their surrounding environment. If any of these situations creates an energy imbalance, it will affect what someone thinks as well as his or her sense of self. It could be argued that energy disruptions at birth lead to certain emotional feelings and thoughts that make you more vulnerable or more likely to have certain negative experiences.

Although knowing the actual cause of the energy disruption is not crucial to resolving the problem, it can help explain many of your problems as well as your behavior. Energy disruptions can have a major impact on your life, and if they are not treated, it is unlikely that the problems will be resolved.

Q: *How can an energy imbalance affect your thinking?*

A: It is well known by scientists that when a person has a thought, a chemical presence or reaction occurs, and *neuropeptides*, the chemical correlates of thought, become detectable. Neuropeptides not only are present in the brain, but also are found throughout the body, including in the stomach, kidneys, and liver. Thus, a thought has a real embodied, physical presence. At the same time, an electromagnetic-like field also can be detected when a person has a thought. This is the energetic presence or manifestation of the thought, which Roger Callahan (Callahan and Callahan 1996) termed a *thought field*.

Negative emotions are created by a disturbance in the thought field, which can be caused by a physical or emotional trauma. The theory is that the disturbance affects specific energy points that, in turn, set off hormonal, physiological, neurological, chemical, and cognitive events that result in the experience of a negative emotion. The disturbances cause energy imbalances that can be experienced as depression, fears, or addictive behaviors.

When a disturbance occurs within a thought field, it always corresponds to specific energy points on the body. This is why energy psychologists have been able to correlate meridian points with specific problems and thus to develop treatments.

Q: *What is a psychological reversal?*

A: It's not really clear what happens to your energy system when you experience a psychological reversal. One theory is that when a traumatic event depletes your energy to a low level, your energy can become negative. This, in turn, elicits self-sabotaging beliefs or behaviors and you end up creating a situation that is the opposite—or reverse—of what you would prefer. Hence, the term *reversal*.

Most often reversals are situation-specific, meaning that they affect only specific areas of your life, such as your ability to achieve a particular goal, overcome a phobia, or get along better with another person. If there was an event in your life that created strong feelings of shame or guilt, for instance, it's possible that this event created a reversal, which partly accounts for why you may not be coping well today with similar situations. Another feature of a psychological reversal is the lack of self-acceptance. For example, when you don't accept a part of who you are, what you did, or what you are doing, there can be a reversal in your energy system. The outcome can be an unconscious act of sabotage against your consciously expressed goals.

For example, you might be reversed about being successful. That is, you may unconsciously think, "I don't deserve to have success in my life." Or, "I am not worthy of having a successful situation in my life." The impact of the reversal is clear when you have the potential to be successful in a particular part of your life, but you are not. Psychological reversal creates the feelings and thoughts that sabotage the parts of your life that you do not accept or feel that you deserve.

Psychological reversals create situations that we've all experienced. In certain circumstances you know what you have to do—or not do—and yet you are unable to act the way in which you know you should. For instance, consider a situation in which it would be best to avoid saying anything. When you have a reversal, what happens is that you say aloud the words that make the situation even worse. Further, if you don't accept yourself and believe that you deserve—or are good enough to have—a specific situation in your life, you will sabotage it.

For example, a woman who doesn't think she deserves to be happily married will continually pick the wrong man as a potential partner. Although other issues are most likely also involved, this type of behavior is a perfect form of self-sabotage. The woman appears to be actively seeking a fulfilling partnership, but in reality she is only reinforcing her belief that she doesn't deserve a suitable life partner. Although this example is specific, self-sabotage can occur and affect any life event that you feel you don't deserve.

Self-sabotaging behavior can ruin years of hard work. Energy psychologists believe that self-sabotaging beliefs are a primary reason why many people experience difficulty in their lives, even though they have the skill and ability to achieve their goals. When you've finished reading this book, you will know how to correct the reversals that sabotage your actions. You also may be able to give helpful advice to your friends and your children about how to overcome self-sabotage.

Q: *How do you correct an energy imbalance?*

A: The process of correcting an energy imbalance usually involves working with an energy therapist who has been extensively trained in the field. The techniques in this book will teach you how to do this without the assistance of a trained therapist.

Typically, once a client has described his or her problem to a therapist, the client is asked to think about that problem and become aware of its associated feelings. For example, if a fear of heights were being treated, the client would be asked to remember the last time she was on a balcony or in a location similar to where the problem occurred.

When you focus your awareness on a problem, all you are doing is thinking about the problem or situation that is distressing you. There is nothing magical or difficult that you have to do other than think about the situation. You don't even have to visualize it (although that may be one way of getting in touch with the problem). Once you focus your attention on the problem at hand, your body-mind will respond in a small way as if you actually were in that situation.

If there are meridian points that need to be treated, you once again bring your energy into that problem pattern or thought field by focusing your attention on the problem you are trying to overcome. Once you've done this, you are ready for the energy psychology treatment techniques to help you overcome your obstacles. Remember that the emotional problems you perceive are mere disturbances in your energy system.

To treat a problem, specific meridian points—which may be different for each problem—need to be stimulated. We use the word *algorithm* to mean treatment sequences. *Treatment sequences* are patterns of places to tap on your face, hands, and upper torso to address specific issues. Through years of experience and testing, these patterns have been proven effective. After you learn the locations of specific meridian points, you will find it easy to use the treatment sequences that are provided. It should be noted that although we offer specific sequences, the treatment usually will be effective, even if the order is changed. And, depending on the problem, other treatment points might also be effective.

Q: *What is applied kinesiology and how is it related to energy psychology?*

A: *Applied kinesiology* is one of the procedures used in energy psychology. It is a unique method of evaluating bodily functions by means of manual muscle testing. Most often, testing is done on an isolated muscle, such as the *deltoid*, a large, strong muscle in the shoulder area. During the procedure, clients are asked to think about a problem while extending an arm parallel to the floor, thus tensing the deltoid muscle. Applied kinesiologists found that when clients mentally tune in to their issue, there may be a momentary weakening of the muscles. This is the result of an energy imbalance. The application of this highly specified procedure pivots on this essential muscle-weakening phenomenon, which allows the energetic aspects of the psychological problem to be diagnosed.

Although the process of energy psychology was developed using applied kinesiology, muscle testing is not required in order to use the techniques in this book. We've analyzed various types of problems and through extensive clinical experience we've provided you with treatment sequences for every issue examined in this book. As you will learn, tapping with your fingers on different meridian points will, in most cases, successfully treat each condition or problem.

Q: *Does energy psychology really work?*

A: Please review the research section in the appendix for more detailed information. A number of studies have found that energy psychology is an effective approach to help maintain weight loss, eliminate phobias, depressive feelings, and resolve traumas. In addition, the testimonials that energy psychology is effective come from a growing number of internationally known experts such as Mark Hansen, as well as Anthony Robbins and Donna Eden, who are using these treatments in their private practice. The president of the Canadian Society of Clinical Hypnosis, Lee Pulos (1999), says "I find energy psychology to be among the most powerful and effective tools in the treatment of all varieties of psychological problems."

Research on energy psychology often uses a measurement called Subjective Units of Distress (SUD) to evaluate success. The term SUD was first used to evaluate a therapeutic technique called "systematic desensitization," developed by Joseph Wolpe (1958). As the term implies, SUD is a subjective evaluation by the person as to the full impact of a problem. When doing the treatment sequences in this book, you will be asked to think about a problem and then rate it as to how much it affects you. For example, if you have a fear of elevators, and you imagine being in an elevator, you would then rate the SUD from 0 to 10, with 0 indicating no impact or distressing feeling at all and 10 indicating the highest possible level of distress. As you will notice in Part II of this book, energy psychology uses a rating scale similar to the SUD scale to determine the magnitude of the emotional problem or challenge that you are addressing.

In 1995, two researchers at the University of Florida, Figley and Carbonell, conducted clinical studies with several *power therapies*, one of which was an energy therapy. Power therapies are those that can rapidly eliminate trauma. The treatments were used to help patients who suffered from post-traumatic stress disorder. The results found that the energy therapy was not only a very effective approach, it worked the fastest.

Additional surveys involved two therapists who treated individuals who called in on radio talk shows. In 1986, Roger Callahan (Callahan and Callahan 1996) treated sixty-eight people on radio shows and had a 97 percent success rate. On average, problems that were presented by callers had an average SUD rating of 8.3; after callers did the treatment prescribed by Callahan, their average SUD rating was reduced to 2.1. Ten years later, Glenn Leonoff replicated Callahan's radio show study (Callahan and Callahan 1996). He also worked with sixty-eight callers and also had a success rate of 97 percent. The average SUD rating was 8.1 before the treatment and 1.5 after the treatment.

Our experience has shown that a problem that has an SUD rating of 8 to 10 has a very powerful impact on an individual's life. Conversely, a problem that has an SUD rating of 1 or 2, is most often being well managed by the individual and has minimal impact on his or her life.

Q: *Will you give an example of someone who has been helped by energy psychology?*

A: Our clinical experiences with energy psychology have resulted in many successes. For instance, one bright, yet depressed, teenage girl who was ready to repeat her senior year in high school was greatly helped by energy psychology. She was not motivated and would not complete the minimal amount of work required for her to graduate. Once she agreed to treatment, there was a smile on her face in less than thirty minutes and a newfound belief that she could succeed. She not only completed her course work for graduation, she was motivated to apply to colleges as well.

Another example is provided by a thirty-two-year-old woman who was raped when she was thirteen and was still tormented by memories of the event. Her self-image was so poor that she perpetually sabotaged her life. After one energy treatment, she was no longer disturbed by the event. She readily changed her view of herself in such a positive direction that she later went on to complete college and graduate school and eventually became a licensed psychotherapist.

Weight loss is another area in which energy psychology has proved to be effective. For example, one middle-aged man was unable to lose weight, despite trying numerous diets. Using energy psychology, he was treated for loneliness and feelings of rejection. After one session, he became motivated to begin a diet. He learned how to appropriately deal with his weight issues and used the treatments on a regular basis to help him maintain his diet and to continue to lose weight.

Q: *How quickly do energy treatments work?*

A: The answer to this important question depends on the type of problem being addressed, as well as on the person who is receiving treatments. Some people will resolve their problem in one treatment; most people will experience significant relief after their first treatment. In general, we recommend two weeks of daily treatments for any problem, although periodic follow-up treatments may also be needed. Once these treatments have been learned, however, they take only a minute to complete and can be done almost anywhere.

Basically, there are two types of problems: those that are based on single events, such as if your house is robbed, and those that are ongoing and interactive, such as relationship issues. If your house has been robbed, you know firsthand that it is a traumatic event. The good news is that it is a single event, that is, your home is not robbed on a regular basis. If you address this event by using the treatment for painful memories (see chapter 10), it is very likely that you can experience significant relief from one treatment. You then can use follow-up treatments to reinforce your success.

Complex, interactive problems are more difficult and are addressed in the last several chapters of this book. You must be patient when treating these types of issues, as they take more time to successfully eliminate. We consider weight loss, relationships, and addictive issues to be complex and interactive problems. They are complex because there can be several reasons why they exist; they are interactive because these situations occur and reoccur on a regular basis, unlike single-event traumas. For example, there can be several reasons for people to be overweight, and yet they encounter situations that can sabotage their dieting plans every day.

The other factor that affects how quickly energy psychology treatment works is *you*. Every person is different. People with multiple problems, severe problems, or long-term problems need to be patient. Although some of you will feel relief quickly, for most, it will take more time and many treatments to help you to better cope with and/or eliminate your issues. If you believe that you have extremely low levels of energy, the healing process will take even longer.

1

Energy Psychology: The Missing Piece to Your Success

Letting go of the emotions that trap you, painful memories, fears, depression, or anger, is the way to a longer and healthier life.

—Deepak Chopra, MD

In the last decade, the use of alternative medicine has made enormous strides as an effective, acceptable tool that helps people prevent or better cope with various health problems. Although the number of leading contributors in this growing area is quite large, the work of Deepak Chopra, Caroline Myss, and Andrew Weil is among the most prominent. Each of these individuals has helped people to better understand themselves and to recognize that they have more control over their lives than they previously may have thought possible. Because of their work, people now have a more thorough understanding of how their bodies are impacted by toxins that can come from air, food, water, and chemicals. These toxins can increase people's vulnerability to disease and even speed up the aging process.

Although all three authors explore and stress the importance of life force or the internal energy system, it is Caroline Myss' (1997) work, especially, that has helped many people understand they can alter their energy system and, by doing so, change their lives. She says that if you spend your energy continually dealing with and holding onto the negative aspects of your life, you will not have enough energy left to ward off disease, to heal from illnesses, or to deal appropriately with other potential problems. Myss, Chopra, and Weil all have developed distinctive approaches to the healing process, although all three stress the importance of letting go of your negative emotions. In the chapters that follow, we will teach you specific techniques that will help you to do this efficiently and effectively.

THE ESSENCE OF ENERGY

Everything you see—the sun, the moon, planet earth, the solar system, the stars—is a form of energy. Whether you are male or female, strong or weak, angry or happy, in the end, when broken down to your simplest structure, you are energy. There is positive and negative energy in our world and it continuously affects us in millions of ways. Our thoughts are energy, our feelings are energy, even the actions required for you to read this book are all based on energy. To read this page, for example, your mind told your hand to open the book and turn the pages; next, your eyes sent the images on the pages to your brain; then, your brain interpreted the images so that you'll understand what you are reading. Now, think about the speed at which this process must take place again and again for you to read. It happens at the speed of energy. In fact, it is the power of energy in our lives that allows us to do most activities and yet, in many areas, energy remains an untapped resource.

Physicist David Bohm (1980) says that energy saturates every inch of space throughout the universe and that it is energy that connects us to each other and everything else in our world. Energy psychology is about the examination and development of techniques that will help you to manipulate and use your life energy to deal more effectively with your physical and emotional problems.

In fact, energy psychology allows you to tap into your own energy system and, by balancing it, eliminate the causes of any psychological problems or impediments. The results: You will feel better about yourself, you will be more confident, you will be better able to cope with a myriad of emotional problems, and you will stop feeling as if you are "stuck" in your life.

> Energy psychology offers techniques that can help you to manipulate and use your life energy to cope more effectively with your emotional problems.

YOUR ENERGY SYSTEM PROVIDES THE SOLUTIONS

Because we all struggle with our personal issues, learning how to better manage our lives has become one of the dominant themes in our society. Energy psychology will help you to understand that the solutions to your problems are to be found within your body's energy system. Often, one of the most perplexing parts of having a problem is that you don't understand why it exists. Individuals are commonly taught to believe that if only they had had more knowledge or if they developed certain skills, their problems would disappear. Unfortunately, this is not always true.

When people don't understand why a problem is affecting them, they are prone to blame themselves. This lowers their self-esteem, makes them feel "stuck," and contributes to their confusion about how they can be helped. One of the most attractive components of energy psychology is that you don't have to understand why you have a problem to treat it. The techniques in this book teach you the skills needed to "tap" your problems away. In energy psychology, we will take you through a step-by-step process that will enable you to treat your problems without having to analyze and dissect every aspect of your life.

Fears and Phobias: A Case Study

The fears and phobias that can be treated with energy range from simple to complex. For example, Bill, a teacher, has a fear of heights. He is successful and competent in most aspects of his life, but he has this fear that he cannot control. It seems as though he has always had it. As a child he became aware of this fear when he couldn't climb high up into a tree without becoming very anxious. As a teenager, he felt embarrassed when he couldn't climb a ladder. He had no idea why he felt this fear, so he just learned to adjust to it, staying away from the situations that he knew would make him anxious.

As an adult, he was faced with many embarrassing moments, such as the time he went to a party in an eighteenth-floor apartment only to find that the people he wanted to socialize with were out on the balcony. He got a drink and walked out onto the balcony, but his fear soon had him feeling paralyzed. He looked for a seat away from the end of the balcony, but once he looked over the railing, his fear began to overwhelm him. First, there was an uncomfortable feeling and then a fleeting thought about jumping, and soon he felt compelled to go back inside.

Although Bill's fear of heights was a situation he believed he could not change, energy psychology helped him to confront and deal with it. Imagine that before attending the party, Bill had thought about his fear of heights and tapped on his eyebrow with two fingers several times, then under his eye, and then under his arm. If he had done that, when he got to the party and went out onto the balcony, he would have found that, although he was not completely comfortable, he was able to stay out there, socialize, and enjoy himself. If later that evening, Bill felt his fear starting to return, he could have used another energy psychology technique. While continuing to feel his fear, he could have discreetly touched the side of his hand, under his eye, under his arm, and under his collarbone. He would have found that when he went out on the balcony again, he would have been able to walk up to the railing, look down, and watch the people walking on the sidewalk, eighteen stories below.

Today, the fear that used to paralyze Bill and force him to go inside no longer affects him. He still doesn't know why he has a fear of heights, nor does he need to. Instead, he has learned what is most important: how to manage his fear. In time, Bill will eliminate his fear of heights altogether. This is the world of energy psychology. Although tapping on your face or hands may seem a little strange, it will open the door for you to make changes in your life that you may not have thought possible.

Relationships: A Case Study

Your energy level affects all aspects of your life, including your relationships. Despite the huge growth in the number of marriage counselors and numerous best-selling books on how to resolve relationship problems, the divorce rate is still extremely high in the United States. One out of every two marriages ends in divorce. What's happening? Are people having difficulty choosing the right person or are they sabotaging good relationships? There are many ways to create problem relationships, including ignoring the right person or chasing the wrong one.

For example, Ann always wants to be in control because she doesn't trust men. She chooses to date men who are needy—similar to children—and who depend on her. In her relationships, she is the caretaker, the person making most of the decisions. Most importantly, however, she is in control. The problem is that her relationships don't last. Although she has control, Ann also does all of the work in the relationship, which leaves her feeling angry and frustrated. She feels like giving up on men entirely, because it appears that the only men she attracts, who are attracted to her, are similar to the men in her past, failed relationships.

Ann really wants to change. She wants to find a man whom she can trust, one who will share the workload with her, and also be able to take care of her. Unfortunately, Ann has an energy imbalance that sabotages her real goal and blocks her from finding the right man. In future chapters, you will learn more about this concept and how to correct it.

> If you pause and reflect for a minute, you can probably think of a time when you sabotaged a situation in your life.

HOW ARE ENERGY IMBALANCES CREATED?

Although it is true that problems can occur due to no fault of yours, we are all still responsible for finding effective solutions for dealing with the challenges in our lives. If you have a chronic problem, do you have the knowledge, skill, or ability to help you to cope with the problem, or is it an energy imbalance? If you do not lack the knowledge, skill, or coping ability, then most likely the cause of your problem is both an energy imbalance and a psychological reversal that prevent you from identifying or implementing appropriate solutions.

For example, millions of people struggle with problems like weight loss, unhappy relationships, depression, and/or addictive behaviors. Our whole society, and too many people in general, seem chronically angry about life's small concerns and issues. Often, people struggle year after year with the same issues. It seems as though many people have accepted the belief that they cannot understand their own problems or develop effective strategies for change. Some experts and authors of self-help books imply that a lack of knowledge or skill creates the problem. Yet, when people sincerely try to develop coping skills and implement self-help strategies, they frequently find that those skills and strategies don't work for them. This type of situation is the hallmark of an energy-related issue: that is, you know how to solve the problems you encounter, but for some reason you can't make yourself do what is needed.

When we examine the beliefs that clients share with us, the word can't is important because, as we contend, it isn't a lack of knowledge or skill that causes your problems. Instead, we believe that an imbalance in your energy system sabotages your ability to achieve certain goals and/or be capable of moving on with your life after a traumatic event has occurred. Once your energy system becomes balanced, however, you will be able to develop the motivation and concentration required to accomplish your goals, and you will do so with much less difficulty.

If you are struggling to accept the ideas that support the effectiveness of energy psychology, remember that new approaches are often confronted with skepticism. For instance, it wasn't that long ago that chiropractic care was viewed as a completely bizarre alternative medical practice. Today, however, it provides treatment to more than fifteen million people a year; it is one of the fastest growing professions in the country; and its services are covered by most insurance plans (Burton Goldberg Group 1993).

> The Chinese believe that all things have chi, are chi. If life is movement, then chi is what makes things move. The ability to increase or decrease this energy is the basis for healing.

HOW ENERGY LEVELS AFFECT YOUR LIFE

Your personality is a complex and changing element of who you are and how you cope with problems. In every situation, you respond with a different set of emotions, some are constructive and others destructive. For example, did you ever wonder about those people who scream at other drivers when they're on the road? Those same people can go to work and deal with a complex situation using trust, clear communication, and under-standing. It is amazing how people can behave differently depending on the particular problem. Much of this depends on a person's balance—or imbalance—of energy.

When you are involved in a situation that involves an energy imbalance, your energy level is not sufficient to cope, and you may resort to behaviors that are associated with low energy. For example, at the moment when people experience "road rage," they are hateful, impatient, and very anxious. In fact, their behavior at the wheel can be both self-destructive and vengeful. At times, they may even try to punish other drivers. Their rage seems to be fueled by the belief that they should be able to drive exactly the way they wish to, which often means driving as fast as they want, without interference. When another driver slows them down, it elicits feelings of rage. What is equally strange is that this behavior most likely is not typical of these individuals' behavior in any other circumstances.

That is, once they step out of their car and go about the business of daily life, they can leave their rage feelings behind and almost immediately behave in a calm and thoughtful manner. The point is, you can behave differently in various situations depending on your level of energy.

Map of Consciousness

To better understand this concept, we use the Map of Consciousness developed by David Hawkins (1985). The map is a theoretical construct and should not be confused with the writings of Callahan and Callahan (1996) or Gallo (1998; 2005), which are based on extensive clinical experience. However, the map is a helpful guide to understanding energy psychology. It identifies emotions and related behaviors that are associated with specific energy levels.

For example, if you have an experience that severely lowers your energy, you are likely to experience lower energy-level emotions and/or behaviors, such as shame or guilt. This can be confusing, because it can be argued that a negative experience makes anyone feel bad and, depending on the experience, anyone would feel shame. It is clear, however, that energy imbalances come about when you can't change, when certain areas of your life are stagnant, or when emotions like shame or anger are a regular part of your daily life.

People also operate at different energy levels for various problems. This is why people can be so angry in one situation and exhibit acceptance and inner strength in another. Hawkins believes that few people reach the higher levels of consciousness and emotions, such as willingness and acceptance. Instead, most people operate at the level of pride and anger. The map should not be used to make judgments. Rather, it should be used as a guide to identify your energy level with regard to a particular problem. It will also help you to identify which issues you may need to address, if you are to move to a higher level.

What follows is a brief explanation of each energy level, as defined by Hawkins (1985). Your goal is to determine the lowest energy level(s) at which you operate when you try to solve a problem. Remember, even if you start at a higher energy level, it is important to identify the lowest energy level at which you operate for the given circumstance. For example, in a tense situation, you may begin by being calm and trustful (neutrality level), trying to empower others to solve a problem. If, however, you get frustrated and eventually blame others for the problem, then for this particular situation, you are operating at the guilt level. This information will be used in the following chapters to help you decide which emotions you may need to treat in order to eliminate a problem.

As you review each of the levels identified below, keep in mind the following two questions:

1. Can you identify a problem you wish to resolve?

2. What is your energy level when you are dealing with that problem?

LOWEST ENERGETIC EMOTIONAL LEVELS

Shame, guilt, apathy, and grief represent the four lowest energy levels. Keep in mind that when your energy is operating at these levels, there are usually multiple issues and problems causing the energetic imbalance. In these circumstances, it generally will take more time and multiple treatments to rebalance your system.

Shame: Early traumatic life experiences, such as sexual abuse and abandonment, can lead to shame. Moreover, in our judgmental society, physical imperfections, sexual orientation, and other unconventional behaviors also can lead to feelings of shame. Situations that deal with shame create many problems with self-acceptance. This is one reason why shame most likely will create a psychological reversal. Shame is the most destructive energy level, often leading to many self-sabotaging behaviors.

Guilt: People whose energy has dropped to the level of guilt tend to develop manipulative and/or punishing personalities. They always behave as if they are victims, and blame is one of their primary weapons. Those who have unconscious guilt or feel responsible for a traumatic situation tend to suffer from psychosomatic diseases.

Apathy: This is a state of helplessness where external energy is sought from caregivers. People operating at this energetic level are often felt to be a burden by those around them, as they are very needy and may discuss their problems endlessly.

Grief: Often felt during times of sadness and loss, grief is a feeling that everyone experiences for short amounts of time during their lives. However, those who grieve for extended periods of time (years) and continually operate within this level are living lives of regret and depression. Grief is also the energy level of habitual losers and chronic gamblers, who accept failure as an integral part of their lifestyle.

MIDDLE ENERGETIC EMOTIONAL LEVELS

The next four levels are fear, desire, anger, and pride. It is possible for people operating at these levels to lead successful lives; the energy level is much higher than in the lowest level, and these individuals tend to exhibit healthier behaviors. These middle levels, however, have their own particular concerns.

Fear: As you probably know, fear can be a healthy emotion, because it protects us from danger. As a life-view or a continual state of being, however, it can lead to jealousy, chronically high stress, or a fear of success. Fear also limits the growth of the personality, because so much energy is expended on dealing with fears.

Desire: The desire for money or power dictates many people's lives and helps to drive the economy. Desire is also the energetic level of addictions, where satisfying a craving becomes more important than any other goal. Unfortunately, as soon as one desire has been gratified, another often quickly replaces it.

Anger: Energy at this level can be either constructive or destructive. Anger may cause people to abandon problem situations or deal with them. But, as a lifestyle, anger expresses itself as resentment or revenge. Angry people are irritable and explosive, can easily fall into a rage, and tend to distance others from themselves.

Pride: People feel positive as they reach the level of pride, as they have attained some level of accomplishment in their lives. If pride originates exclusively from external forces, however, the inflated ego is vulnerable to attack. Also, if a loss of status occurs in regard to pride, this energetic level can quickly move toward shame. This is different from what we call a "healthy pride," which is closer to the description of neutrality that follows.

HIGHEST ENERGETIC EMOTIONAL LEVELS

The last group of emotional levels to be discussed is the beginning of the crossover point, where power—rather than force—is used to make decisions and create change in your life. At this level, there is a realization that your own empowerment and the empowerment of others are the true keys to success. This level includes courage, neutrality, willingness, and acceptance.

Courage: This is where the world starts to look exciting, challenging, and stimulating. At the lower levels, the world is seen as hopeless, sad, frightening, or frustrating. Courage begins the process of empowerment and the ability to cope and handle the opportunities that life presents to us. Courage brings out the capacity to face fear or our own character defects and to grow in spite of them.

Neutrality: At this stage, the world is seen as a complex and changing place without simple answers or rigid positions. The world is no longer viewed as black or white. To be neutral means that not getting one's way is no longer experienced as defeating or frustrating. Rather, the view is, "If I didn't get this, then I'll get something else. Life has its ups and downs and I will be okay if I roll with the punches." People at this level are easy to get along with and aren't interested in conflict.

Willingness: People who have reached the level of willingness are genuinely friendly, and social and economic success is a part of their lives. They have the ability to overcome inner resistance and do not have any major learning blocks. Having let go of pride originating from external forces, they are willing to look at their own defects and learn from others.

Acceptance: Although there are higher levels, acceptance is the level, according to Hawkins (1985), where there is the realization that the source of happiness is within oneself. Love is not something that is given or taken away by another, rather it is created from within. Long-term goals take precedence over short-term goals. Self-discipline and mastery are prominent aspects of these personalities.

The Law of Attraction

The Law of Attraction is a popular concept that holds, "like energy attracts like energy," and if you want something, you must specifically desire it. However, if all you think about is what you don't have in your life, that is what you will attract; even though this is not what you truly desire. Although there is no Law of Attraction in a scientific sense, many of the advocates of this concept believe that if you focus on the positive and on what you specifically want, this is what you will attract. We have little doubt that this is true in a practical sense. As Henry Ford said, "If you think you can, or think you can't, you're right."

It is also important to accept that life itself has no mandate about being fair, so not everyone has either the same opportunities or hurdles to leap in their lives. Moreover, many times people are forced to deal with traumatic events as children when they don't have the resources to cope with their problems. And we certainly don't believe that people who are in car accidents or similarly negative life-changing events brought those experiences upon themselves by attracting that energy.

Our view of attracting what you want in life is different, because first you must resolve the beliefs and behaviors that sabotage your success. Our focus is to help you understand how to use energy psychology to accomplish your goals. For example: Why don't you think positively? Why do you dwell on the negative aspects of your life? Why aren't you happier? We believe that you will be unable to maintain a positive focus and achieve your goals if your energy is unbalanced. You will, in effect, sabotage your efforts to succeed.

If you are able to think consistently about what you want in a positive manner and to get the results you desire, then you need not read any further. But if you struggle to think positively; frequently end up in situations that make you frustrated, angry, or lonely; or struggle to overcome your fears and past traumas, this book will help you to overcome those and other hurdles. Throughout the book, we provide you with strategies to change your negative beliefs and prevail over your problems. As you do this, you will find it easier to focus on the positive in your life and you will attract more joy and success. Guaranteed!

We hope that you will use the concepts and techniques covered in this book and also introduce others to this valuable new approach to getting connected to positive energy. So, with that said, we wish you a joyful journey on the road to better health, great success, and much happiness.

SUMMARY

The goal of this chapter is to introduce you to the development of energy work and provide you with some examples of how your energy may affect your behavior. As you have seen, we believe that most psychological problems are maintained by an energy imbalance. Energy imbalance is the reason why you have had so much difficulty dealing with the problems in your life. The key to eliminating your problems is to balance your energy. After learning and utilizing the energy treatments in this book, you will be able to deal with most of your problems in an efficient and effective manner. Finally, remember that letting go of your negative emotions is one of the keys to good physical health.

2

Your Energy Meridians

*Just because we cannot detect, perceive, or measure forces that
Chinese doctors say are important in managing illness does
not automatically mean that they do not exist.*

—Andrew Weil, MD

There are a number of ways to obtain energetic balance in your body and thus relieve emotional distress. In this book, we specifically cover a simple, highly portable method that can be used by anyone, in practically any place, at almost any time. In most instances, repeating the energy treatments one to three times will eliminate your problem altogether.

ENERGY MERIDIAN POINTS

There are twelve major energy meridians in your body. They run from the top of your head, through your fingers, and down to your toes. *Meridians* are "vessels" or channels that carry subtle energy through the body. *Acupoints* or *meridian points* are specific points on the surface of the skin, many of which evidence lower electrical resistance relative to the surrounding skin surface. These are the points that you will tap on when doing the energy treatments described in these pages. It is thought that subtle energy from the environment enters the body through these portals. The acupoints interconnect along the meridians.

To provide easy access to the treatment points, we will focus on the meridians that are in your face, upper torso, and hands. Starting with the meridian points on your head, we will describe the location of each meridian and the emotions and/or problems that are addressed when stimulating the point on that meridian. We will also provide the meridian points for treating psychological reversals, which will be addressed further in this chapter and in chapter 6. And, we will explore two additional treatments that are often used in conjunction with the primary treatments.

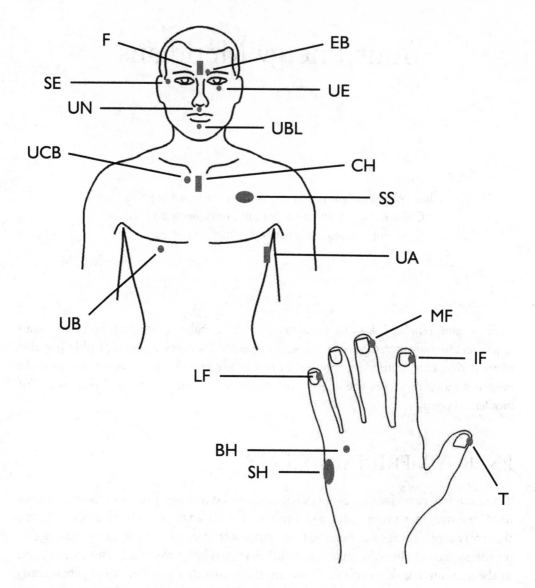

Diagram One: The Meridian Points Used in Energy Psychology

Eyebrow Point

The Eyebrow (EB) energy meridian point is located at the beginning of either eyebrow, near the bridge of the nose. The EB is often important in the treatment of trauma, frustration, impatience, and restlessness.

Side of Eye

The Side of Eye (SE) energy meridian point is located on the bony orbit of the eye socket at the side of either eye, directly below the end of the eyebrow. The SE is frequently helpful in alleviating feelings of rage.

Under Eye

The Under Eye (UE) energy meridian point is located on the bony orbit of the eye socket below either eye, directly under the pupil when the eyes are directed straight ahead. The UE is often used to treat anxiety, nervousness, phobias, and addictive cravings.

Under Nose

The Under Nose (UN) energy meridian point is located directly under the nose in the crevice above the upper lip. The UN is used to treat many conditions and is uniquely helpful for embarrassment. It is also used in treating what is referred to as deep-level psychological reversal.

Under Bottom Lip

The Under Bottom Lip (UBL) energy meridian point is located directly under the bottom lip, in the depression between the lip and the chin. The UBL is also used in the treatment of many problems and is specifically useful for alleviating feelings of shame. Additionally, it is used in treating some types of psychological reversal.

Under Collarbone

The Under Collarbone (UCB) energy meridian point is located directly under either collarbone, next to the sternum or chest bone. The UCB is easily found by placing a finger in the crevice beneath where the Adam's apple is located (above the sternum), sliding the finger down one inch and then to the right or left, approximately one inch.

The indentation is the UCB. The UCB is used in the treatment of many conditions. It has specific relevance for anxiety and insecurity.

Under Arm

The Under Arm (UA) energy meridian is located on the side of the body, six inches under either armpit. The UA is frequently used to treat anxiety, nervousness, and addictive cravings. Sometimes, it is used to treat self-esteem issues as well.

Under Breast

The Under Breast (UB) energy meridian point is located directly under either breast, approximately where the rib cage ends. The UB is often useful for treating feelings of unhappiness.

Little Fingernail

The Little Fingernail (LF) energy meridian point is located on the inside tip of either little (pinkie) finger, where the fingernail joins the cuticle. The LF is easily located by extending the little finger and touching the side of the fingernail that is facing the ring finger. The LF is important in alleviating feelings of anger.

Middle Fingernail

The Middle Fingernail (MF) energy meridian point is located on either middle fingernail, on the side closest to the pointer or index finger. The MF is often useful for treating jealousy and addictive cravings.

Index Fingernail

The Index Fingernail (IF) energy meridian point is located on either index finger, on the side of the fingernail closest to the thumb. The IF is useful in the alleviation of guilt feelings.

Thumbnail

The Thumbnail (T) energy meridian point is located on either thumb, on the side of the nail nearest the body and away from the other fingers. The T is useful in treating feelings of intolerance and arrogance.

Back of Hand

The Back of Hand (BH) energy meridian point is located on the back of either hand between the little finger and ring finger knuckles, in the direction of the wrist. The BH is helpful for treating physical pain, depression, and loneliness. The BH is also used during two additional treatments that are covered in this book: the Brain Balancer (BB) and the Eye Roll (ER), both described later in this chapter.

Side of Hand

The Side of Hand (SH) energy meridian point is located on the little finger side of either hand. The SH is easily located by looking at the palm of your hand, finding the palm crease that is closest to the fingers, and noting where the crease crosses the edge of the hand closest to the little finger. This point is important in the treatment of sadness and in the correction of several types of psychological reversals.

Forehead

The Forehead (F) energy meridian point is located above and between the eyebrows on the forehead. It easily is located by placing a finger between your eyebrows and sliding the finger upward approximately one inch. The F point is useful for treating a wide variety of problems, including trauma, anxiety, addiction, and depression.

Chest

The Chest (CH) energy meridian point is located on the chest, between and slightly down from the Under Collarbone (UCB) meridian points. The CH is useful in improving the functioning of the immune system and a wide variety of other problems.

Sore Spot

On the left side of your chest, at the midpoint of your collarbone and down toward your breast, is a tender spot. Sometimes it's actually quite sore, even painful. This spot is a pressure point or reflex along the lymphatic system, and it is referred to as a *neuro-lymphatic reflex*. For simplicity, however, we call it the Sore Spot (SS). It is not a meridian point, although it seems to affect the energy system. The SS is used to treat certain types of psychological reversals. Instead of tapping on this point, you rub it briskly with your fingertips. After locating the SS, press on it with your fingertips and quickly rub in a clockwise direction for several seconds. Although we identify the location of the SS in each treatment diagram, its location may be a little different for each person. The SS is particularly useful for treating massive psychological reversals.

Summary of Treatment Points

Meridian Point	Treats These Emotions or Symptoms
Eyebrow (EB)	Trauma, Frustration, Restlessness
Side of Eye (SE)	Rage
Under Eye (UE)	Anxiety, Nervousness, Phobias, Addictive Cravings
Under Nose (UN)	Embarrassment, Deep-Level Psychological Reversals
Under Bottom Lip (UBL)	Shame
Under Collarbone (UCB)	Anxiety, Insecurity
Under Arm (UA)	Anxiety, Nervousness, Cravings, Self-Esteem
Under Breast (UB)	Unhappiness
Little Fingernail (LF)	Anger
Middle Fingernail (MF)	Jealousy, Addictive Cravings
Index Fingernail (IF)	Guilt
Thumbnail (T)	Intolerance, Arrogance
Back of Hand (BH)	Depression, Loneliness, Physical Pain
Side of Hand (SH)	Sadness, Psychological Reversals
Forehead (F)	Trauma, Anxiety, Addiction, Depression
Chest (CH)	Improve Function of the Immune System
Sore Spot (SS)	Psychological Reversals

LOCATING AND TAPPING MERIDIAN POINTS

By participating in the following exercise, you will become more familiar with the location of the energy meridian points and how to balance your energy:

Step One

Think of something that causes you a minimal level of emotional discomfort. Do not focus on a complex issue at this time. Perhaps you can think of an old argument that you've had that still causes you to feel a little angry.

Step Two

Now, rate the level of discomfort that you feel while thinking about the situation (for example, the old argument). This should be the level of distress you are experiencing right now as you think about the issue. It may not be the same level of distress that you experienced when you last encountered the situation. Rate your discomfort on a scale from 0 to 10:

- **Zero** means that the issue does not bother you at all; you're completely relaxed.

- **Two** means that the issue causes slight discomfort but you're in control.

- **Four** means that although you can tolerate the distress, you are uncomfortable.

- **Six** means that you're highly uncomfortable.

- **Eight** means that your distress is very severe.

- **Ten** means that the distress is the most extreme imaginable.

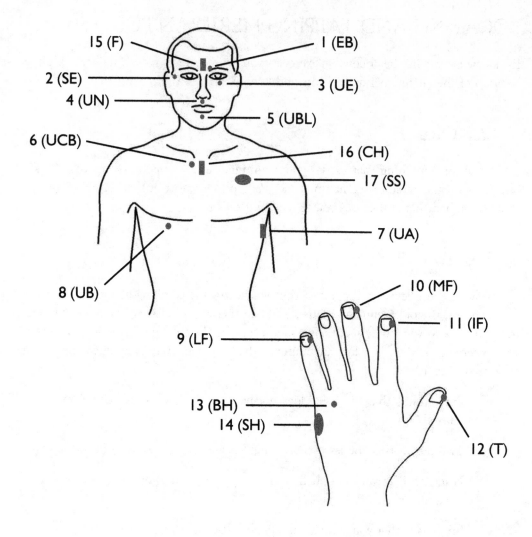

Diagram Two: A Numerical Sequence of the Meridian Treatment Points

Step Three

Use diagram 2 and follow the sequence below. Beginning with number 1, find each energy meridian point and tap lightly with two fingertips on each point five times.

1. Eyebrow (EB)

2. Side of Eye (SE)

3. Eye (UE)

4. Under Nose (UN)

5. Under Bottom Lip (UBL)

6. Under Collarbone (UCB)

7. Under Arm (UA)

8. Under Breast (UB)

9. Little Fingernail (LF)

10. Middle Fingernail (MF)

11. Index Fingernail (IF)

12. Thumbnail (T)

13. Back of Hand (BH)

14. Side of Hand (SH)

15. Forehead (F)

16. Chest (CH)

17. Sore Spot (SS)—Instead of tapping, rub this spot.

Step Four

Next, think about the issue or event that originally caused you some emotional discomfort. Rate the level of your discomfort again on a scale from 0 to 10. Is it lower than it was before you did the treatment sequence above? Usually, it is. If the discomfort hasn't been completely eliminated, you may need to tap the sequence one to three more times. If there is little or no change in the way you feel, this may be due to a number of factors (for example, psychological reversals or switching) that will be addressed later in this chapter.

After doing the above treatment, you may find it difficult to fully think about the issue that caused you discomfort in the first place. That is, it often feels as though the event is simply a vague distraction in your mind. If you take the time to really bring the issue to mind, however, you usually will find that you do not become upset by it. In most instances, this absence of distress persists into the future. Many people come to realize that before doing this simple treatment sequence, they always or almost always felt upset about the issue, and that now it no longer upsets them.

Most people report that after tapping on these seventeen energy meridian points they feel calm and relaxed, or even energized and tingling. As a matter of fact, this tapping sequence is one method you can use to become relaxed whenever you need it. That is, whenever you are feeling stressed, for whatever reason, take a 0 to 10 rating for the issue that is distressing you, and then tap on all of these points, in numerical order, until your stress is entirely gone.

Generally, the relief lasts for an extended period of time. Although tapping on all of the seventeen energy meridian points is often effective in treating many different problems, the process can become somewhat cumbersome. In Part II of this book (chapters 6 through 14), you will learn how to apply concise treatment recipes that are specifically designed to treat various conditions.

PSYCHOLOGICAL REVERSALS

As previously discussed, a psychological reversal is a disruption in your body's energy system that serves to sabotage your efforts at getting what you really want. Although everyone becomes reversed at times, we don't always know why this happens. Unfortunately, whenever there is a psychological reversal present, energy psychology treatments are not effective. As a matter of fact, it is unlikely that any therapy will work when you are in a state of psychological reversal. Therefore, it is extremely important to be able to eliminate these blocks. More details about psychological reversals as well as specific treatment sequences used for eliminating them are discussed and explored further in chapter 6.

SUPPLEMENTAL TREATMENT STRATEGIES

Energy treatments (tapping on meridian points) are often sufficient on their own to treat a given problem. There are, however, three supplemental treatments and an alternative to tapping on the meridian points. They are discussed below. The Brain Balancer (BB) and Eye Roll (ER) are referenced in each of the treatment sequences provided in this book.

The Brain Balancer

The Brain Balancer (BB) is a treatment often used in combination with tapping on meridian points. The purpose of the BB is to activate various areas of your brain so that an energy treatment for a specific problem will work more effectively. For instance, each of the following three behaviors—moving your eyes in different directions, humming a tune, and counting, tends to stimulate different areas and functions of the brain.

The BB involves tapping on the Back of Hand (BH) meridian point (located on the back of either hand between the knuckles of the little finger and ring finger, midway between the knuckles and the wrist) while performing the following actions:

- rolling your eyes clockwise 360 degrees

- rolling your eyes counterclockwise 360 degrees

- humming a tune

- counting to five

- humming again

The BB is not always needed to bring about a therapeutic result. However, as a matter of routine and because, sometimes, it can make the tapping more effective, we include it in all of the treatments described in this book. Although you may personally determine whether it is useful or necessary when you do a tapping sequence, it takes only a few seconds to do and it certainly can't hurt. Give it a try now.

Eye Roll

Another treatment used throughout this book is the Eye Roll (ER). The purpose of this treatment is to strengthen the results of treatment sequences and reduce any feelings of stress. The ER, like the Brain Balancer, also involves tapping on the BH. This time, however, as you are tapping, slowly and steadily move your eyes vertically down and up from looking down at the floor to looking up toward the ceiling (without moving your head). Like the Brain Balancer, the ER is not always necessary, but we routinely include it in the treatment sequences. It takes only a few seconds to do and it usually feels good. The ER is a helpful, quick stress reducer. Try it now.

Switching

Sometimes, treatments will not work to alleviate psychological issues due to a pervasive energy disruption referred to as *neurologic disorganization* or *switching*. When this condition exists, your energy system is disrupted significantly enough so that the treatment sequences either will not work at all or will work far too slowly.

Some people experience a chronic degree of switching that requires ongoing and intensive treatment. In most cases, however, switching occurs directly in relation to specific problems that are being treated. It also can occur temporarily for other reasons, such as high levels of stress; exposure to substances to which you are sensitive, like specific foods and chemicals; or improperly executed physical exercises. For example, running with improperly fitted shoes or on highly irregular surfaces sometimes causes switching.

Indications that your energy system is switched may include physical awkwardness and difficulties with coordination and spatial relations. Also, a tendency to confuse words and concepts can be present. For example, saying "impossible" when you mean "possible," or saying "hot" when you mean "cold." As noted previously, another sign of switching being present may occur when you are trying to implement a treatment sequence and it produces results very slowly or not at all.

There are a number of ways to treat switching, some of which are more complicated than others. One of the easiest is to do the Over-Energy Correction (or Hook-Up) exercise. After doing this exercise for about two minutes, you can repeat treatment recipes and determine whether switching influenced their effectiveness. You may prefer to do this exercise routinely before attempting any treatment sequence, just in case you are switched at the time.

OVER-ENERGY CORRECTION METHOD (OR HOOK-UP)

1. Sit down in a comfortable chair.

2. Cross your legs at the ankles, left over right.

3. Extend your arms in front of you with the palms of your hands facing each other. Then, turn your hands over so that your thumbs are pointing down.

4. Raise your right hand up and over the left hand, and intertwine your fingers.

5. Bend your arms so that your enfolded hands are now resting on your chest.

6. Place your tongue at the roof of your mouth, slightly behind the center ridge.

7. While maintaining this position, breathe deeply with your eyes closed for about two minutes.

Alternative to Tapping

Although we believe that tapping is the most effective way to stimulate a meridian point, there is a less noticeable alternative. This can be very helpful as there may be times when you need to treat a problem, but you are at work or in a public area in which you don't feel comfortable physically tapping your meridian points. As an alternative, you can touch each meridian point while breathing deeply. That is, you can think about the specific problem or emotional distress you are treating, and then touch each meridian point with some pressure. At the same time, you take in a deep breath, hold it for a few seconds, and then release it.

This method is also effective for treating energy reversals. As you touch the reversal treatment points, think to yourself, "I accept myself even though (name problem)." Again, we do not recommend this method in place of tapping, but as an alternate treatment method when you may feel uncomfortable tapping in public.

Another technique that has been effective for many of our clients is Imaginary Tapping, which is best used after becoming familiar with physical tapping. That is, you can think about the specific problem or emotional distress and then imagine tapping each meridan point.

SUMMARY

In this chapter we've provided an overview of the treatment points (acupoints) used in energy tapping. Additionally, a comprehensive treatment was introduced that can help you reduce stress and assist you in becoming familiar with all of the acupoints. Psychological reversals and other detailed treatment routines that are used throughout the book were introduced, including the Brain Balancer, the Eye Roll, Switching, and the Over-Energy Correction (Hook-Up). To stimulate the acupoints, you can use an alternative technique called Touch and Breathe if you are in public areas where you feel uncomfortable tapping (Diepold 1999). You can also use the power of your imagination by applying Imaginary Tapping. Before going into more detail about how to use energy psychology treatments for a wide array of problems, we will first present and discuss the important phenomenon of energy toxins in the next chapter.

3

Energy Toxins

Aging is accelerated by the accumulation of toxins in your body ... eliminating
those toxins will influence your biological clock in the direction of youth.

—Deepak Chopra, MD

Deepak Chopra (1993) believes that our biological system is continually eavesdropping on our thoughts. He also believes that how we feel about ourselves can and will alter our immune systems and make us more or less vulnerable to disease. Feelings of hopelessness, says Chopra, can increase the risk of heart attacks and cancer, while joy and fulfillment will help to extend our lives. Andrew Weil (1995) supports this theory. In his approach to health and wellness, Weil encourages people to let go of their anger and express forgiveness to those who have made them feel angry. Weil also believes that healing depends on the efficient operation of our bodies' healing system, and that the toxins in our water, air, and food can create emotional and physical problems.

If your energy system is in balance, you will feel well, achieve your goals, and maintain healthy relationships. On the other hand, if your body's energy system is disturbed, many other areas of your life will be affected negatively. It is important to maintain a balanced energy system. Although painful emotional or physical experiences are among the more obvious causes of energetic disturbance, even the foods you eat can be another energy disrupter.

Interestingly, some of the foods that you may find most enticing may be the very ones that disrupt your energy system so profoundly that you sabotage your life. That is, a food you really enjoy eating may affect your internal thought process and cause you to make unhealthy emotional choices. (This issue is addressed further in chapter 6.) In short, certain foods and beverages may send you on self-sabotaging missions.

One of the goals of this chapter is to help you to identify and guard against some of the environmental pollutants and substance sensitivities or toxins that may be interfering with your emotions, your relationships, and the achievement of your goals. This chapter also introduces the tools that you need to stabilize your body's energy system whenever it is out of balance.

Our bodies' energy systems can go out of balance for a variety of reasons. Painful experiences or traumas are one of the major causes of imbalance. In these instances, treatment to restore balance simply involves focusing on past events and other triggers while tapping on the appropriate energy meridian points. With this method, the negative emotions associated with memories and other triggers are completely eliminated so that distress does not return again at any future time. In energy psychology, we call this the *cure*.

Heredity can be another cause of energy imbalance. For example, some people have a tendency to become anxious or depressed. Often, this tendency is seen in several members of one family, and it is not due simply to distressing childhood experiences. Rather, the tendency for the energy system to become imbalanced is inherited. In this respect, it appears that there are two kinds of heredity: genetic, which is related to genes and chromosomes; and energetic, which is related to disturbances in the energy system.

Just as there are genes within the chromosomes of cells, the energy system can contain inherited energetic matter, that is, "genes" of the energy system. **Note:** Even when the cause of an energetic disturbance is inherited, in most cases, it can be treated successfully by the methods taught in this book.

THE IMPACT OF TOXIC SUBSTANCES

Energy toxins are another cause of energetic imbalance. This involves substances that, upon exposure, alter your energy system. Toxins are found in certain foods, beverages, and other substances, such as perfumes and cleaning products. Exposure to electromagnetic pollution, such as high tension wires and the positive ions found in electromagnetic fields, also seems to disrupt the body's energy system.

As you know, each individual is unique. What affects one person may not necessarily affect another. Or as the old saying has it: "One man's meat is another man's poison." Therefore, it is important to pay attention to how the foods and beverages that you consume affect you. Generally, within thirty to sixty minutes after consuming or being exposed to an energy toxic substance, symptoms of anxiety, nervousness, or fatigue will emerge. Substances that are especially toxic, such as nicotine and alcohol, will commonly disrupt your energy system even faster.

There are three concerns related to energy toxins. The first is that problems that have been successfully treated by energy psychology may reemerge after exposure to the toxin, thus undoing successful treatments. A second concern is that toxins, initially, may prevent energy treatments from being effective, and you may mistakenly conclude that this approach doesn't work for you. Finally, the toxin itself can be causing the problem, whether it is anxiety, depression, on any other emotional symptoms. Although abstract, intangible concepts are sometimes difficult to understand, the case study below demonstrates how toxins may be impacting your energy system.

Sarah: A Case Study

Sarah had a severe fear of driving on freeways, which began shortly after she was involved in a car accident. Since the accident, sometimes Sarah experienced panic attacks while driving on a freeway, especially if she was driving in heavy traffic. During these attacks, she would have to pull over to the side of the road. Sarah came in for energy treatments because her fear was becoming an increasingly debilitating problem, preventing her from traveling any distance and often interfering with her work and family responsibilities.

After Sarah was treated with energy psychology methods, she was able to easily imagine driving in heavy traffic on a freeway without experiencing any anxiety. When she tried to actually drive in traffic, however, the anxiety and panic attacks returned. Each time Sarah was treated, she would feel much better, but then the symptoms would return.

It became increasingly clear that something else was interfering with her treatments, as they are usually highly effective for relieving phobias, anxiety, and panic. We discussed the various foods and beverages that Sarah loved to consume. One of her favorite foods was corn and she also drank a lot of a particular kind of tea.

We determined that the corn and tea were somehow interfering with Sarah's energy system. Her assignment was to eliminate these substances from her diet for some length of time until the accumulated energy toxins in her body had been adequately reduced. Approximately three weeks later, the energy treatments provided the results we wanted: no more anxiety and panic while driving. Furthermore, after this last treatment, it was possible for Sarah to eat corn and drink tea occasionally without creating an energetic disturbance in her system.

IS TOXICITY A PROBLEM FOR YOU?

There are numerous symptoms that are a result of toxins, but you need focus only on those that are chronic. Some chronic symptoms include constant sneezing, runny nose, headaches, frequent mood swings, insomnia, bad breath, blotchy skin, blocked sinuses, fatigue, anxiety, and chronic aches or pains. If you have been experiencing any of these symptoms for a month or longer, you may want to consider the possibility that a food or inhalant toxin (for example, certain perfumes or tobacco smoke) is negatively affecting you.

Identifying Energy Toxins and Allergens

Although each person is unique, there are a number of substances commonly known to disrupt the energy system. The list below includes some of these substances. **Please note:** Do not assume that each item on the list will negatively affect you.

Refined Sugar	Coffee
Artificial Sweetener	Tea
Alcohol	Caffeine
Wheat	Rice
Corn	Peas
Nicotine	Pepper
Legumes	Eggs
Tomatoes	Shellfish
Eggplant	Herbs
Detergents	Artificial Fibers
Pesticides	Cosmetics
Mold	Dust
Gasoline Fumes	Aftershave Lotion
Formaldehyde	Toiletries
Perfumes	

If you suspect that a substance is energy toxic to you, one of the simplest things to do is avoid it altogether. As we have noted, there are certain symptoms that will appear shortly after you consume a food that is toxic to you. The best way to identify these foods is to make mental notes (or better yet, written ones) after you eat. You can usually identify these substances by observing the patterns of emotional and physical effects they create. After consuming a food or beverage you suspect to be toxic, you may want to ask yourself the following questions:

- How did that food item make you feel?

- Did it energize you or did it make you feel tired?

- Did any other symptoms appear that made you think this food may not be the best for you?

- Did your pulse rate increase significantly within thirty to sixty minutes after consuming the food? If it did increase, one or more of the foods or beverages you consumed may be an allergen or energy toxin.

Although toxic substances are often the very foods or beverages to which you feel addicted, it should be noted that cravings can occur for good physiological reasons as well. Such reasons include low blood sugar; the need for minerals, like iron and sodium; and hormonal fluctuations in the brain. Aside from these types of reasons, however, the foods and beverages that you crave the most intensely are often those that can most readily disrupt your energy system. You may also find that these foods are the ones that you consume when you sabotage other goals in your life. Simply put, these foods weaken you and your body.

Eliminating Energy Toxins and Allergens

The goal is not to remove all the fun foods from your life, but rather for you to be aware of their impact. You may determine that it is better for you to cut back on— rather than completely eliminate—toxic foods. For most people, however, consuming toxins is a way of life. The good news is that your body has a high-functioning natural detoxification system.

Your liver is one of the hardest-working organs in your body, but it can use some assistance. Our recommendation is that if you have no additional health problems (if in doubt, consult your physician), you should detoxify your system. We are not suggesting anything radical. Most health food stores can recommend pills or powders that contain the fibers and herbs needed to detoxify your system without you having to severely change your diet. If you don't want to use any supplements, then you must increase the amount of fruit and water you consume, and reduce the amount of protein from foods such as red meat. There are a number of books you can find at your local library or bookstore that address the topic of detoxifying the body.

Foods and other substances that cause allergic reactions are invariably energy toxic to the allergic person. An energy toxin by itself, however, does not necessarily cause an allergic reaction. That is, although allergen equals energy toxin, energy toxin does not always equal allergen. An *allergen* disrupts your immune system, causing your body to react as though the substance is a dangerous viral invader. On the other hand, an *energy toxin* disrupts your energy system. In most instances, however, both allergens and toxins are examples of a threshold phenomenon: That is, as the amount of the substance accumulates in your system, it reaches a point where the allergy or energy toxicity surfaces. This is why many people develop allergies later in life.

This concept is known as the *barrel effect*, according to Doris Rapp (1991), the noted environmental physician who has seen a connection between allergies and conditions such as depression and attention-deficit/hyperactivity disorder (ADHD). According to this concept, you can think of your body as a barrel. An allergy does not occur until the barrel (your body) is overflowing with the allergic substance. If you occasionally eat corn, for example, it is usually not a problem. If you regularly eat a lot of corn, however, in time, your barrel will overflow and you may develop an allergy to it.

One simple approach for detoxifying your system is offered by Andrew Weil (1995). He believes an effective approach is to drink a lot of water each day, take vitamins C and E and, at a different time of day, take selenium.

SUMMARY

The main purpose of this chapter was to make you aware that toxins can affect energy work, including the energy psychology treatment methods provided in this book. This doesn't mean that you must detoxify your system. If you have any of the above-noted symptoms of toxicity, however, it might be a healthy choice for you to seek more information and advice about this topic. Keep in mind, too, that you need to recognize and avoid the foods or beverages that weaken you. If you continually consume substances that are toxic to you, they may negatively affect your entire energy system.

4

Beliefs That Hold You Back

Believe in yourself! Have faith in your abilities! Without a humble but reasonable confidence in your own powers you cannot be successful or happy.

—Norman Vincent Peale

The quote above was written more than thirty-five years ago in Norman Vincent Peale's best-selling book, *The Power of Positive Thinking* (1996). Peale was one of the first authors ever to encourage people to realize that their beliefs can affect their lives. His book emphasizes the fact that success is largely a function of your expectation. He challenged readers to closely examine their lives and to believe in their ability to make a difference.

Peale's ideas were a step away from the more prevalent, traditional beliefs of the time, which said that hard work—don't count on luck—was the way to make a difference in your life, and that confidence came from your work being recognized and rewarded by others. Instead, Peale said that you must first believe in yourself and this belief will set the stage for your work to succeed. Although there is truth to Peale's adage, the problem with it is that although believing in yourself sounds great, it's difficult to sustain that belief when important parts of your life are not going well or as you planned.

WHAT IS A BELIEF?

Beliefs don't have to be either true or fact-based; they are merely perceptions. Amazingly, beliefs can be extremely complex, and yet operate with the precision of a surgeon's scalpel, defining your behavior in each situation. Appearance, for instance, is one way your beliefs operate. That is, when you meet someone, you may treat that person differently than you might otherwise, based purely on his or her appearance. Most of us have experienced situations where two people behave exactly the same way, yet our response to each is very different.

Every activity in which you participate is accompanied by a conscious or unconscious belief, positive or negative. A belief can be *global*, "I will fail at whatever I attempt"; *focused*, "I can parallel park a car in a small space"; or *subjective*, "He always acts like a jerk." Your beliefs affect every aspect of your life. The beliefs you hold about your own life will be explored in later chapters.

Your parents were an early source of your beliefs. One of their goals as parents was to create beliefs within you that would protect you from danger. For example, "Don't talk to strangers!" is a belief that almost everyone remembers learning as a child. Someone you trusted told you that it was dangerous to talk to or accept rides from people you did not know. You listened to stories about what happened to children who did speak to strangers: They were taken away and never seen again. These stories instilled in you the belief that strangers who offered you a ride or wanted to give you gifts were dangerous. Most likely, you were also told, "Don't take candy from strangers." You responded by not trusting strangers and taking your parents' advice about whom to trust.

As you got older, you learned to modify these beliefs and, based on your experiences and adult approval, you increased the circle of strangers whom you could trust. This is an example of a complex belief about human behavior that affects you throughout your life. For example, as an adult, you may still believe that if a stranger wants to give you a gift, he or she wants something from you in return. As an adult, however, you ought to be able to determine when it is safe and reasonable for you to talk with and/or accept gifts from people you don't already know.

SOCIAL CHANGE AND YOUR BELIEFS

Radical social changes can affect your beliefs. The events that occurred in the 1960s, for example, created and altered the beliefs of people for several generations. The trauma associated with the assassinations of John F. Kennedy, Martin Luther King Jr., and Robert Kennedy altered our society's beliefs about safety and created a feeling of national grief that can still be felt more than forty-four years later. Many other events from the 1960s still reverberate within the belief systems of modern society: The feminist movement sought equality for women in the workplace but, in the process, often created anger and alienation between the sexes. For the first time, a drug, marijuana, rivaled alcohol in popularity as a mind-altering substance. "Free love" and a safe contraceptive for women—the pill—changed socially acceptable sexual behaviors and left many people feeling confused about what was morally comfortable. The war in Vietnam divided younger and older generations, as hundreds of thousands of young men and their families were traumatized in a war that had no obvious noble purpose.

These events of the 1960s coincided with the soaring divorce rate and the breakup of millions of families, a trend that continues to the present day. Furthermore, while those events were taking place, television was becoming a dominant cultural force. It created more passive interaction among family members, parents spent less time learning about the beliefs governing their children's behavior and their children's role models were suddenly television stars—not family members or community leaders as had formerly been the case.

Traumas that affect our society as a whole can create significant energy imbalances. This is particularly true when events are dividing our country and individual beliefs are under attack, making self-acceptance much more difficult. Perhaps this is one reason why, in a time of tremendous affluence, many people struggle even harder to be happy than in the past, and why, as a nation, we seem angrier and less respectful of others.

> It has been said that if you were to identify and write down all of your beliefs, you would see your life being played out before you.

MOVING TOWARD AN ENERGY APPROACH

Modern psychology supports the position that your beliefs can hold you back and prevent you from achieving your goals in life. Many popular self-help books exhort you to believe in yourself. When authors are on target, you may even experience an emotional cleansing while you are reading about a problem in your life and how you can overcome it. It's exciting to believe that your problem can be resolved; as long as the book is believable, it may help you to move in a positive direction, and reading it may be enjoyable. But did you really change? For a short time you may feel new energy, but in many instances, your old habits of thinking, feeling, and behaving eventually return.

A book can be intriguing, but it can't do the actual work that must be accomplished to change your life or make the process of change interesting. That takes time and effort. Generally, self-help books are designed to give you knowledge and help you develop the skills that are required for you to change some aspect of your life. If you can follow through on the suggestions, you will most likely succeed. Too many people, however, give up and don't implement the solutions that are provided by these secular bibles of our modern age. The reason most individuals don't follow through is due to an energy problem or energetic imbalance that must first be corrected before their efforts can succeed.

ALTERNATIVE APPROACHES TO CHANGING BELIEFS

Many therapeutic strategies that are designed to help clients deal with their problems are effective. In fact, we believe your energy can be positively altered by other treatments; however, energy work is one of the most efficient, effective approaches available. In talk therapy, you are in the presence of a person who cares about you and is guiding you through a difficult situation. In effect, this person helps you to stop the negative habits that may be continually re-creating your original problem. A good therapist is very supportive and provides you with a lot of positive energy. Over time, the goal of talk therapy is to change the energy around your issue from negative to positive.

Additionally, if you talk about your problem, you focus on the issues at the crux of it. Learning to reframe your problems or think differently about them frequently balances energy in a positive direction. The process, however, takes much longer and demands a lot more effort than energy psychology requires.

The following is a brief exploration of several strategies that can help you to deal with your problems more efficiently. These approaches can be very effective, especially when they are used in conjunction with energy psychology. One of the common goals is to remove the beliefs that create self-sabotage. People often find themselves unable to stop their self-sabotaging behaviors. This is commonly caused by an energy imbalance that is at the source of their issue and can be identified by the presence of self-defeating beliefs and behaviors.

Energy imbalances also prevent many people from ever implementing new strategies or even taking the time to learn them. This is where most self-help approaches fail. Psychological reversals commonly leave people unable to use these approaches. As you learn how to treat your energy imbalances, traditional therapeutic strategies can be used to help eliminate your less desirable habits.

While you explore problems and/or try to change any of the habits that may be creating your energy imbalances, we encourage you to use the strategies discussed in the following sections, which include cognitive therapy, visualization, behavior and belief assessment, and releasing personal myths. Note that, although energy treatments can correct a problem, imbalances can reoccur; especially if you don't alter your old habits.

Cognitive Therapy

Cognitive therapy is currently one of the most popular strategies—especially in self-help books—that can help you to change your beliefs. Simply stated, this approach maintains that what you think affects how you feel and act. This strategy follows the logic that the mind controls our feelings and actions. With cognitive therapy, besides a stimulus (an event) and a response (your reaction to that event), a third intervening component—internal processing or self-talk (your interpretation of the event)—is added.

According to cognitive therapy, your self-talk is what creates the self-defeating belief and subsequent behaviors that prevent you from finding a solution to your problem. The therapeutic strategy is to identify and change your internal self-talk. This strategy, like many others, is much more difficult to accomplish than is energy work. Once your energy is balanced, however, you may find that these strategies are easier to implement and to use for help in changing old habits.

For example, let us say that your boss's reaction to most problems is to become angry and yell, and your position in the company makes you a prime target for his behavior. When he behaves in this manner, you respond by withdrawing and feeling depressed. A cognitive therapist such as Albert Ellis (1995) would want to know what you believe about this situation. Most often your response would be similar to "My boss should not (or must not) yell at me for every problem."

Ellis believes that it is not simply the situation, but rather your irrational beliefs, that block your ability to change. The irrational belief is operating when you tell yourself that a situation should not occur when, in fact, it is happening. For example, while you are thinking that your boss must not yell at you, he still yells at you. Ellis says that once you trap yourself with a "must" or a "should" thought, it leads to negative feelings, such as anxiety and depression, that, in turn, prevent you from exploring effective solutions to your problem.

In Ellis' view, the first step is to identify and dispute your irrational belief. That is, instead of saying, "My boss must not yell at me," you rationally reframe the belief and say, "It would be better for me, or it would be nice, if my boss did not yell at me. But if he does, it is his problem and it does not reflect on me." Ellis believes that once you eliminate the irrational belief, it frees you to move toward solutions.

The core of Ellis' work is to remove the block, that is, the irrational belief that prevents you from changing. Cognitive therapy in general focuses on the idea that problems are created or perpetuated by a person's interpretation of a situation. By changing your beliefs, you can find most aspects of life acceptable and, therefore, not experience terrible unhappiness. It's helpful to become aware of the beliefs that trap you, and to realize that you can negate some of their effect by changing the way you think about and react to a situation.

Visualization

Visualization is another way to examine and affect your beliefs. This strategy is based on the idea that unless you can clearly imagine a situation, for example., completing a task or being promoted, then it is highly unlikely to happen. Conversely, if you *negatively* visualize a situation, this speaks volumes about how your internal beliefs and feelings generate your self-sabotaging.

One of the most interesting studies in the area of visualization and sports was presented at the Ericksonian Approaches to Hypnosis and Psychotherapy Conference in 1986. After interviewing professional tennis players, Swedish psychologist Lars-Erik

Unestahl (1988) studied videotapes of their game to determine what strategies they used to serve the ball on a consistent basis. In the interview, he asked them to close their eyes and describe what they did to serve well. Each described the position of their arm and body and exactly how they tossed the ball into the air to begin the serve.

When the videotapes were examined, the psychologist met with the players again and told them that many times they served just the way they had described. At other times, however, the players' bodies were in different positions than they thought and yet, the ball still went to the corner where they were aiming. It was as if their bodies naturally compensated for the changes that occurred in their serving style.

Upon closer investigation, the psychologist found that the tennis players visualized where the ball was going before they actually hit it. He also found that the average player was less confident and often visualized the ball going into the net or going out of bounds. The professional players believed that they could hit the ball over the net, so they could easily visualize and see the ball going over the net. The players who did not perform well were less confident about their ability to serve and hit the ball over the net, so their minds and bodies were not working together in harmony.

This doesn't mean that if you can visualize and see the ball going over the net and into the corner, you will reach the skill level of a professional player. We are limited by our natural abilities. What we are talking about, however, is reaching peak performance. To be at your best, you must believe that you can do what you are trying to achieve. As long as you choose realistic goals and are able to truly visualize them, you greatly increase your chances for success.

Visualization is simple, but it takes some work—you must visualize yourself achieving your goal. It's best to be specific, rather than simply thinking about the overall situation or end point, such as scoring the winning point in a game. Instead, you spend time visualizing each component required for you to succeed. For example, professional golfers may walk a golf course while visualizing each swing.

Visualization is a tool to help you identify a problem and/or improve yourself once you have treated your underlying belief issues. If anxiety is blocking your success, combining relaxation strategies with visualization can help you to improve your skills and more easily overcome problems.

Belief and Behavior Assessment

In the 1980s, Steve de Shazier (1988) wrote several books on therapeutic change that explored an interesting approach to looking at problems. He wanted to know how people "did" their problems. That is, he wanted to determine what the beliefs and/or behaviors were that people used to perpetuate problems in their lives. He believed that individuals are often unaware of the specific beliefs or behaviors that create a problem, and focus instead on the problem itself.

For example, if you want to lose weight, being overweight is the problem. The solution is diet and exercise. The question posed by de Shazier would be, "What beliefs or behaviors prevent you from succeeding in losing weight?" The better you understand what beliefs and/or behaviors create the behaviors that comprise how you "do" the problem, the easier it will be for you to use energy psychology to resolve it.

TEACHING APPROACH

One strategy for understanding how you create or maintain problems comes from a teaching approach. Although this may seem odd, imagine that someone wants to have your problem and they don't know how to "do" it. Using your life experiences as an example, your goal is to teach them how to re-create your problem. Normally, when you share a problem with someone, the person listens and then solutions are offered on how you can solve it. In this situation, however, after you have shared your problem in detail, imagine your friend saying "Wow! That's a great problem. I wish I had that problem. How do you 'do' it?"

For example, if you are overweight, imagine talking to a thin woman who claims that no matter how hard she tries or how much she eats, she can't gain a pound. You would say, "But have you tried my approach?" At that point, you provide the detailed strategy you use to gain weight. Don't forget to include any negative beliefs that you use to diminish your self-esteem, or behaviors you use to put yourself in situations where you are likely to overeat or eat fattening foods. Once you have created this list of strategies, you will be consciously aware of the approach you use to create your problem.

OBSERVING EXCEPTIONS

Another strategy of de Shazier's is to look for the exceptions to your problem. The goal is to identify an exception when your problem doesn't occur. If you are helping to create or maintain your problem, then there should be a time when you behave in a manner that doesn't support it. For example, if you are eating too much of the wrong foods, determine when you are best able to stay on your diet. Who are you with and what are you doing? Sometimes exceptions are hard to recognize, but they usually exist. Once you identify an exception, you need to do more of that behavior. Note that for the teaching approach and exception strategies to succeed, you must take the time to write down the details.

Releasing Personal Myths

Caroline Myss (1997) explores people's beliefs by looking at the personal myths they hold on to, such as "My life is defined by my wound." She believes that after people experience a traumatic event, there is a tendency for them to look at their lives through the lens of the wound that was created by the event. Holding onto negative or traumatic events long after they have ended greatly diminishes a person's vital life energy. Interestingly, Myss also believes that holding onto good times as well as bad times can be costly. One common example might be the high school football star who still lives in the past and doesn't accept the fact that he is fifty years old, overweight, and a couch potato.

In Myss' view, accepting who you are is one key to maintaining your healthy energy. No matter which stage of life you're in, you must consciously accept it and fully live it. This doesn't mean the high school football star has to accept being a couch potato; he can still exercise and be a competitive athlete. He must let go of the mind-set, however, that he is somehow still eighteen years old and a football star. Once you consciously accept your life the way it is now, you will stop wasting your energy and find many ways to enjoy being who you are.

SUMMARY

This chapter explored how your beliefs may contribute to your problems. Beliefs are divided into two groups: sabotaging beliefs that are the result of energy reversals, and beliefs that are bad habits. Although you most likely developed bad habits because of an energy imbalance, you can use the suggestions provided in this chapter to help you deal with your problems.

In energy psychology, you can often treat a problem without understanding its roots. Nevertheless, the better you understand the beliefs or behaviors that create that problem, the better equipped you will be to direct the energy treatments to their specific causes, and the less likely it will be that an energy imbalance will reoccur. This is especially true of complex problems, such as alcoholism, where multiple beliefs and behaviors are at the source of the problem.

In conjunction with using energy psychology, you may want to use the following self-help strategies:

1. Examine your internal self-talk and dispute any irrational beliefs.

2. Use visualization to test your internal beliefs about a situation.

3. Determine how you "do" a problem via your behaviors or beliefs.

4. Accept who you are at this time in your life.

5

Identifying Problems That
You Want to Resolve

Insecurity is the negative expected. What are you doing about what bothers you?

—Merle Shain

To use energy psychology effectively, you need to be clear and specific about each problem that you want to change in your life. Although believing that your entire life is a mess may be a real feeling, it is too generalized and abstract a belief to be affected by energy psychology techniques. Don't worry that there should be a specific order in which your issues must be addressed. What often happens is that, as you treat one problem, another problem reveals itself that also affects the specific situation.

As you identify and treat each problem, you will begin to see a change in your life, and your outlook on related situations will improve. Although some problems are very straightforward, such as a fear of insects, others, such as addictive behaviors, are far more complicated.

Once you learn the process of energy psychology, you will be able to treat each problem in a fast and efficient manner.

DEVELOPING YOUR PERSONAL PROFILE

The goal of developing a personal profile is to identify each situation, behavior, or belief that you believe is creating disruptions in your life. A personal profile also provides a solid opportunity to identify any ongoing themes or chronic problems you may have. Your personal profile is not a comprehensive, onetime list of every issue affecting your life. In our experience, we've found that whatever issue you think of first should be treated first. Then, once you've successfully treated those problems, you can repeat the process. While you are engaged in this process, problems that you were not consciously aware of may become apparent.

Review the areas of concern that are listed below and write down any that you feel you need to treat. Do not rely on your memory. Sometimes important problems are elusive; that is, they surface to your conscious awareness, but then are quickly forgotten. The impact they have on your behavior, however, can remain active and significant.

1. **Childhood memories.** Can you identify any childhood memories or events that you feel might be creating problems in your life? If you have a specific memory, but you aren't sure how or if it is affecting your present life, list and treat the memory anyway. As we've mentioned, you don't have to remember all the details at once. Memories will surface when you are ready to treat them.

2. **Associated beliefs.** Can you identify any beliefs you have that were created as a result of these childhood memories?

3. **Fears.** Can you associate any fears you have with any of the problems in your life? Remember, fears can be straightforward, such as a fear of snakes or public speaking; or they can be more complex, such as a fear of being intimidated, or relationship and/or sports performance fears. Note that there should be at least one fear on your list, because everyone is fearful of something.

4. **Controlling your emotions.** Can you identify any uncomfortable, yet common, emotions that you experience regularly? For example, do you often find yourself in situations in which you respond with anger, or feel alone or lonely? Other emotions of which to be aware include embarrassment, shame, rejection, frustration, and guilt.

5. **Painful memories.** In addition to your childhood memories, are there painful events that you've experienced as an adult? Identify any that you believe are related to or are negatively affecting your adult behaviors or beliefs.

6. **Depression.** This feeling is usually the culmination of many other unresolved issues. You can treat depression with energy psychology. To prevent depression from continually reoccurring, however, it is most important to identify and treat the underlying problems causing it.

7. **Eating.** Your inability to control what you eat is often related to unresolved emotional problems. What beliefs or behaviors are blocking you from achieving your goals regarding your eating or weight concerns?

8. **Addiction problems.** Smoking, alcohol, drugs, and gambling are the most common addiction problems. You can use the treatments in this book to treat these and any other addictions, such as an addiction to sex. For long-term success, however, it is important to identify what is missing in your life, as addictions are usually filling a void of some sort.

9. **Relationships.** This is the most complex issue presented in this book, because the source of relationship problems can be related to any of the previous problems you've listed. The goal here is to identify your current relationship situation, what you would like the relationships in your life to actually be, and what relationship-specific concerns currently exist.

10. **Common issues or patterns.** Identify any patterns or reoccurring situations that can help to guide you and determine which of your problems need to be treated.

USING ENERGY PSYCHOLOGY FOR YOUR SPECIFIC ISSUES

After reviewing the questions above, you should now have a *written* personal profile (list) of the problems you hope to address as well as some idea of how these problems have an impact on your life.

Treatment Sequence Overview

In the chapters that follow, you will learn specific treatment sequences that address various types of problems. Generally, the process is very simple: Each sequence includes the following steps:

1. Identify a problem, such as a fear of heights, or a feeling, such as being angry. Now, rate the amount of distress the problem causes you on a scale of 0 to 10, with 0 indicating no distress and 10 indicating the most amount of distress.

2. Identify and treat any self-sabotaging beliefs (that is, reversals).

3. Identify the appropriate treatment and tap those meridian points using a number-sequenced diagram. All you have to do is look at the diagram and tap the numbered meridian points in the indicated order.

4. Again, rate your distress on a 0 to 10 scale (a number should just pop into your mind). If there has been no decrease, repeat steps 2 and 3.

5. Next, do the Brain Balancer (BB), which is explained in each treatment sequence.

6. Repeat the treatment sequence.

7. Again rate your distress on a 0 to 10 scale. It should be lower yet. When your distress is within the 0 to 2 range, go to step 9. Sometimes, the treatment must be repeated several times before relief is felt from the distressful situation.

8. As long as the distress continues to decrease, continue with the treatment sequence until there is no distress remaining. If the treatment stalls at any point, this indicates a mini-reversal. Treat this by tapping on the Side of Hand (SH) while saying three times "I deeply accept myself, even though I still have some of this problem."

9. When the distress is in the 0 to 2 range, consider doing the Eye Roll, this technique will also be explained in each treatment sequence.

The basic steps listed above are generally all you will have to do to eliminate most problems. Again, it is normal to repeat the treatment sequence two to three times to completely eliminate the problem. The entire process, however, rarely takes more than five minutes once you know what you are doing.

SUMMARY

By this point, you should have developed a profile of your problems and have some idea of how they are contributing to the creation of certain situations in your life. As you engage in energy work, more unresolved issues that have been affecting your life will become part of your conscious memory. Eventually, you will eliminate the impact these problems have and will have to deal only with current issues in your life. We must emphasize: Do not avoid the process of identifying a personal profile. Your problems affect you in many ways and are connected to all aspects of your life. Although in many cases it is true that a specific treatment will eliminate the associated problem, developing a profile and working on all of your issues is the best way for you to achieve success with this approach.

PART II

Energy Treatments for Specific Problems

6

Understanding Psychological Reversals and Self-Sabotage

We cannot change anything unless we accept it.
Condemnation does not liberate, it oppresses.

—Carl Jung

This chapter begins the treatment section of *Energy Tapping*, where specific problems are examined and appropriate treatment sequences are provided. The first step in applying energy psychology is to eliminate any psychological reversals. The simplest definition of a *psychological reversal* is that your energy system elicits thoughts and behaviors that are the opposite of what one would normally believe about life situations. For example, if you were asked if you want to be happy, the expected response would be "yes." But experience has proven that when people are psychologically reversed, deep within themselves they are choosing (unconsciously) to be miserable. There is a conflict between their internal beliefs and what they are trying to achieve. For instance, perhaps you don't believe that you deserve to be happy or perhaps you did something you are ashamed of and can't accept in yourself.

When people are psychologically reversed, they sabotage their lives. For example, they may try to resolve a problem with someone they love and, in the process, behave in a manner that is destructive and needlessly hurtful. Or, when psychologically reversed people apply for jobs for which they are qualified, they may freeze up and act confused during their interviews.

Although what takes place physically when your energy is reversed is not readily apparent, it is clear that when you have sabotaging beliefs or behaviors, you literally act in opposition to what you are consciously trying to attain. Sabotaging beliefs, for example, are probably a major reason why people stay in abusive relationships, and they also explain why partners are abusive in the first place. If an abused individual's underlying beliefs (such as, "I am not good enough") were treated with the techniques provided in this book, that person would realize she or he needs to leave the abusive situation; similarly, the abusive partner would realize that his or her anger is with themselves. (See chapter 17 for a thorough discussion on relationships.) *An energy reversal blocks you from seeing solutions even when you have the knowledge, or it prevents you from implementing the solution even though you have the ability.* This is a core point of energy psychology.

It is a reversal in your energy that prevents you from accomplishing your goal and it is an energy imbalance that creates faulty ideas or weak willpower. Once reversals are treated, you will experience the difference. In theory, when you correct a psychological reversal you are reconnecting the mind (beliefs) with the body (energy) so that you can again create positive energy in the previously reversed areas of your life. Once this is done, you will stop making the wrong decisions and start moving toward a successful life.

> An energy reversal blocks you from seeing solutions even when you have the knowledge, or it prevents you from implementing the solution even though you have the ability.

SIX TYPES OF SELF-SABOTAGE

Throughout these pages, we will stress the importance of identifying and treating psychological reversals. There are six common types of reversals at the core of all sabotaging beliefs or behaviors. When an energy treatment doesn't work, a psychological reversal is frequently the culprit, and it must be treated. Following is a brief description of these six types of reversals. Once you are familiar with them, you can assess yourself to determine whether you are reversed in relation to a particular problem. You will find that you can be psychologically reversed with one problem and not another. Remember, energy treatments are not effective until reversals are corrected.

Massive Reversal

Massive reversals affect major areas of your life, especially in those aspects where everything seems to go wrong all of the time. People who experience this type of reversal may appear as if they want to lead miserable lives. Although they consciously believe that they want a happy life, their behaviors create the opposite of what they seek. People who are massively reversed often reject or pass up potentially good opportunities. Unfortunately, they can't recognize them and instead often focus on the one negative aspect of that opportunity. They are unable to identify situations and people that are good for them and, in the worst cases, they actively seek out negative situations. People who continually experience bad relationships, chronic depression, or ongoing addiction problems are usually massively reversed.

Deep-Level Reversal

Deep-level reversal affects people who want to change, but believe that their problem is too powerful or too much a part of their lives for them to eliminate. With this type of reversal, the person expresses a sincere desire to deal with and eliminate the problem, yet at an unconscious level he or she holds the belief that "There is no way I'm going to get over this problem." Usually, a lack of confidence and the inability to visualize a life without this problem helps to perpetuate it.

Specific Reversal

Specific reversals are the most common and are usually limited to particular situations, such as a fear of heights or of public speaking. With specific reversals, there are no other major issues to address, except the particular problem you wish to eliminate (for example, fear of heights). The central question of specific reversals is whether you are ready to eliminate the problem *now*. Although you might want to get over the problem, at the present time, you may be blocked on letting it go. You also may be blocked on whether you are ready to eliminate the problem in its entirety.

Criteria-Related Reversal

The fourth type of reversal, criteria-related reversal, also deals with specific issues or beliefs. This type of reversal centers on issues such as whether you believe you *deserve* to get over a problem or whether you will *allow* yourself to get over a problem. For example, people who suffer from severe guilt may want to get over the guilt, but unconsciously they may believe that they deserve to feel guilty. In this case, the issue of what they believe they *deserve* must be treated before further treatments can be effective.

Mini-Reversal

A mini-reversal can occur after there has been some treatment progress. In this situation, you experience considerable progress in getting over a problem but then, at some point, your progress comes to a halt. Some of the problem remains and the treatment sequence stops being effective. Most likely, you are not yet ready to completely let go of the problem. Mini-reversals can appear in the form of specific, deep-level, or criteria-related reversals. In these situations, you must determine which of the reversals is preventing you from completely eliminating your problem.

Recurring Reversal

When you experience significant progress in eliminating a problem but then a resurgence of your original level of distress occurs, that frequently indicates a recurring reversal. This is not merely a halt in progress, as is the case with mini-reversals, but rather a recurrence, often at the level of distress that existed prior to the treatment. This is important to recognize because you can make the mistake of thinking that a treatment process isn't effective. With recurring reversals, patience is required because you must start again and complete the entire treatment sequence from the beginning to the end. You must also reexamine the possibility of each type of reversal and treat any reversal that you believe is blocking your success.

Once you understand the various types of reversals, you will be able to identify the specific ways that you sabotage situations in your life. The mind-body relationship is very concrete. Therefore, the more specific you are, the better the results will be. In general, repeated treatment for psychological reversal is necessary for addictive problems, for very competitive people, or when the problem has resulted in a very low energy level. Actually, if your problem has been resistant to change, regardless of ongoing efforts on your part, you are probably reversed in that area. If your problem involves shame, guilt, apathy, or long-term grief, your energy level is most likely very low, and it is likely that you are reversed. This will require you to have patience. You must be willing to treat yourself on a daily basis for several weeks to eliminate the problem. While you are doing this, however, you will continue to receive some benefits from the treatment.

TREATING PSYCHOLOGICAL REVERSALS

As we have been discussing, before using one of the treatment sequences in the chapters that follow, you need to determine if a psychological reversal exists, as it will block the successful elimination of a problem. When you are reversed, the first step is to accept yourself and the fact that you have the problem. This doesn't mean that you aren't going to change. Before you can change, however, you must accept yourself with your flaws.

The following questions are designed to help you to determine which type of reversal may be affecting you. Many of these questions are directed at your unconscious mind, so don't allow yourself to hesitate when responding. The first answer you choose is most likely to be the correct one. The purpose of completing this analysis is to help you understand the underlying beliefs that may be preventing you from achieving your goals. If you have an energy reversal in a particular area, it will impede your treatment. It is essential that these beliefs be explored with each problem you try to eliminate. Note that you may find you have different beliefs associated with different problems.

Once you have completed the analysis for a particular problem, use the treatments that are provided to correct any reversals that are sabotaging your life. Then, immediately locate and use the treatment sequence for that particular problem. If you wait— even for five or ten minutes—before using the treatment sequence, the reversal may reoccur and block the treatment. Once you treat the imbalance in your energy, it is far less likely that the reversal will reoccur. If there is a delay after you treat a reversal, just treat it again before using the appropriate treatment sequence.

> After you treat a reversal, you must immediately begin the treatment sequence and treat the problem that is causing you distress.

Determining Massive Reversal

1.   Think about your life in general over the last year. Do you feel you have been miserable?

2.   Are two or more major parts of your life negative, such as your work or your relationships?

3.   Have you been chronically depressed?

4.   Do you have a long-term addiction or an "addictive personality"?

5.   Are feelings of shame, guilt, apathy, or long-term grief major problems for you?

If you answered "yes" to anyone of the questions, this may indicate that you have a massive reversal (whole-life reversal), in which many aspects of your life are negatively impacted. A massive reversal's presence is supported by the fact that the problems are chronic and multifaceted.

TREATMENT

Find the Sore Spot (SS) on the left side of your chest (see diagram 3). Rub that spot while thinking or saying to yourself three times, "I deeply and profoundly accept myself with all of my problems and limitations." Even if you don't believe it right now, say it to yourself anyway. In fact, the more you don't believe it, the more important it is that you do this treatment. You need to repeat this treatment daily and always before you use any of the treatments in the following chapters.

Once a massive reversal is treated, it is common for other reversals that must also be treated to become apparent. It will take many treatments of massive reversals before the energy remains increasingly positive. You will, however, feel some progressive relief and change each time you treat the reversal. The concern is that massive reversals tend to reoccur repeatedly. They also require numerous treatments. In fact, daily treatments for massive reversal are needed before you can be sure you have eliminated this problem.

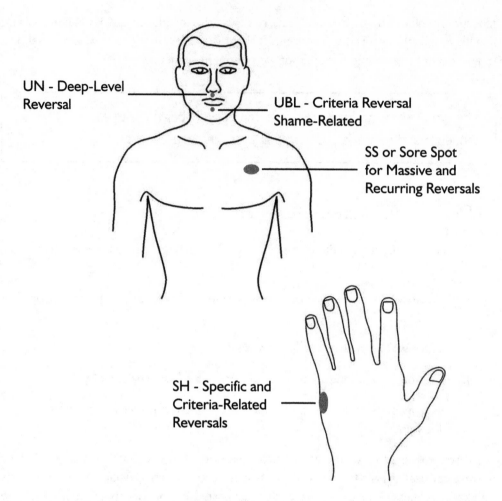

UN - Deep-Level Reversal

UBL - Criteria Reversal Shame-Related

SS or Sore Spot for Massive and Recurring Reversals

SH - Specific and Criteria-Related Reversals

Diagram Three: The Treatment Points for Specific Types of Reversals

Determining Deep-Level Reversal

Which of the statements below accurately defines your belief about the problem you want to treat?

_____ I will get over this problem.

_____ I will continue to have this problem.

If your answer was "I will continue to have this problem," a deep-level reversal may be present. This means that at a deep level you may believe you are unable to get over your problem. To help you change this belief, you must build your sense of pride and your self-confidence.

TREATMENT

While you are thinking about a situation where your problem occurs, tap above your upper lip, directly under your nose (UN), and say three times, "I accept myself even if I never get over this problem."

Determining Specific Reversal

Which of the statements below accurately defines your belief about the problem you want to treat:

_____ I am ready to eliminate this problem.

_____ I am not ready to eliminate this problem.

Sometimes, there are several problems going on at once. In some instances, you may not be ready to eliminate one of them. If you answered "I am not ready to eliminate this problem," you may want to make a list of your problems, ranking them in the order you think would be best to solve them. Don't necessarily start by treating the problem that annoys you the most. It may be easier to begin by treating the less frustrating issues.

TREATMENT

Think about a problem or situation where this problem occurs and then tap on the Side of Hand (SH) while thinking or saying to yourself three times, "I deeply accept myself even though I have this problem."

Determining Criteria-Related Reversals

Determine which of the following statements accurately define your beliefs about the problem you want to treat.

1. _____ I deserve to get over this problem.

    _____ I don't deserve to get over this problem.

2. _____ I feel it's safe to get over this problem.

    _____ I feel it's not safe to get over this problem.

3. _____ I am scared to try to deal with this problem.

    _____ I am not scared to try to deal with this problem.

4. _____ I will feel deprived if I get over this problem.

_____ I will not feel deprived if I get over this problem.

5. _____ I will allow myself to get over this problem.

_____ I will not allow myself to get over this problem.

6. _____ I will do what is necessary to get over this problem.

_____ I will not do what is necessary to get over this problem.

TREATMENTS

Select the belief questions above that you feel best identify your problem and match their number to the statements below. While thinking about your problem or about a situation where your problem occurs, tap on the Side of Hand (SH) and think to yourself three times:
"I deeply accept myself even if":

1. I deserve to have this problem.

2. It's not safe for me to get over this problem.

3. I'm scared to get over this problem.

4. I will feel deprived if I get over this problem.

5. I will not allow myself to get over this problem.

6. I will not do what is necessary to get over this problem.

Psychological Reversal Sample Treatment

Imagine that you have experienced too much rejection in your personal life and you are feeling frustrated or angry about a current social event. After reviewing the belief questions on reversals, you decide that not only are you feeling rejected, but you believe that you will continue to have this problem (deep-level reversal). Your reasoning is that although you are experiencing rejection, you are confused because you don't know why it occurs or how to stop it. Not understanding what you are doing wrong or how to change a problem is very common when you are reversed.

To treat a deep-level reversal, tap above your upper lip directly under your nose (UN) and say to yourself three times, "I accept myself even if I never get over this problem." You can personalize the statement and say, "I accept myself even if I never stop being rejected."

Although this sounds like an odd treatment, you must accept your situation, that is, getting rejected, before you can create change in your life. Once you have treated yourself for the reversal, you are ready to use the specific treatment sequences for rejection, and eliminate the energy imbalance that is causing your problem. If you are still feeling angry about past situations, you will need to use the treatment sequence for anger as well.

You may need to repeat this treatment to ensure long-term, permanent success, although you will immediately become more confident and less likely to seek out people who will reject you. You will also be better able to handle rejection and to focus on supportive people and situations in the future.

Once you have identified any of the above reversals and treated yourself for them, you may be able to identify other beliefs that may be blocking you from changing. Once again, identify the type of reversal and treat it.

SUMMARY

You cannot change a problem in your life unless you are willing to accept that, to some degree, you are involved in creating it. It is true that a problem can occur in your life without it being your fault; however, your response to it is key to your ability to cope with that problem. The core of a psychological reversal is that if your energy levels become very low due to problems in your past, your energy about a specific situation can become negative. Once that happens, your view of that or another situation and your idea of how to resolve a problem can become distorted. If you are reversed, you will actively sabotage a goal that you are consciously seeking to achieve. Your behaviors and beliefs at the time, however, will feel appropriate. That is why it is essential to treat any possible reversals before you employ a specific energy treatment.

If an energy treatment is not effective, a psychological reversal is usually the culprit. This chapter has examined the main types of reversals and their matching treatments. Once you learn how to treat reversals, you are ready to read the chapters about specific problems and to use the corresponding treatment sequences to eliminate them. Remember, if you are reversed, the energy treatments for specific problems will not be effective. Therefore, always treat yourself for reversals before using other treatment sequences to eliminate specific problems.

Everyone Is Scared of Something

*There are two fears really. The original wound from way back when and
the fear of giving up our defenses and having to face the pain, so our fear
becomes a roadblock that we service and maintain.*

—Merle Shain

"No Fear!" and "Just Do It!" are two popular product slogans that exemplify a commonly accepted cultural idea that you aren't supposed to think of yourself as phobic or as having fears. The message is that you should be able to handle your situation, block out the fear, get out there, and make it happen. We have learned, however, that being fearless in one part of your life doesn't mean that you are immune to fears in other areas. For example, a firefighter will voluntarily enter a burning building to save another person's life, which is admirable and courageous. The same firefighter, however, may become paralyzed with fear at the thought of flying in an airplane.

Many situations, such as flying, which can easily be handled by most children, can cause serious panic for individuals who are fearless in most other areas of their lives. This is the nature of fears and phobias: What causes panic in one person has no effect on another. Fears and phobias have little to do with whether a person is weak or lacks courage. Instead, they are about energy imbalances. Once these imbalances are treated, you will be able to better cope with the presence of fear in your life.

A common strategy for coping with fears is learning to avoid the situations that create them and trying to accept this part of yourself. Unfortunately, your fears and phobias are not overcome easily, and their reason for existing has very little to do with logic. The result is that people tend to feel ashamed because they can't overcome their fears, especially if their fears are not socially acceptable. In truth, most people are not going to learn how to overcome their fears without some form of therapeutic help.

In this chapter, we will help you conquer your fears using energy psychology. We will address common phobias, such as a fear of flying, as well as the fears that affect your ability to be successful in sports, at work, and in various intimidating situations.

HOW DO FEARS GET STARTED?

Some fears can be traced to a single traumatic incident, others seem to be learned, and still others exist as part of our natural defense mechanisms. You might be able to trace the origins of a fear, such as imagining monsters in the bedroom closet. When you are in the dark, your diminished ability to interpret noises and the shapes created by shadows or objects can elicit a fear response because your primary sense—vision—is incapable of determining whether you are safe. Isn't it mysterious that children who have never seen a monster (and no matter how many times you check the closet) believe that something dangerous exists? Most people have a natural fear of the unknown, a defensive guard that is designed to protect us.

Fears can also be generated by a single traumatic incident. If someone is in a car accident, for example, he or she may develop a fear of driving or even riding in a car. This type of fear is easily understood. That is, if the person has been in a severe car accident, being in a similar situation understandably re-creates feelings that existed at the time of the initial trauma.

Other fears are learned and are commonly reflective of societal beliefs. For example, some people have a fear of alien abduction. In these cases, accurate information and experience can often help to erase the fear. All too often, however, people are ashamed and don't seek outside help that can help them to eliminate their fears.

An energy-related theory about fears is that they can be inherited by way of subtle energy. One way of looking at this is to imagine that your great-great-great-great grandfather suffered a traumatic event that has been passed on to you as a phobia or fear. For example, if your ancestor had a fall from the top of a tree and from then on avoided high places, your fear may have initiated with that incident. Generations later, you now have a fear of heights for no good reason of which you are consciously aware.

William McDougall (1938) conducted one of the longest experiments in the history of psychology. It lasted more than fifteen years and strongly suggested that animals can inherit fears. So why not people, too? Whether or not you believe in subtle energy transference, do keep in mind that it's often impossible to determine the cause of any fear or phobia. No matter what theory you try to employ, you will find many holes in it. What holds true for one person often doesn't affect another.

Have you ever thought about why your fears exist? In some cases, fears prevent people from achieving important goals in their lives. For example, having a fear of success may be reflected in the fear of behaving responsibly. That is, once a certain income or position is achieved, the person may feel that he or she will be obligated to assume greater responsibilities. So, by avoiding the success as well as the responsibilities, the fear becomes a vehicle for self-sabotage.

Although the origin of your fears and phobias can be complex, the good news is that with energy psychology, you don't need to understand your problems to successfully eliminate them. If you simply treat your fears one at a time, you will eventually get to the root of your problem, and eventually you will eliminate that as well. Energy psychology doesn't require you to reexamine your life. Instead, it is a simple process done by rote that will be effective once you identify the fears in your life.

IDENTIFYING YOUR FEARS

Generally, identifying and dealing with fear is a lifelong process. As you deal with one fear, your growth and development will lead inevitably to other fears that you must address and deal with as well.

There are a number of ways to identify the fears that block your growth. Jeffers (1987) divides fears into three levels:

1. Level one includes fears of normal events that you experience, such as aging or dying, and fears that require action, such as test taking.

2. Level two fears involve your sense of self, and include fears such as rejection or having to deal with intimidating people.

3. The last level is what underlies all fears: the belief that you can't handle the situations in your life.

According to Jeffers, level three is the core of all fears. She uses the phrase, "I can handle ..." to examine fears. For instance, if someone is going on a job interview and fears not getting the job, this is translated as, "I can't handle not getting this job." According to Jeffers, it is your fear of not being able to handle the situation that creates your fear sensations. Although we agree with this position to some extent, we also believe that it is an underlying energy disruption that ultimately causes fear and fearful thoughts. The goal of this chapter is to help you learn to eliminate the anxiety and the sensations that are associated with your fears.

From an energy psychology viewpoint, people who become stuck in levels one and two may have criteria-related or specific reversals, while the level-three person is most likely reflective of a massive reversal. The reversals at the root of these levels must be treated before using the energy treatments. Otherwise, as noted previously, the treatment sequences won't be effective.

You should first identify and then write down the fears that are affecting your life, as well as writing a brief example of the specific fear situation. It can be as simple as, "I'm embarrassed that I can't do (whatever it is)." Or, it can be a fear that is blocking you from achieving an important goal. If your fear is complex with many parts, identify and write down all of the fears that contribute to the overall totality of your complex fear.

For example, if you are afraid of getting old, you may also fear dying, lost opportunities, or the reality that certain desired events are not going to happen in your life. Note that with complex fears, you may be required to treat each problem individually to experience relief.

Four Phobias and Fears

In the following pages, fear is divided into four groups and each is addressed individually. These groups are not radically different from each other. However, to achieve results with energy psychology treatments, it is important to be as specific as possible. The four groups of fears include:

1. Basic phobias, that is, fear of insects, animals, elevators, heights, flying

2. Related fears, that is, test taking, fear of success, public speaking, meeting new people

3. Intimidating situations

4. Panic attacks

The treatment section is also divided into four areas. Although they overlap, our goal is to provide treatments that encompass most of the fears that people encounter. If your specific fear is not listed, locate the group that best matches your fear and then use that group's treatment sequence to address your specific fear. It is important to note that energy psychology will rid you only of *unrealistic* fears. Feeling fear when you are in dangerous or truly life-threatening situations is a healthy reaction.

BASIC PHOBIAS AND FEARS

The first group of fears includes fear of insects, animals, heights, elevators, and flying. The treatment for each of these is identical. We will briefly discuss each situation and then provide the relevant treatments.

Fear of Insects

It is embarrassing when a warm day arrives and you inevitably find an insect in your house or, worse, it finds you. If you are allergic to insect bites, such as bee stings, to some extent your fear is natural and understandable. We still assume that your goal is to not panic, because panicking only increases your chances of getting stung. However, if your fear extends to all insects, even those that cannot harm you, your fear is irrational. Most fears regarding insects are irrational.

Fear of Animals

This fear is very similar to fearing insects, especially in that it's an unrealistic or irrational fear. It's natural to be nervous about large, barking dogs that can physically reach you, but panic will not help you and most likely will make the situation worse. So, you have to evaluate the situation. Can the animal you are fearing hurt you? Is it probable that the animal will hurt you? Remember, energy psychology will rid you only of *unrealistic* fears. For example, large, dangerous, barking dogs will still be cause for concern. The good news is that you can eliminate the unrealistic fears you have about animals, such as mice, cats, and/or dogs that are not dangerous.

Fear of Heights

The fear of heights is a very common fear that most people manage by avoidance. In fact, sometimes people have trouble getting in touch with their feelings of fear because they have avoided heights so well. In that case, you may need to find a safe situation that sparks your fear again to help you treat it. What generally happens with a fear of heights is that when you go out on a balcony and get near the railing, you start to feel sensations that (to you) imply that you are losing control.

One reason for this feeling may be that as you peer over the edge, lines from the structure from which you are looking down converge as they approach the ground. These converging lines of perspective can create disturbing sensations. At the same time, you may have intrusive thoughts of falling or jumping. These sensations create the negative thoughts that scare you.

The goal of treating the fear of heights is to eliminate the negative feeling associated with this sensation. Once you have accomplished this, the negative thoughts will be less likely to appear. You can use the same sequence that is provided for all phobias and fears. However, you will not only treat for fear of heights in general, but will also treat the disturbing sensations you experience, such as your fear of jumping or falling and your fear of losing control. If you think about each one and rate your feelings, you can judge which needs to be treated.

The outcome will be different for each person. For some people, ongoing treatments are needed because the visual stimulus that creates the fear of heights is very strong. Regardless, the treatment, which takes only one minute to complete, will provide relief. If you know that you are going to be in a situation that involves heights, be sure to treat yourself beforehand. And, as always, treat yourself for reversals first.

Fear of Elevators

You must clearly identify your fear of elevators. Is it a matter of being out of control? Are you afraid of being in an enclosed space (claustrophobia)? Is your fear based on the sensation that occurs while riding in an elevator? Are you imagining that something bad will happen, such as getting stuck between floors and being trapped? The better you are at identifying the thoughts and beliefs associated with your fear, the faster and more thoroughly you can resolve it by employing energy psychology treatments.

Fear of Flying

This situation is similar to fear of elevators, although a number of additional elements come into play. You should treat each possible reason for your fear, such as the fear of taking off and landing, fear of being out of control, fear of flight turbulence, fear of feeling trapped in an enclosed area, or any form of catastrophic thinking. Although some people think that fear of flying is the same as fear of heights, actually, they are quite distinct. Most people who have fear of heights are amazed that they do not experience that fear when looking out the window of an airplane. This is because the proximity of converging lines of perspective (which is the primary cause of fearing heights) is not present.

Treatment Sequence for Basic Fears

1. Think about a situation that scares you. It should be a single, specific event, such as a bee flying around your bedroom, being in an enclosed place, or riding in a car. Try to be as specific as possible. For example, it is more effective to treat a fear of German shepherds rather than treat a fear of all dogs. Rate your level of fear on a scale of 0 to 10, with 10 representing the highest level of distress and 0 indicating no stress at all.

2. Treat for the possibility of reversal by tapping repeatedly on the Side of Hand (SH) or rubbing the Sore Spot (SS) while thinking or saying three times, "I deeply accept myself even though I am scared of (name your fear)." It also may be helpful to tap the SH or rub the SS while saying, "I accept myself with all my problems and limitations."

3. Look at diagram 4 and the treatment sequence for basic phobias and fears directly under the diagram to identify the locations for the meridian points for Under Eye (UE), Under Arm (UA), and Under Collarbone (UCB). While thinking about the feared item (don't get into it so much that you experience any major discomfort during the process), tap five times at each of these meridian points. Tap them in the following order: 1 → 2 → 3. Tap only hard enough to feel it. The tapping shouldn't cause any pain.

4. Again, rate your distress on a 0 to 10 scale (a number should just pop into your mind). If there is no decrease, go back to step 2 and cycle through the sequence again. If there is not a decrease after three attempts, this is

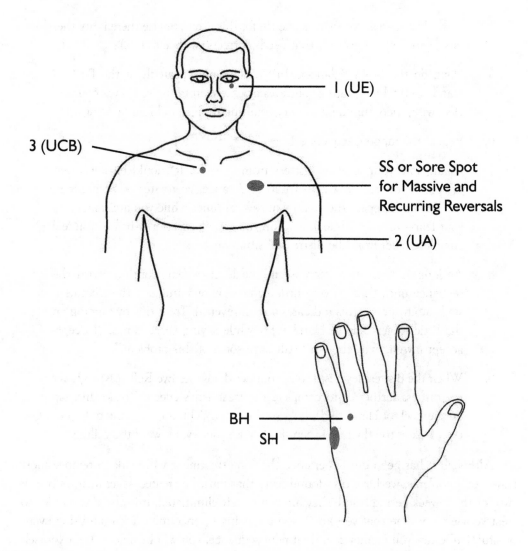

Diagram Four: Fear of Insects, Animals, Heights, Elevators, and Flying

Treatment Sequence for Basic Phobias and Fears

Meridian		Location
Under Eye (UE)	1	Under the center of the eye on tip of bone
Under Arm (UA)	2	Six inches below and under the armpit
Under Collarbone (UCB)	3	One inch under collarbone near throat

probably not an appropriate sequence for this event, or else there is another sabotaging belief (reversal) that needs correction. (See step 8.)

5. Next, do the Brain Balancer (BB) by tapping repeatedly at the Back of Hand (BH) while rotating your eyes clockwise, rotating your eyes counter-clockwise, then humming a tune, counting to five, and humming again.

6. Repeat the tapping sequence 1 → 2 → 3.

7. Again, rate your level of distress from 0 to 10. It should be lower yet. When the distress is within the 0 to 2 range, go to step 9. Sometimes, you'll need to repeat the treatment several times while you are imagining your fear—or even while you are in the actual situation—before you feel complete relief from the distressful situation.

8. As long as there is a decrease in the level of fear, continue with the sequence until there is very little or no fear remaining. If the treatment stalls at any point, this indicates a mini-reversal. Treat this by tapping on the little finger Side of Hand (SH) while saying three times, "I deeply accept myself, even though I still have some of this problem."

9. When the distress level is 0 to 2, consider doing the Eye Roll (ER) to lower the distress further or to complete the treatment's effects. To do this, tap on the Back of Hand (BH), hold your head straight, and, moving only your eyes, look at the floor and then slowly raise your eyes toward the ceiling.

Although it has been our experience that one treatment will work to remove most fear-based problems, we have also found fears that must be treated several times over a two- or three-week period before they are completely eliminated. It is also a good idea to treat yourself any time that you know you are going to encounter a fear-arousing event or situation. Once you memorize a treatment sequence, you will be able to treat yourself for that event or situation even if your fear starts to return.

The first step is always to try to treat the fear/phobia itself. If, after several attempts, the treatment sequence doesn't create the results you want, then we encourage you to examine your beliefs: What are you telling yourself about your fear? Do you believe you can be hurt? Are you imagining the worst that can happen to you in a fear-based situation? Being aware of your beliefs will help you to break any habits that are helping to perpetuate the problem. However, it will be much easier to change your beliefs once you have completed energy treatments on the most obvious aspects of your fear.

Testing Treatment Effectiveness

It is important to test the effectiveness of a treatment. For most situations, you can easily do this with a friend. For example, once you have treated a fear, place yourself in a situation where it is comfortable for you to test it. If you have a fear of elevators, for example, you can get on an elevator with a friend and ride the elevator up or down only one floor. Of course, airplanes are an exception to this strategy. In this instance, you can prove the effectiveness of this technique by using it for another fear and testing that result. Or, you can go to an airport and think about flying while you are watching planes take off and land. Once you see the positive results of energy treatments, your confidence will grow and you'll soon realize that you have a technique that can help you, even in the most anxiety-provoking situations, such as flying. **Please note:** Reversals are very common with fears, especially fears that you don't have the opportunity to experience regularly. Therefore, always treat yourself for a reversal before each treatment.

Treatment for Special Considerations

There are specific phobias that may require a more vigorous treatment approach. These include claustrophobia, fear of spiders, and anxiety related to flight turbulence. You may need to repeat this sequence three times before you feel complete relief from your distress. You still use the same treatment points listed on diagram 4, but you need to tap the points in the following order:

Treatment Sequence for Special Consideration Phobias and Fears

Meridian		Location
Under Eye (UE)	1	Under the center of the eye on tip of bone
Under Collarbone (UCB)	2	One inch under collarbone near throat
Under Arm (UA)	3	Six inches below and under the armpit
Under Collarbone (UCB)	4	One inch under collarbone near throat
Under Eye (UE)	5	Under the center of the eye on tip of bone

RELATED PHOBIAS AND FEARS

The second group of fears includes test taking, public speaking, and meeting new people. Each of these situations involves a fear of how we will be evaluated or judged by others.

Test Anxiety

Tests are a very real and powerful tool that can have a strong impact on your life. They are also a huge business For example, every year millions of students take college entrance exams, such as the Scholastic Aptitude Test (SAT), Graduate Record Exam (GRE), Law School Admission Test (LSAT), and Medical College Admission Test (MCAT). Many people must take exams that are required to obtain specific licenses, certifications, and, in some cases, employment.

Unfortunately, simply complaining that tests are "unfair" won't help you. At some point, tests are going to have an impact on your life. Don't allow anxiety to prevent you from doing your best.

First, determine which of the following statements about test anxiety apply to you:

1. You know the material, but when you take the test you freeze.

2. You don't know the material and you freeze when you take the test.

The first statement indicates pure test anxiety. In this situation, you know the material, you may have taken preparation courses (for the SAT, LSAT, etc.), and you have studied on your own. You have evidence that you know the material, but when you take the test, your mind seems to go blank. The result is that you can answer the easier questions, but you cannot focus and solve the moderate and difficult questions. This means that anxiety is blocking you from taking the test to the best of your ability and you should treat yourself for test anxiety.

If your text anxiety is caused by the fact that you don't know the material and you don't study for the test, you must determine what life circumstances and/or beliefs cause you to behave in this manner. There are several possible reasons for your behavior, and you must examine each before you can ascertain which one is blocking you. It is entirely appropriate to experience some anxiety when you must take a test for which you have not studied and don't know the material.

Our experience indicates that a number of issues may exist that create test anxiety in these categories. In the first situation, it may be pure test anxiety, because you know the material, but start to panic in a test situation. In the other situation, however, you may be sabotaging your chances for success by not studying for tests, by being impatient, or by fearing success. If you find it difficult to study for extended periods of time, it may be helpful to do the following treatment sequence before treating yourself for test anxiety.

TREATMENT FOR IMPATIENCE WHEN STUDYING FOR A TEST

Imagine you are going to study for two hours. Tap under your nose (UN on diagram 5) and say three times, "I accept myself even though I can never study for two hours at one time." Then, tap the Side of Hand (SH) or rub the Sore Spot (SS) and say three times, "I accept myself even though I get impatient with studying and quit." Next, tap five times on your Eyebrow (EB). If this does not significantly reduce your impatience, then use the treatment for impatience and frustration in chapter 12. Lastly, complete the treatment sequence for test anxiety.

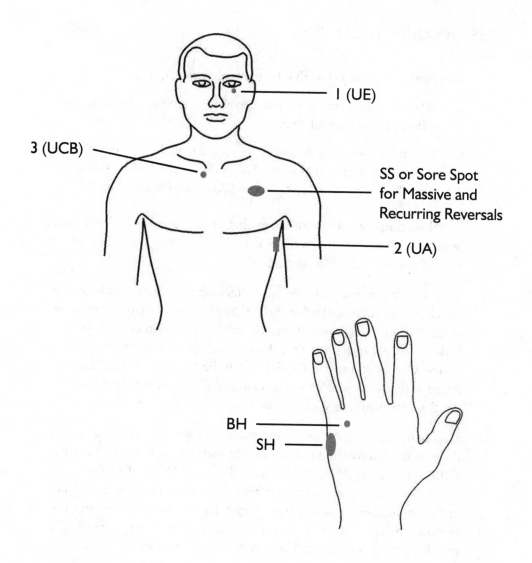

Diagram Five: Fear of Tests, Public Speaking, and Meeting New People

Treatment Sequence for Test Anxiety

Meridian		Location
Under Eye (UE)	1	Under the center of the eye on tip of bone
Under Arm (UA)	2	Six inches under the armpit
Under Collarbone (UCB)	3	One inch under collarbone near throat

TEST ANXIETY TREATMENT

1. Identify the example below that best describes your situation:

    a. When you take the test, you become so anxious that you can't perform to your actual ability.

    b. You anticipate failing at some level or will not accept yourself if you score below a certain number. For example, you believe this statement: "If I don't score 1100 on the SAT, then I am a failure."

    Now, think about the situation that creates anxiety and rate your level of test anxiety on a scale of 0 to 10, 10 representing the highest level of distress and 0 indicating none.

2. Treat for the possibility of reversals by tapping repeatedly on the Side of Hand (SH) or rubbing the Sore Spot (SS) while thinking or saying three times, "I deeply accept myself even though I freeze when I take tests." Or, "I deeply accept myself even if I don't score high enough on this test." It also may be helpful to tap the SH or rub the SS while saying, "I accept myself with all my problems and limitations." It is always best to try to put the statement into your own words.

3. Look at diagram 5 and the treatment sequence for test anxiety under the diagram to identify the locations for the meridian points for Under Eye (UE), Under Arm (UA), and Under Collarbone (UCB). While thinking about your test anxiety (don't get into it so much that you experience any major discomfort during the process), tap five times at each of these meridian points. Tap them in the following order: 1 → 2 → 3. Tap only hard enough to feel it. The tapping shouldn't cause any pain.

4. Again, rate your distress on a 0 to 10 scale (a number should just pop into your mind). If there is no decrease, go back to step 2 and cycle through the sequence again. If there is not a decrease after three attempts, this is probably not an appropriate treatment sequence for this situation, or else there is another sabotaging belief (reversal) that needs correction. (See step 8.)

5. Next, do the Brain Balancer (BB) by tapping repeatedly at the Back of Hand (BH) while rotating your eyes first clockwise, then rotating your eyes counterclockwise, then humming a tune, counting to five, and humming again.

6. Repeat the tapping sequence 1 → 2 → 3.

7. Again, rate your level of distress from 0 to 10. It should be lower yet. When the distress is within the 0 to 2 range, go to step 9. Sometimes, you'll need to repeat the treatment several times while you are imagining your fear—or even while you are in the actual situation—before your test anxiety no longer affects your performance.

8. As long as there is a decrease in the level of test anxiety, continue with the treatment sequence until there is very little or no anxiety remaining. If the treatment stalls at any point, this indicates a mini-reversal. Treat this by tapping on the little finger Side of Hand (SH) while saying three times, "I deeply accept myself, even though I still have some of this problem."

9. When the distress level is 0 to 2, consider doing the Eye Roll (ER) to lower the distress further or to complete the treatment effects. To do this, tap on the Back of Hand (BH), hold your head straight and, moving only your eyes, look at the floor and slowly raise your eyes up toward the ceiling.

Public Speaking and Meeting New People

Although we have not directly addressed public speaking or meeting new people, the formula and treatments are identical to those used for treating other kinds of anxiety. As we briefly address each topic below, remember that a fear of success is a reversal and should be treated as such because it blocks you from succeeding and may be how you sabotage yourself.

PUBLIC SPEAKING

When you speak in public, you are taking a risk and allowing yourself to be evaluated by the audience. You may also have had a negative experience in the past, such as freezing up or feeling your mind go blank. You may fear that this will happen again or you may be concerned that the audience will not like your speech. You must identify and treat each sabotaging belief before you begin the treatment sequence. For example, tap on the Side of Hand (SH) while saying three times, "I deeply accept myself even though I am afraid the audience will not like my speech." Then think about the situation of speaking in public and rate your anxiety. Next, use the treatment sequence for test anxiety, substituting the test anxiety statements with statements specific to your public speaking engagement.

MEETING NEW PEOPLE

When you meet a new person, you are evaluated. You also must decide what *you* want from this encounter. Do you want to be liked by the person or do you want him or her to do you a favor? Although a date is different from a business meeting, often the feelings are the same. Again, the first step is to identify any self-sabotaging beliefs, such as, "I'm not good enough." Or, "This never works for me." Once you treat any reversals, employ the treatment sequence for test anxiety. If you don't experience any decrease in your distress, it may be because you feel intimidated when you meet new people in a particular setting. In that case, use the treatment sequence for intimidation that is outlined in the following section.

Intimidating Situations

One of the hardest situations to overcome is not being true to yourself when you're in an intimidating situation. This covers many types of circumstances, but they are essentially caused by the same idea: You believe that you can get hurt. It is easy to feel embarrassed or ashamed when you believe that you have not been true to yourself. Most likely, however, these feelings are caused by old, unresolved emotional wounds.

Typically, emotional wounds occur when you are, or think you are, helpless. Later, even if you've developed the resources and/or skills to deal with similar situations, you react the same way you did when you were traumatized during the original experience. It's important to remember that emotional wounds create an energy imbalance that prevents you from being the most that you can be in these situations. In fact, you are quite likely to be better able to cope well with intimidating situations than you may believe.

A secondary consideration for successfully dealing with intimidating situations is that an unidentified fear has affected your sense of self, which has, in turn, produced an ongoing roadblock in your life. In this case, you must identify the fear or intimidating situation that has prevented you from achieving. You should treat any related problems that you can identify.

TREATMENT FOR INTIMIDATION

As always, you must try to be as specific as possible when using energy psychology treatments. You may want to think about "how you do" intimidating situations. That is, what are the ingredients that create intimidation for you? Here are some examples:

- Someone has power over you emotionally or physically.

- Someone has the ability to provide you with something you want.

- You give a person power over you and respond accordingly.

- Someone is aggressive and not respectful toward you.

- You believe that you cannot be successful.

1. Think about a situation that you find intimidating. The first question to ask yourself is: How do I respond to an intimidating situation? Do I

respond with anger, sit quietly, do what I am told, or become an active participant in something I don't want to do. There are many scenarios that could be examined, but the treatments are the same. This is about you and how you respond to a situation. There will always be intimidating situations in life, but once you identify your fears and the beliefs associated with them, you can eliminate these roadblocks to a better life.

Select a specific problem and rate your feelings of intimidation on a 0 to 10 scale, with 10 indicating the highest distress and 0 indicating none.

2. Below are some examples of intimidating situations/beliefs. Treat for the possibility of a reversal by tapping on the Side of Hand (SH) or rubbing the Sore Spot (SS) while thinking or saying one of the following statements three times:

   a. "I accept myself even if I think people with power are better than me."

   b. "I accept myself even if I am not myself when I am trying to achieve/obtain what I want."

   c. "I accept myself even if I believe I will get hurt."

   d. "I accept myself even if I give them (or whoever) power over me."

   e. "I accept myself even if I am not good enough to succeed in (name/describe)."

   If you can identify any other intimidating situations/beliefs, include them. Treat for the possibility of reversals by tapping on the Side of Hand (SH) or rubbing the Sore Spot (SS) and saying three times, "I accept myself even though (describe intimidating situation)." It also may be helpful to tap the SH or rub the SS while saying, "I accept myself with all my problems and limitations."

3. Look at diagram 6 and the treatment sequence for intimidation under the diagram to identify the locations for the meridian points for the Eyebrow (EB), Under Eye (UE), Under Nose (UN), Under Collarbone (UCB), and Little Finger (LF). While thinking about the intimidating situation (don't get into it so much that you experience any major discomfort during the process), tap five times at each of these meridian points. Tap them in the following order: 1 → 2 → 3 → 4 → 5. Tap only hard enough to feel it. The tapping shouldn't cause any pain.

4. Again, rate your distress on a 0 to 10 scale (a number should just pop into your mind). If there is no decrease, go back to step 2 and cycle through the sequence again. If there is not a decrease after three attempts, this

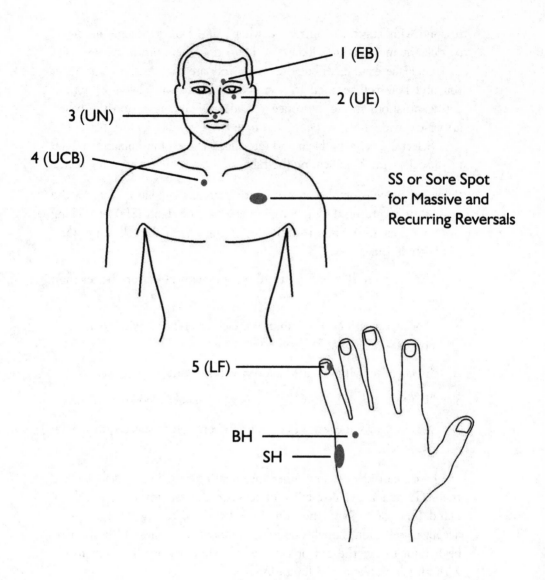

Diagram Six: Intimidating Situations

Treatment Sequence for Intimidation

Meridian		Location
Eyebrow (EB)	1	Beginning of the eyebrow near bridge of nose
Under Eye (UE)	2	Under the center of the eye on tip of bone
Under Nose (UN)	3	Above upper lip and below the center of nose
Under Collarbone (UCB)	4	One inch under collarbone near throat
Little Finger (LF)	5	Inside tip of little fingernail on the side

is probably not an appropriate sequence for this event, or else there is another sabotaging belief (reversal) that needs correction. (See step 8.)

5. Next, do the Brain Balancer (BB) by tapping repeatedly at the Back of Hand (BH) while rotating your eyes clockwise, rotating your eyes counterclockwise, then humming a tune, counting to five, and humming again.

6. Repeat the tapping sequence 1 → 2 → 3 → 4 → 5.

7. Again, rate your level of distress from 0 to 10. It should be lower yet. When the distress is within the 0 to 2 range, go to step 9. Sometimes, you'll need to repeat the treatment several times while you are imagining your intimidation—or even while you are actually in the actual intimidating situation—before the problem is completely resolved.

8. As long as there is a decrease in the level of intimidation, continue treating with the sequence until there is very little or no distress remaining. If the treatment stalls at any point, this indicates a mini-reversal. Treat this by tapping on the little finger Side of Hand (SH) while saying three times, "I deeply accept myself, even though I still feel some of this intimidation." Another type of reversal that occurs with intimidating situations deals with shame. If you have been demeaned in a situation, then you should treat for the possibility of a reversal. Tap under your bottom lip (UBL) while saying to yourself three times, "I deeply accept myself even though I feel ashamed."

9. When the distress level is 0 to 2, consider doing the Eye Roll (ER) to diminish your distress further or to complete the treatment effects. To do this, tap on the Back of Hand (BH), hold your head straight and, moving only your eyes, look at the floor and then slowly raise your eyes toward the ceiling.

Panic Attacks

One of the most frightening events that can occur in a person's life is to have a panic attack. As with most fears and phobias, there is often no rational reason why a particular situation causes a panic attack, or why a panic attack sometimes occurs "out of the blue." Yet the experience is very real for those who suffer from panic attacks and who commonly lose control over many of their physical functions. The physical responses people have during panic attacks are similar to what people experience when in completely real terrifying situations. The symptoms can be numerous and diverse depending on the situation or the type of attack the person experiences. Common symptoms include shortness of breath, rapid heart rate, disorientation, tightening of the chest, a feeling of losing control, inability to breathe, intense feelings of anxiety, and thoughts of dying or going crazy while the person is rapidly pacing.

These symptoms are part of the natural survival mechanism for dealing with imminent danger. This mechanism has been widely referred to as the "fight-or-flight syndrome." At such times, the adrenal glands rapidly secrete adrenaline to speed up your heart, allowing extra oxygen and nutrients to become available to specific areas of your body, such as your arms and legs. The tingling sensations experienced during panic indicate that blood is being drawn away from the surface of your body, so that if you were to incur a physical injury, you would not readily bleed to death. Stomach discomfort at such times is indicative of the digestive process slowing down to divert needed energy to your legs for running, arms for fighting, and so forth. A wide array of other symptoms in line with the intention of survival also takes place. During a panic attack, however, these survival mechanisms are triggered erroneously because the looming danger is being greatly exaggerated.

What appears to cause panic attacks is that anxiety-produced sensations and thoughts are interpreted catastrophically. Those false interpretations allow your thoughts and feelings to spin out of control. For example, it is normal to feel strange sensations while driving at high elevations, especially on curves where your view of the elevation is panoramically clear. Also, it is not that unusual to have a scary thought at these times, such as the thought of crashing or falling off the bridge. The problem occurs, however, when you take such notions seriously, can't let go of them, and they start to occur.

The actual thoughts that cause a panic attack may not be at a conscious level. Sometimes a frightening thought occurs, such as the possibility of losing someone dear to you, and the thought gets suppressed before you've had a chance to register it consciously. However, your survival mechanisms noticed it and interpreted it seriously as a danger, thus triggering anxiety sensations. In turn, you misinterpret the anxiety sensations as a sign that there is something dangerously wrong with you. This adds to your frightening thoughts, resulting in your thought process spinning wildly out of control and producing a panic attack.

Although scary thoughts are an aspect of panic attacks, such thoughts do not invariably produce panic. Many people have such thoughts and do not succumb to panic. The key is the energy imbalance, which allows such thoughts to become terrifying.

TREATMENT FOR PANIC ATTACKS

1. Think about a situation when you had a panic attack. It should be a single, specific memory, maybe your first panic attack or the worst one. For example, it might be a memory of feeling frozen and not being able to move. Try to be as specific as possible. The goal is to focus on an isolated, specific event, but not to focus on it so much that it could trigger an actual panic attack. Rate your level of distress about the panic attack on a scale of 0 to 10, with 10 representing the highest level of distress

and 0 indicating no stress. (Note that this treatment can be used to eliminate a panic attack while it is occurring.)

2. Treat for the possibility of reversals by tapping repeatedly on the Side of Hand (SH) or rubbing the Sore Spot (SS) while thinking or saying three times, "I deeply accept myself even though I have this panic problem." It may also be helpful to tap the SH or rub the SS while saying, "I deeply accept myself with all my problems and limitations."

3. Now look at diagram 7 and the treatment sequence for panic attacks under the diagram to identify the locations for the meridian points for Under Eye (UE), Under Arm (UA) Eyebrow (EB), Under Collarbone (UCB), and Little Finger (LF). While thinking about the panic attack (don't get into it so much that you experience any major discomfort during the process), tap five times at each of these meridian points. Tap them in the following order: 1 → 2 → 3 → 4 → 5. Tap only hard enough to feel it. The tapping shouldn't cause any pain.

4. Again, rate your distress on a 0 to 10 scale (a number should just pop into your mind). If there is no decrease, go back to step 2 and cycle through the sequence again. If there is not a decrease after three attempts, this is probably not an appropriate sequence for this event, or else there is another sabotaging belief (reversal) that needs correction. (See step 8.)

5. Next, do the Brain Balancer (BB) by tapping repeatedly at the Back of Hand (BH) while rotating your eyes clockwise, rotating your eyes counter-clockwise, then humming a tune, counting to five, and humming again.

6. Repeat the tapping sequence 1 → 2 → 3 → 4 → 5.

7. Again, rate your level of distress from 0 to 10. It should be lower yet. When your distress is within the 0 to 2 range, go to step 9. Sometimes, you'll need to repeat the treatment several times while you are imagining your problem—or even be in the actual situation—before you feel complete relief from your panic attacks.

8. As long as there is a decrease in the level of distress, continue with the treatment sequence until there are minimal feelings of panic. If the treatment stalls at any point, this indicates a mini-reversal. Treat this by tapping on the little finger Side of Hand (SH) while saying three times, "I deeply accept myself, even though I still have some of this panic problem." Then repeat the treatment sequence.

9. When the distress level is 0 to 2, consider doing the Eye Roll (ER) to lower the distress further or to complete the treatment effects. To do this, tap

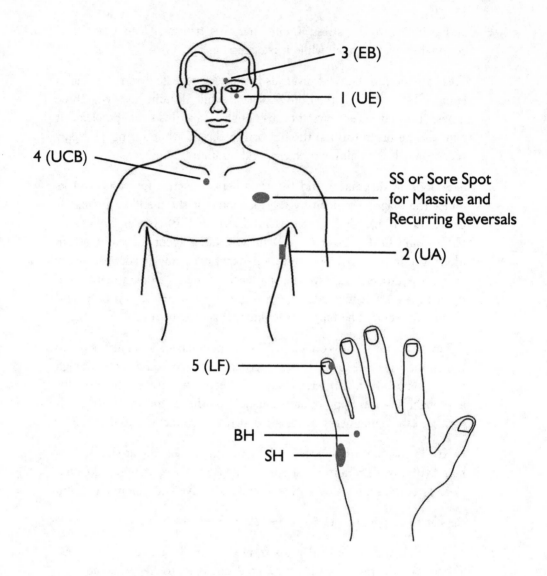

Diagram Seven: Panic Attacks

Treatment Sequence for Panic Attacks

Meridian		Location
Eyebrow (EB)	3	Beginning of the eyebrow near bridge of nose
Under Eye (UE)	1	Under the center of the eye on tip of bone
Under Arm (UA)	2	Six inches under armpit
Under Collarbone (UCB)	4	One inch under collarbone near throat
Little Finger (LF)	5	Inside tip of little fingernail on the side

on the Back of Hand (BH), hold your head straight and, moving only your eyes, look at the floor and then slowly raise your eyes toward the ceiling.

If after three attempts, your distress level is not lower, there are two recommendations. First, your panic attacks may be based on a previous traumatic experience. If this is the case, you must use the treatment for trauma in chapter 10 before the treatment sequence for panic will be effective. Second, the alternate cluster of meridian points listed below may be required to effectively treat your panic problem.

ALTERNATIVE PANIC TREATMENT

Look at diagram 7 to identify the locations for the meridians for the Under Arm (UA), Under Eye (UE) Eyebrow (EB), Under Collarbone (UCB) and Little Finger (LF). Use the same steps 1 through 9 listed above, but use the alternate sequence order of $2 \rightarrow 1 \rightarrow 3 \rightarrow 4 \rightarrow 5$.

TREATING YOURSELF IN PUBLIC PLACES

In some instances, you may be uncomfortable tapping a sequence when you are in public. Once you have successfully treated yourself using the suggested tapping treatment sequences, you can use the Touch and Breathe (Diepold 1999) technique briefly discussed in chapter 2. Instead of tapping, you can simply touch the meridian points to treat reversals and to eliminate your feelings of fear.

When you use this technique, you will be in the situation that actually causes the distress, so there is no need to rate it. Inhale, touch the Side of Hand (SH), exhale, and say to yourself, "I deeply accept myself even though I still have (name your problem)." Then, inhale and touch under your eye (UE) and exhale, then inhale and touch under your arm (UA) and exhale, and then inhale and touch under your collarbone (UCB) and exhale. Repeat this sequence until there is no more distress.

You can use this approach with any of the treatment sequences in this book; remember, however, that your problem must initially be treated by using the tapping treatment approach.

FURTHER READING

There are a number of books that go into great detail about how fears and phobias are created. Although you don't have to understand where your fears come from to successfully treat them, you may be interested in more information. We recommend *Anxiety Disorders and Phobias* by Beck and Emery (1985). Although this book is designed for clinicians, it does provide well-written explanations of the functions and relationships between anxiety and phobias. A more general book is *Feel the Fear and Do It Anyway* by Jeffers (1987).

SUMMARY

There are many fears in our lives that can hold us back. If you still feel embarrassed about any of your past behaviors or beliefs, it's time to treat them and move on with your life. Your fears have never meant that you are any less of a person. Rather, fears indicate that you have had an energy imbalance that prevents you from being at your best in certain situations. Although some people have more fears than others, what is important is that you identity your fears and treat them. The more you grow and develop, the more new fears there will be to overcome. By learning the treatment sequences in this chapter, however, you have gained a new tool that will help you to clear those hurdles successfully.

8

Overcoming Anger, Rage, Guilt, Shame, Embarrassment, Jealousy, Loneliness, and Rejection

*Anger is a passion that makes people feel alive and that they matter
and are in charge of their lives. So people often feel a need to renew their anger
long after the cause of it has died. It is a protection against the helplessness . . .
and for a while makes them feel less vulnerable.*

—Merle Shain

In this chapter we explore the emotions of anger, rage, guilt, shame, embarrassment, jealousy, loneliness, and rejection, along with treatments for each. In addition, we introduce a unique treatment that can be used with almost any problem. These treatments can be used alone or in combination with resolving other problems you want to eliminate.

All of the treatments in this book are only as effective as your willingness and commitment to apply them consistently to achieve the results you desire. If you read about a particular treatment and then apply it haphazardly, you won't experience much in the way of results. The treatments depend entirely on your *dedication*. If you have a tendency to not be diligent, you ought to suspect that you have a psychological reversal (see chapter 6). As always, it's advisable for you to test for and correct psychological reversal before attempting any treatment sequence.

RELEASING ANGER

It's possible that anger is America's number one emotion. A survey done nearly a decade ago found anger to be a significant problem within the work setting (*Wall Street Journal* 1999). If anything, the problem has only worsened. When people get together with friends, they often share stories about the situations that upset them at work that week. These conversations are frequently a way to find relief by sharing feelings, and they give people the opportunity to find some humor in their situation. For some people, however, anger is a chronic problem. Many situations at work or at home can instantly provoke their anger. Usually, such individuals see themselves as victims of the events in their lives, and their anger is a response to their feelings of helplessness. This does not mean that all anger is unjustified; there is no shortage of unfortunate situations that cause legitimate anger, such as people whose behavior is rude or cruel.

The best strategy for interacting with anger is to accept and deal with the situations that caused it. Some people, however, once angered, behave irrationally, leaping into the fight, and often making the situation worse. It is clear that the more time you spend being angry about situations you can neither control nor change, the more you reinforce your tendency to use anger—even if this solution never works to your advantage.

Carol and Helen: A Case Study

What follows is a description of how energy treatments helped a family situation that was creating a great deal of anger. Carol was angry with her mother-in-law, Helen, whom she believed was extremely self-centered and who often made cruel remarks about Carol's husband Mark. The real issue was that Mark had a poor sense of self-esteem and he drank too much, especially when he had to deal with family problems. Carol largely blamed Helen for her husband's behaviors. Also, during the years of their marriage, Helen had often excluded Carol and the children from extended family gatherings. The situation got so bad that even the mention of Helen's name immediately made Carol defensive.

Carol's resentment toward Helen was also interfering with her marriage, and possibly preventing Mark from dealing with his alcohol problem. At the very least, it gave him an excuse to go out drinking, because they had so many arguments about his mother.

The solution was not to be found in simply discussing the reasons why Carol ought to overcome her anger. Any attempts to talk along these lines were met with a tremendous amount of resistance, as would be expected. Therefore, it was suggested to Carol that energy treatments might help to at least take the edge off the emotional upset she felt toward Helen. That way, if Carol absolutely had to be around Helen for some unforeseen reason, she would be better able to cope. Carol agreed.

After taking Carol through a rather extended energy treatment for this problem—about twenty minutes—her response to her thoughts about Helen changed rather dramatically. The change occurred in stages: Initially, she felt only anger and resentment;

after a few rounds of the anger-releasing treatment, she felt a reduced degree of irritation; next, her irritation dissolved into feelings of sorrow; and, finally, she felt a sense of relief. After the energy treatment had been completed, Carol said, "I guess Helen just can't help herself. I wonder if she's struggled with this problem, too?" From then on, Carol found it much easier and more comfortable to be around Helen. In time, even their relationship improved and Carol and Mark were regularly invited to family events. Carol also learned how to apply energy treatment to her relationship issues with Mark, and their relationship improved as well.

Forgiveness

Many people who have experienced trauma and other negative experiences understandably harbor anger about those events and those who caused them. Once a person has been violated, every conscious and even unconscious review of the event causes emotional upset. Anger is one of the principal emotions here; it is associated with blaming, as well as with an inability to forgive the circumstances, the other people involved, and even oneself.

It's normal to object to the idea of forgiving someone who has wronged you. In fact, you may feel that your forgiveness would be equivalent to saying that what the person did was okay. However, this is not what forgiveness is about. When you forgive someone, you still recognize that what the other person did was wrong—otherwise, forgiveness would make little sense. When you forgive, you don't condone the other person's behavior. The behavior is obviously wrong. You would not condone the behavior of someone who severely mistreated you anymore than you would condone the behavior of a burglar or a rapist. It might be possible, however, to achieve another level of understanding and to forgive the person. When we forgive, there is a clear distinction between the person and the deed.

Still, you may strongly object to forgiveness. You may wonder, for instance, how you can forgive someone for violating you or for committing an atrocity. How do you let go of your anger when it seems so justified? The idea of forgiving under such circumstances may cause you to shudder. Nonetheless, there is another way to think about forgiveness.

Comedian Buddy Hackett said that he couldn't understand being angry at someone because, "While you're angry at them, they're out dancing." Guess who gets to suffer? Certainly not the person who did you wrong. Rather, you are the one stuck with the emotional consequences of remaining angry. And, as we all know, feeling angry isn't a pleasant or beneficial situation.

Emotions like anger deprive you of your emotional, psychological, and physical wellbeing. There is even evidence that chronic anger can lead to cardiovascular problems, such as heart attacks and stroke (Johnson 1990). Therefore, for all intents and purposes, it is best to alleviate your anger. One way to accomplish this is through the acts of releasing and letting go; forgiveness can be a part of this.

Treatment for Anger

The following treatment sequence has been found to be highly effective in diminishing or even eliminating the feeling of anger. This treatment addresses the principal meridian involved in anger and forgiveness. When you are in a state of anger, this meridian is often out of balance. When you experience forgiveness, the imbalance in this meridian is removed. In addition, balancing this meridian makes way for forgiveness.

1. Think about the person (it might be yourself) or a situation that angers you. It should be a single, specific person or event. Rate your level of anger from 0 to 10, with 10 representing the highest level of distress and 0 indicating no stress.

2. Treat for the possibility of reversal by tapping repeatedly on the Side of Hand (SH) or rubbing the Sore Spot (SS) while thinking or saying three times, "I deeply accept myself even though I'm angry at/about (person's name or event)." It also may be helpful to tap the SH or rub the SS while saying, "I accept myself with all my problems and limitations."

3. Look at the treatment sequence for anger under diagram 8 to identify the locations for the meridian points for Little Finger (LF) and Under Collarbone (UCB). While thinking about the anger item (don't get into it so much that you experience any major discomfort during the process), tap repeatedly on LF while saying the following statement three times, "I release myself of this anger." (Alternative statements, depending on your preference, include the following: "I forgive (name the person, place, or circumstance), I know he/she/it couldn't help it." Or, "There is forgiveness in my heart." If you are angry at yourself, consider using the following alternative statement, "I forgive myself, I'm doing the best that I can.") Next, tap on the UCB point five times. Tap the meridian points in the following order 1 → 2. Tap just hard enough to feel it. The tapping shouldn't cause you any pain.

4. Again, rate your anger on a 0 to 10 scale (a number should just pop into your mind). If there is no decrease, go back to step 2 and cycle through the sequence again. If there is not a decrease after three attempts, this is probably not an appropriate sequence for this event, or else there is another sabotaging belief (reversal) that needs correction. (See step 8.) Also consider the treatment for rage, which follows this exercise.

5. Next, do the Brain Balancer (BB) by tapping repeatedly at the Back of Hand (BH) while rotating your eyes clockwise, rotating your eyes counterclockwise, then humming a tune, counting to five, and humming again.

6. Repeat the tapping sequence 1 → 2.

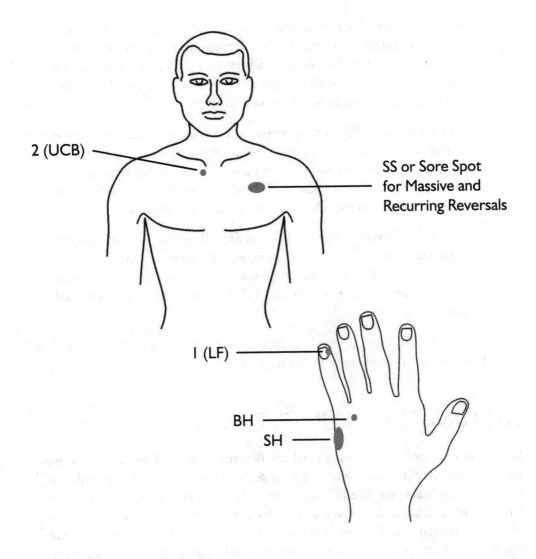

2 (UCB)

SS or Sore Spot
for Massive and
Recurring Reversals

I (LF)

BH

SH

Diagram Eight: Anger and Forgiveness

Treatment Sequence for Anger

Meridian		Location
Little Finger (LF)	1	Inside tip of little fingernail on the side
Under Collarbone (UCB)	2	One inch under collarbone near throat

7. Again, rate your level of distress from 0 to 10. It should be lower yet. When the distress is within the 0 to 2 range, go to step 9. Sometimes, you'll need to repeat the treatment several times while you are imagining your anger—or even while you are in the actual situation—before you feel complete relief from the distressing situation.

8. As long as there is a decrease in your level of anger, continue with the sequence until there is very little or no anger remaining. If the treatment stalls at any point, this indicates a mini-reversal. Treat this by tapping on the little finger Side of Hand (SH) while saying three times, "I deeply accept myself, even though I still have some of this problem."

9. When the distress level is 0 to 2, consider doing the Eye Roll (ER) to lower the distress further or to complete the treatment effects. To do this, tap on the Back of Hand (BH), hold your head straight and, moving only your eyes, look at the floor and then slowly raise your eyes toward the ceiling.

If the anger should return at a later time, repeat these treatments. In time, anger about this issue will become less and less frequent.

PUTTING OUT THE RAGE FIRE

Rage is an even more intense emotional reaction than anger. Often, a different meridian is involved in rage when compared to anger, and this meridian can be balanced by tapping on the Side of the Eye (SE; see diagram 9). Some people who have experienced a traumatic event experience chronic rage about the event itself and toward the people who were involved in it. If an event is involved, it is important to use the most complex trauma treatment for healing (see chapter 10), and then to specifically focus on and treat the rage with the following rage treatment sequence.

Rage can occur in many situations, but the most commonly discussed form of rage is called road rage. In this situation, people act as though they own the road and as if the other people driving on it are disobeying their driving rules. The reality is that most drivers are only vaguely aware of other drivers on the road. Drivers cut each other off or drive too slowly without even realizing it. Often what happens is that the person who is in a rage has a set of expectations about driving, and when those expectations are not met, that person blames the other driver. It's true that some people drive too slowly or are confused about where they are going, and they do slow other drivers down. However, there are also drivers who become impatient and honk if someone hesitates for a fraction of a second once the light turns green. It goes both ways, but the real issue is that road rage is about taking what other drivers do as a personal affront. It's not personal but, unfortunately, road rage has gotten out of hand and become dangerous. People have *shot* at other drivers.

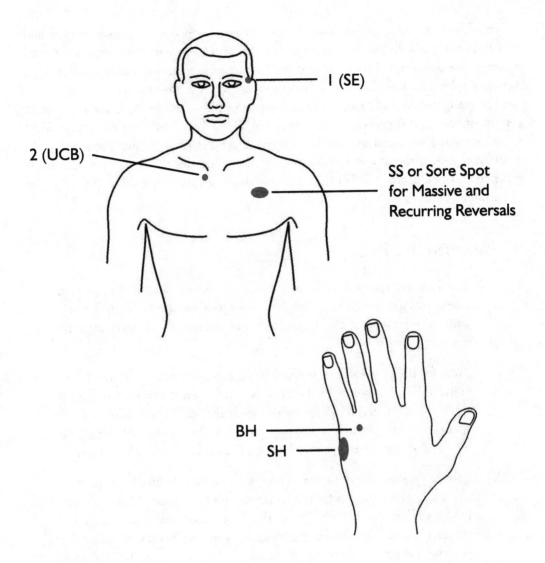

Diagram Nine: Rage

Treatment Sequence for Rage

Meridian		Location
Side of Eye (SE)	1	Side of eye on the bony orbit near temple
Under Collarbone (UCB)	2	One inch under collarbone near throat

In addition to treating rage with the treatment sequence that follows, imagery and visualization are also helpful. For example, the next time you start to feel a sense of rage, imagine that the person causing your emotional upset is someone you care about, such as your mother or a friend. This may help to break up your rage trigger.

For many people, road rage and other forms of rage are a habit. Once they are in certain situations, it triggers their rage response. However, if you use the rage treatment consistently and with dedication, you can break up this problem and eliminate it. As mentioned earlier, the key word here is *dedication*. The treatment for rage, like many other treatments, can be used both to prevent situations that typically trigger rage and to curtail an actual state of rage.

Treatment for Rage

1. Think about the person or situation that enrages you. It should be a single, specific person or event. Rate your level of rage between 0 to 10, with 10 representing the highest level of distress and 0 indicating no stress at all.

2. Treat for the possibility of reversal by tapping repeatedly on the Side of Hand (SH) or rubbing on the Sore Spot (SS) while thinking or saying three times, "I deeply accept myself even though I'm enraged at/about (person's name, event)." It also may be helpful to tap the SH or rub the SS while saying, "I accept myself with all my problems and limitations."

3. Look at diagram 9 and the treatment sequence for rage under the diagram to identify the locations for the meridian points for Side of Eye (SE) and Under Collarbone (UCB). While thinking about the rage item (don't get into it so much that you experience any major discomfort during the process), tap repeatedly on SE while saying the following statement three times, "I release myself of this rage." Then tap on the UCB point five times (see the treatment sequence for rage under diagram 9). Tap the meridian points in the following order: 1 → 2. Tap only hard enough to feel it. The tapping shouldn't cause any pain.

4. Again, rate your rage on a 0 to 10 scale (a number should just pop into your mind and it should be a measure of the intensity of your distress). If there is no decrease, go back to step 2 and cycle through the sequence again. If there is not a decrease after three attempts, this is probably not an appropriate sequence for this event, or else there is another sabotaging belief (reversal) that needs correction. (See step 8.)

5. Next, do the Brain Balancer (BB) by tapping repeatedly at the Back of Hand (BH) while rotating your eyes clockwise, rotating your eyes

counterclockwise, then humming a tune, counting to five, and humming again.

6.   Repeat the tapping sequence 1 → 2.

7.   Again, rate your level of distress from 0 to 10. It should be lower yet. When the distress is within the 0 to 2 range, go to step 9. Sometimes, you'll need to repeat the treatment several times while you are thinking about your rage—or even while you are in the actual situation—before you feel complete relief from the distressing situation.

8.   As long as there is a decrease in the level of rage, continue with the sequence until there is very little or no rage remaining. If the treatment stalls at any point, this indicates a mini-reversal. Treat this by tapping on the little finger Side of Hand (SH) while saying three times, "I deeply accept myself, even though I still have some of this problem."

9.   When the distress level is 0 to 2, do the Eye Roll (ER) to lower the distress further or to complete the treatment effects. To do this, tap on the Back of Hand (BH), hold your head straight and, moving only your eyes, look at the floor and then slowly raise your eyes toward the ceiling.

If rage should return at a later time, repeat these treatments. In time, rage about this issue will become less and less frequent.

OVERCOMING GUILT

When our guilt system is operating properly, we feel guilt only for violating a deeply felt value or moral. When we've done something wrong, the congruent feeling is that of guilt, which tells us to pay attention and change our behavior for the better. Often, however, guilt is not as simple as this indicates. Sometimes, guilt is not triggered when it should be, and sometimes it is triggered when it is no longer necessary, or for reasons that do not warrant guilt feelings. There is also evidence that certain medications, such as some blood pressure treatments, can cause a feeling of guilt or even, more deeply, shame, when we're really innocent. For that reason, if the treatments we suggest here do not alleviate your guilt feelings, and you are taking prescription medications, you may want to consult your health care professional.

Although the treatment that follows is frequently effective in alleviating guilt feelings, it will not make you immune to guilt feelings altogether. Some people never feel guilt and, hence, take advantage of others. Many people with this condition are clinically referred to as antisocial personalities, sociopaths, or psychopaths. Many of these individuals end up in prison because they don't have much of a conscience; they violate laws and the rights of others without any sense of remorse. Our intention is not to encourage such tendencies in our readers. Today more than ever, values and morals are urgently important, and societies need to reinforce appropriate values in their citizens. To suffer chronic guilt, however, is an entirely different matter and serves no useful purpose. Once a lesson has been learned, ongoing guilt feelings only get in the way of healthy psychological functioning.

Treatment for Guilt

1. Think about the person or situation about which you feel guilty. It should be a single, specific person or event. Rate your level of guilt on a scale of 0 to 10, with 10 representing the highest level of distress and 0 indicating no stress.

2. Treat for the possibility of reversal by tapping repeatedly on the Side of Hand (SH) or rubbing the Sore Spot (SS) while thinking or saying three times, "I deeply accept myself even though I feel guilty about (person's name, event)." It also may be helpful to tap the SH or rub the SS while saying, "I accept myself with all my problems and limitations."

3. Look at diagram 10 and the treatment sequence for guilt under the diagram to identify the locations for the meridian points for Index Finger (IF) and Under Collarbone (UCB). While thinking about the guilt item (don't get into it so much that you experience any major discomfort during the process), tap repeatedly on IF while saying the following statement three times: "I release myself of this guilt." (Alternative statements, depending on your preference, include the following: "I forgive myself, because I didn't do anything wrong." Or "There is forgiveness in my heart." Or "I forgive myself. I'm doing the best that I can.") Next, tap on the UCB point five times. Tap the meridian points in the following order 1 → 2. Tap only hard enough to feel it. The tapping shouldn't cause any pain.

4. Again, rate your guilt on a 0 to 10 scale (a number should just pop into your mind). If there is no decrease, go back to step 2 and cycle through the sequence again. If there is not a decrease after three attempts, this is probably not an appropriate sequence for this event, or else there is another sabotaging belief (reversal) that needs correction. (See step 8.)

5. Next, do the Brain Balancer (BB) by tapping repeatedly at the Back of Hand (BH) while rotating your eyes clockwise, rotating your eyes counterclockwise, then humming a tune, counting to five, and humming again.

6. Repeat the tapping sequence 1 → 2.

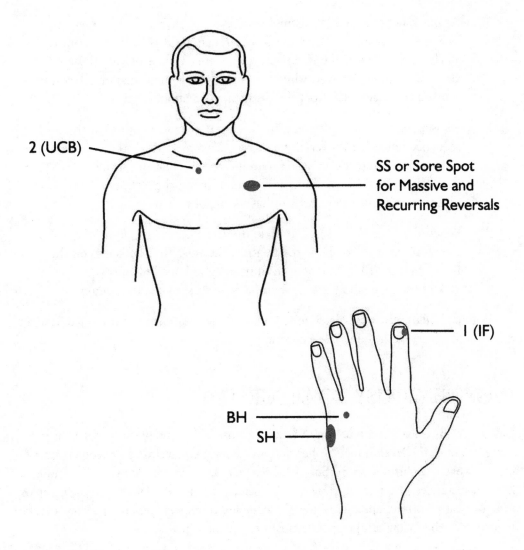

2 (UCB)

SS or Sore Spot for Massive and Recurring Reversals

I (IF)

BH

SH

Diagram Ten: Guilt

Treatment Sequence for Guilt

Meridian		Location
Index Finger (IF)	1	Inside tip of index fingernail on the side
Under Collarbone (UCB)	2	One inch under collarbone near throat

7.   Again, rate your level of distress from 0 to 10. It should be lower yet. When the distress is within the 0 to 2 range, go to step 9. Sometimes, you'll need to repeat the treatment several times while you are thinking about your guilt—or even while you are in the actual situation—before you feel complete relief from the distressing situation.

8.   As long as there is a decrease in the level of guilt, continue with the sequence until there is very little or no guilt remaining. If the treatment stalls at any point, this indicates a mini-reversal. Treat this by tapping on the little finger Side of Hand (SH) while saying three times, "I deeply accept myself, even though I still have some of this problem."

9.   When the distress level is 0 to 2, do the Eye Roll (ER) to lower the distress further or to complete the treatment effects. To do this, tap on the Back of Hand (BH), hold your head straight and, moving only your eyes, look at the floor and then slowly raise your eyes toward the ceiling.

If guilt should return at a later time, repeat these treatments. In time, guilt about this issue will become less and less frequent.

FROM JEALOUSY TO SECURITY

Jealousy seems to be a combination of fear, hurt, insecurity, and anger, and sometimes it can escalate to the level of rage. When you are jealous, you feel that someone is intruding on what is rightfully yours. Sustained jealousy is often associated with a trauma. In such instances, the trauma should be targeted and treated with the most complex trauma treatment in chapter 10. After the complex treatment, residual jealousy can be treated with the following therapeutic treatment sequence.

Treatment for Jealousy

1.   Think about the person or situation about which you feel jealous. It should be a single, specific person or event. Rate your level of jealousy on a scale of 0 to 10, with 10 representing the highest level of distress and 0 indicating no stress.

2.   Treat for the possibility of reversal by tapping repeatedly on the Side of Hand (SH) or rubbing the Sore Spot (SS) while thinking or saying three times, "I deeply accept myself even though I feel jealous about (name the person or event)." It also may be helpful to tap the SH or rub the SS while saying, "I accept myself with all my problems and limitations."

3.   Look at diagram 11 and the treatment sequence for jealousy under the diagram to identify the locations for the meridian points for Middle Finger (MF), Under Arm (UA), and Under Collarbone (UCB). While thinking about your jealousy (don't get into it so much that you experience any major discomfort during the process), tap repeatedly on the MF while saying the following statement three times: "I release myself from this jealousy." Then tap on the UA and UCB five times. Tap them in the following order: 1 → 2 → 3. Tap only hard enough to feel it. The tapping shouldn't cause any pain.

4.   Again, rate your jealousy on a 0 to 10 scale (a number should just pop into your mind). If there is no decrease, go back to step 2 and cycle through the sequence again. If there is not a decrease after three attempts, this is probably not an appropriate sequence for this event, or else there is another sabotaging belief (reversal) that needs correction. (See step 8.)

5.   Next, do the Brain Balancer (BB) by tapping repeatedly at the Back of Hand (BH) while rotating your eyes clockwise, rotating your eyes counterclockwise, then humming a tune, counting to five, and humming again.

6.   Repeat the tapping sequence 1 → 2 → 3.

7.   Again, rate your level of distress from 0 to 10. It should be lower yet. When the distress is within the 0 to 2 range, go to step 9. Sometimes, you'll need to repeat the treatment several times while you are thinking about your jealousy—or even while you are in the actual situation—before you feel complete relief from the distressing situation.

8.   As long as there is a decrease in the level of jealousy, continue with the sequence until there is very little or no jealousy remaining. If the treatment stalls at any point, this indicates a mini-reversal. Treat this by tapping on the little finger Side of Hand (SH) while saying three times, "I deeply accept myself, even though I still have some of this problem."

9.   When the distress level is 0 to 2, do the Eye Roll (ER) to lower the distress further or to complete the treatment effects. To do this, tap on the Back of Hand (BH), hold your head straight and, moving only your eyes, look at the floor and then slowly raise your eyes toward the ceiling.

If jealousy should return at a later time, repeat these treatments. In time, jealousy about this issue will become less and less frequent.

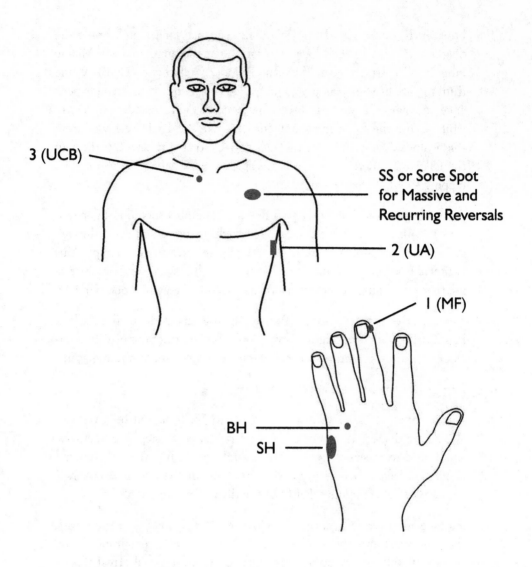

Diagram Eleven: Jealousy

Treatment Sequence for Jealousy

Meridian		Location
Middle Finger (MF)	1	Inside tip of middle fingernail on the side
Under Arm (UA)	2	Six inches under armpit
Under Collarbone (UCB)	3	One inch under collarbone near throat

WHY BE EMBARRASSED?

Mark Twain famously said "Man is the only animal that blushes. Or needs to." You tend to feel embarrassed when you are caught in the act of doing something that you would rather others didn't know you were doing. That is, when you are embarrassed, others have seen you make a mistake, or they've gotten a glimpse of something about you that you would rather keep private. Although Mark Twain's wit and wisdom are profound, we believe that most instances of embarrassment are based on "greatly exaggerated" thoughts about your normal human frailties. But even if embarrassment is warranted, why blush about something that has already occurred? It's over and done with. You might as well learn a needed lesson from your embarrassment and then tap the unwanted emotion away. The following treatment sequence eliminates embarrassment.

Treatment for Embarrassment

1. Think about the person or situation about which you feel embarrassed. It should be a single, specific person or event. Rate your level of embarrassment on a scale of 0 to 10, with 10 representing the highest level of distress and 0 indicating no stress.

2. Treat for the possibility of reversal by tapping repeatedly on the Side of Hand (SH) or rubbing the Sore Spot (SS) while thinking or saying three times, "I deeply accept myself even though I feel embarrassed." It also may be helpful to tap the SH or rub the SS while saying, "I accept myself with all my problems and limitations."

3. Look at diagram 12 and the treatment sequence for embarrassment under the diagram to identify the locations for the meridian points for Under Nose (UN) and Under Collarbone (UCB). While thinking about your embarrassment (don't get into it so much that you experience any major discomfort during the process), tap five times on each of these meridian points. Tap them in the following order 1 → 2. Tap only hard enough to feel it. The tapping shouldn't cause any pain.

4. Again, rate your embarrassment on a 0 to 10 scale (a number should just pop into your mind). If there is no decrease, go back to step 2 and cycle through the sequence again. If there is not a decrease after three attempts, this is probably not an appropriate sequence for this event, or else there is another sabotaging belief (reversal) that needs correction. (See step 8.)

5. Next, do the Brain Balancer (BB) by tapping repeatedly at the Back of Hand (BH) while rotating your eyes clockwise, rotating your eyes

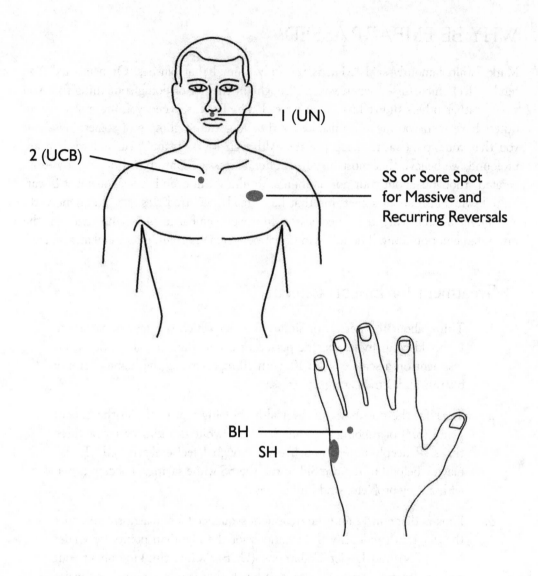

Diagram Twelve: Embarrassment

Treatment Sequence for Embarrassment

Meridian		Location
Under Nose (UN)	1	Above upper lip and below the center of nose
Under Collarbone (UCB)	2	One inch under collarbone near throat

counterclockwise, then humming a tune, counting to five, and humming again.

6. Repeat the tapping sequence 1 → 2.

7. Again, rate your level of distress from 0 to 10. It should be lower yet. When the distress is within the 0 to 2 range, go to step 9. Sometimes, you'll need to repeat the treatment several times while you are thinking about your embarrassment—or even while you are in the actual situation—before you feel complete relief from the distressful situation.

8. As long as there is a decrease in the level of embarrassment, continue with the sequence until there is very little or no embarrassment remaining. If the treatment stalls at any point, this indicates a mini-reversal. Treat this by tapping on the little finger Side of Hand (SH) while saying three times, "I deeply accept myself, even though I still have some of this problem."

9. When the distress level is 0 to 2, do the Eye Roll (ER) to lower the distress further or to complete the treatment effects. To do this, tap on the Back of Hand (BH), hold your head straight, and, moving only your eyes, look at the floor and then slowly raise your eyes toward the ceiling.

If embarrassment should return at a later time, repeat these treatments. In time embarrassment about this issue will become less and less frequent.

OVERCOMING SHAME

Shame is different from embarrassment or guilt. With guilt, you feel that you've *done* something wrong; when you experience shame, you feel that there is something essentially wrong about *you*, that is, something is wrong at the core of your being. This emotional state is also more profound than embarrassment. Many deep-seated psychological problems involve the sharp edge of shame.

When you experience profound shame, it is difficult—if not impossible—to look others in the eyes. The inclination is to hide, to avoid socializing. Experiencing feelings of shame can also be a side effect of certain medications, such as some that are used to regulate blood pressure. If you suspect that this may be the case, please check with your health care provider. Most shame, however, is rooted in experiences from your childhood. Somehow, you learned to be ashamed of yourself. Perhaps it is necessary to reach back into those formative experiences and eliminate the effects of the traumas. Additionally, you can use the following therapeutic treatment sequences to dissipate feelings of shame.

Treatment for Shame

1. Think about your feelings of shame. Rate your level of shame on a scale of 0 to 10, with 10 representing the highest level of distress and 0 indicating no stress.

2. Treat for the possibility of reversal by tapping repeatedly on the Side of Hand (SH) or rubbing the Sore Spot (SS) while thinking or saying three times, "I deeply accept myself even though I feel shame." It also may be helpful to tap the SH or rub the SS while saying, "I accept myself with all my problems and limitations."

3. Look at diagram 13 and the treatment sequence for shame to identify the locations for the meridian points for Under Bottom Lip (UBL) and Under Collarbone (UCB). While thinking about your shame (don't get into it so much that you experience any major discomfort during the process), tap five times on each of these meridian points. Tap them in the following order 1 → 2. Tap only hard enough to feel it. The tapping shouldn't cause any pain.

4. Again, rate your shame on a 0 to 10 scale (a number should just pop into your mind). If there is no decrease, go back to step 2 and cycle through the sequence again. If there is not a decrease after three attempts, this is probably not an appropriate sequence for this event, or else there is another sabotaging belief (reversal) that needs correction. (See step 8.)

5. Next, do the Brain Balancer (BB) by tapping repeatedly at the Back of Hand (BH) while rotating your eyes clockwise, rotating your eyes counterclockwise, then humming a tune, counting to five, and humming again.

6. Repeat the tapping sequence 1 → 2.

7. Again, rate your level of distress from 0 to 10. It should be lower yet. When the distress is within the 0 to 2 range, go to step 9. Sometimes, you'll need to repeat the treatment several times while you are thinking about your shame—or even while you are in the actual situation—before you feel complete relief from the distressful situation.

8. As long as there is a decrease in the level of shame, continue with the sequence until there is little or no shame remaining. If the treatment stalls at any point, this indicates a mini-reversal. Treat this by tapping on the little finger Side of Hand (SH) while saying three times, "I deeply accept myself, even though I still have some of this problem."

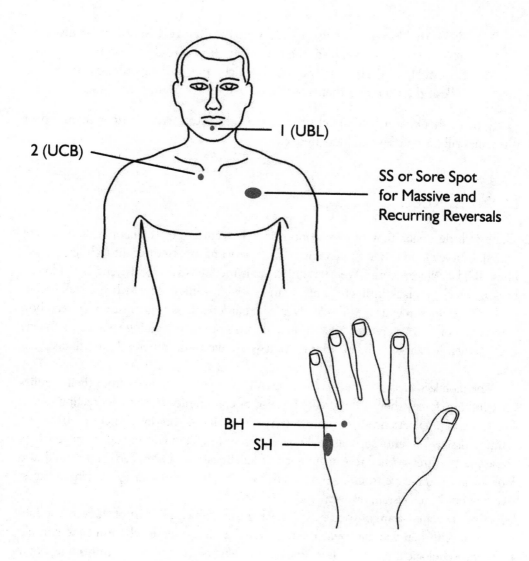

Diagram Thirteen: Shame

Treatment Sequence for Shame

Meridian		Location
Under Bottom Lip (UBL)	1	Under bottom lip in chin cleft
Under Collarbone (UCB)	2	One inch under collarbone near throat

9. When the distress level is 0 to 2, do the Eye Roll (ER) to lower the distress further or to complete the treatment effects. To do this, tap on the Back of Hand (BH), hold your head straight and, moving only your eyes, look at the floor and then slowly raise your eyes toward the ceiling.

If shame should return at a later time, repeat these treatments. In time, shame about this issue will become less and less frequent.

LONELINESS

There is little doubt that human contact is an essential part of happiness. A recent national survey found that 36 percent of all Americans reported recent feelings of loneliness (Olds, Schwartz, and Webster 1996). Loneliness has two forms: emotional loneliness, in which you lack intimate contact, and social loneliness, in which you lack friends to share activities in your life. To clearly affect your loneliness, you must understand how your beliefs or actions create it in your life. This is not about blaming yourself or anyone else. Rather, it is about understanding what you have to do differently to change your life.

The mobile society in which we live often moves people far away from their families and, in part, forces them to re-create a sense of community to ward off feeling lonely. For those who experience a chronic pattern of loneliness, however, there probably are multiple issues present, such as feelings of depression, shame, and rejection. Each of these must be treated before your pattern of loneliness can be broken. You should also look at how you escape from loneliness. For example, do you use drugs, watch an excessive amount of television, or even read too much?

If you become aware of your escape mechanisms, which are part of the way you sabotage yourself, then you can treat them as well. These escape mechanisms are another form of psychological reversals. Loneliness is not always a response to being alone. Some people feel habitually lonely even in the company of others, whereas other people feel quite comfortable being alone.

Treatment Sequence for Loneliness

1. Think about your feelings of loneliness. Rate your level of loneliness on a scale of 0 to 10, with 10 representing the highest level of distress and 0 indicating no stress.

2. Treat for the possibility of reversal by tapping repeatedly on the Side of Hand (SH) or rubbing the Sore Spot (SS) while thinking or saying three times, "I deeply accept myself even though I'm lonely." It also may be helpful to tap the SH or rub the SS while saying, "I accept myself with all my problems and limitations."

3. Look at diagram 14 and the treatment sequence for loneliness to identify the locations for the meridian points for Back of Hand (BH) and Under Collarbone (UCB). While thinking about your loneliness (don't get into it so much that you experience any major discomfort during the process), tap on the BH twenty to fifty times and then tap on the UCB five times. Tap them in the following order 1 → 2. Tap only hard enough to feel it. The tapping shouldn't cause any pain.

4. Again, rate your loneliness on a 0 to 10 scale (a number should just pop into your mind). If there is no decrease, go back to step 2 and cycle through the sequence again. If there is not a decrease after three attempts, this probably is not an appropriate sequence for this event, or else there is another sabotaging belief (reversal) that needs correction. (See step 8.)

5. Next, do the Brain Balancer (BB) by tapping repeatedly at the Back of Hand (BH) while rotating your eyes clockwise, rotating your eyes counterclockwise, then humming a tune, counting to five, and humming again.

6. Repeat the tapping sequence 1 → 2.

7. Again, rate your level of distress from 0 to 10. It should be lower yet. When the distress is within the 0 to 2 range, go to step 9. Sometimes, you'll need to repeat the treatment several times while you are thinking about your loneliness—or even while you are in the actual situation—before you feel complete relief from the distressful situation.

8. As long as there is a decrease in the level of loneliness, continue with the sequence until there is very little or no loneliness remaining. If the treatment stalls at any point, this indicates a mini-reversal. Treat this by tapping on the little finger Side of Hand (SH) while saying three times, "I deeply accept myself, even though I still have some of this problem."

9. When the distress level is 0 to 2, do the Eye Roll (ER) to lower the distress further or to complete the treatment effects. To do this, tap on the Back of Hand (BH), hold your head straight and, moving only your eyes, look at the floor and then slowly raise your eyes toward the ceiling.

If the feelings of loneliness should return at a later time, repeat these treatments. In time, recurrence of loneliness symptoms will become less and less frequent.

Once you have treated the reversals surrounding your loneliness and their accompanying feelings and behaviors, it is time to make some changes in your life. That is, it's time to replace the behaviors you use to escape loneliness with healthy, more productive activities. If you like to read, for example, attend author events at your local bookstore and spend a few hours there some evenings. In time, you will begin to recognize other

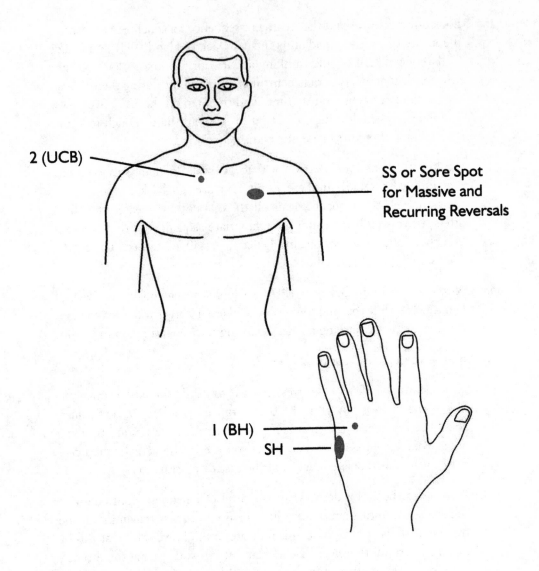

2 (UCB)

SS or Sore Spot
for Massive and
Recurring Reversals

I (BH)

SH

Diagram Fourteen: Loneliness

Treatment Sequence for Loneliness

Meridian		Location
Back of Hand (BH)	1	Back of hand between little and ring fingers
Under Collarbone (UCB)	2	One inch under collarbone near throat

customers. Because you already have a common interest in reading, it will be easier to start a conversation or even a book club. Another option might be to take a class that teaches a topic in which you are interested. There are numerous classes available on almost every subject. The goal is to get out there and meet people who have similar interests as you. Once you do, you will expand your social life—and reduce your feelings of loneliness considerably.

REJECTION

There is little doubt that rejection is one of the hardest feelings to accept, even though it happens to everyone. You can feel rejected when you are trying to sell a product for your business or an idea to your boss. Feelings of rejection can also surface when you ask someone out for a date or when you are not asked out for dates. Regardless of when the feeling arises, no one likes being rejected; it feels like you just got slapped and it hurts. The treatment sequence that follows will help you soothe feelings of rejection. If rejection is a pattern in your life, however, other issues are at hand and you need to figure out what you are doing to help create it.

Treatment for Rejection

1. Think about the situation for which you are feeling rejected. It should be a single, specific person or event. Rate your level of rejection on a scale of 0 to 10, with 10 representing the highest level of distress and 0 indicating no stress.

2. Treat for the possibility of reversal by tapping repeatedly on the Side of Hand (SH) or rubbing the Sore Spot (SS) while thinking or saying three times, "I deeply accept myself even though I feel rejected." It also may be helpful to tap the SH or rub the SS while saying, "I accept myself with all my problems and limitations."

3. Look at diagram 15 and the treatment sequence for rejection under the diagram to identify the locations for the meridian points for Eyebrow (EB), Under Eye (UE), Under Arm (UA), and Under Collarbone (UCB). While thinking about the rejection (don't get into it so much that you experience any major discomfort during the process), tap five times at each of these meridian points. Tap them in the following order: 1 → 2 → 3 → 4. Tap only hard enough to feel it. The tapping shouldn't cause any pain.

4. Again, rate your rejection on a 0 to 10 scale (a number should just pop into your mind). If there is no decrease, go back to step 2 and cycle through the sequence again. If there is not a decrease after three attempts, this

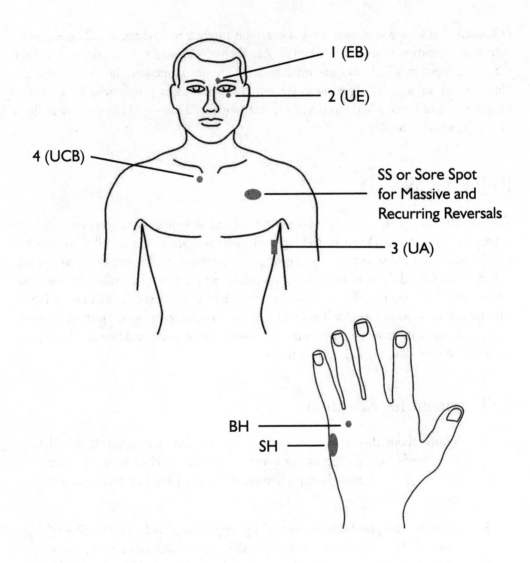

Diagram Fifteen: Rejection

Treatment Sequence for Rejection

Meridian		Location
Eyebrow (EB)	1	Beginning of eyebrow near bridge of nose
Under Eye (UE)	2	Under the center of eye on the tip of bone
Under Arm (UA)	3	Six inches under armpit
Under Collarbone (UCB)	4	One inch under collarbone near throat

probably is not an appropriate sequence for this event, or else there is another sabotaging belief (reversal) that needs correction. (See step 8.)

5. Next, do the Brain Balancer (BB) by tapping repeatedly at the Back of Hand (BH) while rotating your eyes clockwise, rotating your eyes counterclockwise, then humming a tune, counting to five, and humming again.

6. Repeat the tapping sequence 1 → 2 → 3 → 4.

7. Again, rate your level of distress from 0 to 10. It should be lower yet. When the distress is within the 0 to 2 range, go to step 9. Sometimes, you'll need to repeat the treatment several times while you are thinking about your rejection—or even while you are in the actual situation—before you feel complete relief from the distressful situation.

8. As long as there is a decrease in the level of rejection, continue with the sequence until there is little or no feelings of rejection remaining. If the treatment stalls at any point, this indicates a mini-reversal. Treat this by tapping on the little finger Side of Hand (SH) while saying three times, "I deeply accept myself, even though I still have some of this problem."

9. When the distress level is between 0 to 2, do the Eye Roll (ER) to lower the distress further or to complete the treatment effects. To do this, tap on the Back of Hand (BH), hold your head straight and, moving only your eyes, look at the floor and then slowly raise your eyes toward the ceiling.

If your feelings of rejection should return at a later time, repeat these treatments. In time, recurrence of rejection symptoms will become less and less frequent.

Once you have treated your feelings of rejection and any other related problems, you are ready to develop your new strategies. This may mean acquiring more knowledge or new tactics. The question you are always trying to answer is "Am I doing anything to sabotage myself and create this problem?" Once you treat any related reversals concerning rejection, you should be able to see new alternatives to your old approach.

ERASING THOSE NEGATIVE FEELINGS

The treatment sequences in this chapter are effective, but there is another treatment sequence that, in many cases, quickly erases negative feelings. This treatment is referred to as the Midline Energy Treatment (MET). The basic approach is similar to earlier sequences with which you are already familiar.

Midline Energy Treatment (MET)

1. Think about the problem you want to treat. It should be a single, specific problem (a behavior, emotion, or limiting belief). Rate your level of distress on a scale of 0 to 10, with 10 representing the highest level of distress and 0 indicating no stress.

2. Treat for the possibility of reversal by tapping repeatedly on the Side of Hand (SH) or rubbing the Sore Spot (SS) while thinking or saying three times, "I deeply accept myself even though I have this problem." (Be specific.) It also may be helpful to tap the SH or rub the SS while saying, "I accept myself with all my problems and limitations."

3. Look at diagram 16 and the Midline Energy Treatment (MET) Sequence under the diagram to identify the locations for the meridian points for Forehead (F), Under Nose (UN), Under Bottom Lip (UBL), and Chest (CH). While thinking about the problem (don't get into it so much that you experience any major discomfort during the process), tap ten times at each of these meridian points. Tap them in the following order 1 → 2 → 3 → 4. Tap only hard enough to feel it. The tapping shouldn't cause any pain.

4. Again, rate your problem from 0 to 10 (a number should just pop into your mind). If there is no decrease, go back to step 2 and cycle through the sequence again. If there is not a decrease after three attempts, this is probably not an appropriate sequence for this problem, or else there is another sabotaging belief (reversal) that needs correction. (See step 8.)

5. Next, do the Brain Balancer (BB) by tapping repeatedly at the Back of Hand (BH) while rotating your eyes clockwise, rotating your eyes counterclockwise, then humming a tune, counting to five, and humming again.

6. Repeat the tapping sequence 1 → 2 → 3 → 4.

7. Again, rate your level of distress from 0 to 10. It should be lower yet. When the distress is within the 0 to 2 range, go to step 9. Sometimes, you'll need to repeat the treatment several times while you are thinking about your problem—or even while you are in the actual situation—before you feel complete relief from the distressful situation.

8. As long as there is a decrease in the level of distress, continue with the sequence until there are few or no feelings of distress remaining. If the treatment stalls at any point, this indicates a mini-reversal. Treat this by tapping on the little finger Side of Hand (SH) while saying three times, "I deeply accept myself, even though I still have some of this problem."

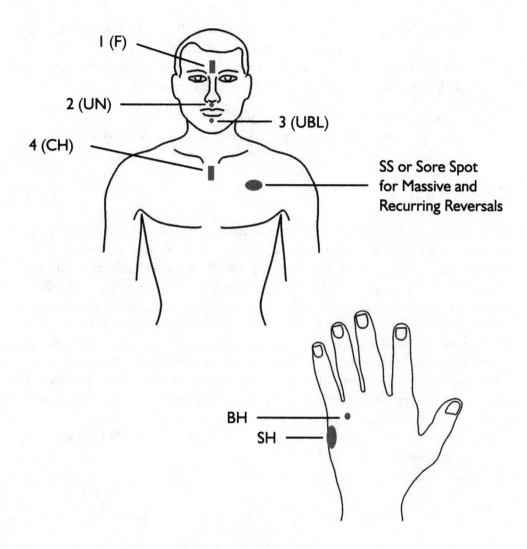

Diagram Sixteen: Midline Energy Treatment

Midline Energy Treatment (MET) Sequence

Meridian		Location
Forehead (F)	1	One inch above and between eyebrows
Under Nose (UN)	2	Under nose and above upper lip
Under Bottom Lip (UBL)	3	Depression between lip and chin
Chest (CH)	4	Upper section of your chest

9. When the distress level is 0 to 2, do the Eye Roll (ER) to lower the distress further or to complete the treatment effects. To do this, tap on the Back of Hand (BH), hold your head straight and, moving only your eyes, look at the floor and then slowly raise your eyes toward the ceiling.

If the distress associated with the issue should return at a later time, repeat the MET sequence. In time, recurrence of the problem will become less and less likely.

SUMMARY

The treatments in this chapter can be used alone or with other treatments described in this book. Traumatic events, for example, often involve feelings of anger, guilt, or shame. After treating the trauma with the treatments outlined in chapter 10, if you should continue to experience some negative emotion, the treatments in this chapter will help you to apply the finishing touches. Also, after treating any problem, such as a panic attack, you may feel guilty or angry with yourself for having had the problem in the first place. This can occur when the problem affects other areas of your life. If this is the case, you should treat these negative feelings with the treatments described in this chapter.

Remember, if you don't treat these secondary negative emotions, over time, they can cause the original problem to return. This is especially true when dealing with anger or forgiveness. After successfully treating a problem, you may find it helpful to routinely forgive yourself for having had the problem in the first place. To do this, follow the treatment sequences for anger and guilt.

9

Feeling Good Again

*The opposite of depression is not happiness, but vitality. Depression is not
so much about feeling incredibly sad, but feeling incredibly devitalized, and
not having any of the essential energy that constitutes being alive or any
of the feelings that make up our day-to-day experience.*

–Andrew Solomon

Although millions of Americans seem to be unhappy and may believe that they are depressed, there is a significant difference between clinical depression and what might be referred to as a "low mood." For the most part, the difference is determined by the degree of severity and longevity. A low, dreary blue mood for a day, regardless of its depth, doesn't qualify as clinical depression. Life invariably has its ups and downs. An unrelenting mildly low mood, however, can qualify as a clinical depression. For example, if a low mood persists for at least two weeks and includes symptoms such as those listed below, clinical depression may be present and professional treatment is advisable. Generally, the longer you are depressed, the greater the effort that will be required to resolve the depression.

Symptoms of clinical depression include the following:

- Difficulty concentrating

- Fatigue

- Low energy, or anergia

- Difficulty making decisions

- Trouble falling asleep

- Frequent awakening

- Early morning awakening

- Excessive sleeping

- Low appetite

- Excessive appetite

- Loss of pleasure in previously enjoyable activities

- Feelings of hopelessness

- Feelings of worthlessness

- Ongoing guilt feelings

- Excessive thoughts of death

- Suicidal thoughts

THE DRUGGING OF AMERICA

There are a number of options for treating depression. Some physicians tend to rely heavily on antidepressant medication, including Tofranil, Sinequan, Prozac, Zoloft, Paxil, Serzone, Remeron, and other drugs. Psychiatric medications, in fact, have become so popular and are in such high demand that many physicians may feel compelled to prescribe them even when they may not be entirely necessary. In addition to conventional medications, alternative antidepressants, such as *hypericum perforatum* or St. John's wort, have been reported to be effective in treating clinical depression (Lockie and Geddes 1995; Linde and Ramirez 1996).

Used properly, medication can be a useful adjunct for treating certain kinds of depression. In most instances, however, depression can be treated successfully without antidepressant medication, or with very little or only short-term use. Most commonly, antidepressants do not *cure* depression because they address only one of its causes—a chemical imbalance. As a result, the depression frequently returns after the medication is discontinued, even when it is discontinued gradually. In the majority of cases where medication is deemed necessary, the best approach is to receive psychological treatment in conjunction with the medication.

Be aware: Certain physical illnesses are known to produce feelings and behaviors similar to depression. For example, an underactive thyroid gland, anemia, or nutritional deficiencies can cause sluggishness and fogged awareness. Before concluding that you are clinically depressed, be certain to examine all the possible causes that might be implicated in determining how you are feeling.

WHAT CAUSES DEPRESSION?

A number of factors affect depression. Certain areas of the brain, for instance, are intricately involved in depression, such as those that are instrumental in regulating emotional responses (for example, the *amygdala* and *thalamus*). Additionally, there are chemical aspects to depression, such as the disruption of the neurotransmitters (for example, *serotonin* and *norepinephrine*); produced in the brain the neurotransmitters serve as chemical messengers that facilitate communication between the nerve cells within our nervous system. Too low a level of these neurotransmitters and you become sluggish, uninterested, and perhaps anxious; you may also have a tendency to worry excessively. This is the cause of depression that antidepressant medications address.

But the level of neurotransmitters can often be increased by means other than medication, including aerobic exercise, proper nutrition, vitamins, full-spectrum light, and certain herbal remedies. The question, however, is what triggers depression in the first place? Surely, the brain and chemical changes associated with depression don't happen all by themselves. Something must set the proverbial ball in motion, rolling it down the hill toward the valley of depression.

In most instances, depression is triggered by recent or past events that are traumatic to some degree and involve real or anticipated loss of some sort. For example, the death of a loved one, the loss of a job, health problems, and the possibility of financial ruin all can instigate the onset of depression. For depression to result, however, you must believe that the events occurring are significantly negative. For instance, if you lost a job that you disliked very much, rather than feeling down or depressed about it, you might actually feel relief or joy. Conversely, when you feel depressed, you have negative, perhaps catastrophic thoughts about the loss. What you think about a situation, therefore, greatly affects your depression probability. (This is the core of cognitive therapy, which assumes that what you *think* directly influences how you feel.) So far, the depression chain of causes looks something like this:

1. A loss event occurs.

2. You have frequent unsettling thoughts about this event.

3. Next, certain instrumental areas of the brain that govern emotion become activated to produce negative emotions.

4. Additionally, certain body chemicals become imbalanced as disturbing thoughts are increased.

5. Depression results.

This formula, however, is incomplete. *Energy* is involved somewhere. Energy operates the nervous system. For depressive thoughts to have an impact on certain areas of your brain and your neurochemistry, the thoughts must have within them certain electrical or electromagnetic features. These features, in turn, stimulate the brain centers and cause the depletion of neurochemicals. Energy (that is, thought) is real; it interacts with your body in profound ways.

For an example, vividly imagine biting into a lemon or a lime. What happens? Most people report that they experience a bitter sensation on their tongue, even though, in reality, there is no citrus fruit; it is only there in thought. How does this happen? Where is the lemon or the lime? Your thinking about the citrus sends a message to your brain analogous to sending electricity through a wire, which results in a puckering sensation. The same is true for experiences of anger, guilt, jealousy, anxiety, and even depression.

Given this, depression isn't simply a matter of the situation, the brain, the chemistry, or even your thoughts, although all four are important and can greatly affect the probability of depression. Instead, the thinking must carry certain electromagnetic charges so that the entire depression chain of causes can take place. Then, the specifically charged thought carries messages to your senses, throughout your body. The formula for depression, therefore, might be revised as follows:

1. A loss event occurs.

2. You have frequent unsettling thoughts about this event.

3. The thoughts are unsettling since they contain certain *disrupted energy* characteristics.

4. The electromagnetic features in thoughts produce negative emotions that activate certain areas of the brain involved in emotion.

5. Neurochemicals become imbalanced as disrupting thoughts deplete them.

6. Depression results.

Of course, this is not the only causal chain that leads to depression. In some instances of depression, there are hereditary factors involved. In fact, some studies of identical twin siblings indicate that heredity is the predominant predisposing factor of depression (Kendler et al. 1994).

ENERGY PSYCHOLOGY HELPS TO RELIEVE DEPRESSION

When you feel depressed, your energy system is out of balance. It can be returned to balance by energy psychology treatments. These serve to remove the most basic cause of the depression, which is within the realm of energy. By tapping on specific energy points in specific ways, negative energetic features of thoughts are removed, your energy system becomes balanced, and the depression is relieved. Think of depression as being caused by an energy field—much like the magnetic impressions on an audiotape that produce the music when you play the tape. Stimulating the energy system causes that field to be erased, thus erasing the depression. Following are some examples of how this has worked for others.

Love, Fear, and Depression: A Case Study

David had been experiencing depression for more than six months. Although his physician put him on an antidepressant medication regime, he found that it wasn't helping him much, if at all. He took the Beck Depression Inventory (BDI) test, which determined that his level of depression was severe. He decided to participate in psychotherapy, something he had not done before.

After discussing the various issues involved in his depression, David was advised to explore energy therapy. In David's first session, he was reminded that although there are chemical aspects involved in a depression, which is why his physician had chosen to prescribe medication, depression is fundamentally caused by our disturbing thoughts about the events in our lives. Furthermore, he was told that his thoughts are not disembodied and that the electrical or electromagnetic aspect of negative thoughts can be relieved quite rapidly with certain techniques. It was also emphasized that David did not have to be caught in his depression-producing thoughts. (This is an important consideration to take into account with any psychological problem.) In this regard, we emphasized that continuing to focus on negative issues causes energy imbalance, negatively affects the nervous system, produces a chemical imbalance, and other more subtle effects.

David took this advice to heart as he openly engaged in the energy treatment sequence for depression (provided later in this chapter). In less than five minutes, David's depression was gone. After the original treatment sequence was over, the importance of David not getting caught up again in depressive thinking was reemphasized, and the treatment sequence was reviewed so that he could repeat it, if necessary, during the coming week.

When David returned for his session the following week, he took the depression inventory (BDI) again, and notable improvement was evident. He no longer was severely depressed, although a mild depression remained evident. The treatment sequences from the previous week were repeated and again the residual depression vanished.

During his third appointment, the depression inventory was administered again. At this point, there was no evidence of clinical depression. He was amazed at what had transpired in such a short period of time. He said, "It's uncanny!"

With the assistance of his physician, David's antidepressant medication was discontinued. A follow-up telephone contact six months later revealed that there was no recurrence of depression. David was doing quite well.

The Death of a Boyfriend: A Case Study

Jennifer was a high school junior. She had been dating nineteen-year-old Chris for more than two years when he developed a serious respiratory condition and deteriorated rapidly, eventually dying. Jennifer grieved deeply and soon became clinically depressed. She missed Chris, felt lost without him, and was plagued by images in her mind of him in his debilitated condition, suffering. Her physician put her on antidepressant medication. She also saw a therapist who encouraged her to discuss her grief, to review many of the events that transpired during Chris's illness, and to focus on her positive memories of him prior to his illness. Unfortunately, none of this helped Jennifer and, in fact, she became increasingly depressed. Psychiatric hospitalization was considered.

With energy psychology, Jennifer didn't have to focus on events from the past. The first objective was to have her briefly tune into the images that were contributing to her depression, including symptoms of sleeplessness, loss of pleasure, crying, and poor appetite. At the time, she rated her distress at the highest level possible. Her visual image was one of Chris lying on the couch suffering while he was having difficulty breathing. Jennifer was taken through the highly complex trauma treatment (see chapter 10) and, within a matter of ten minutes, that image no longer caused her great distress.

Next, we focused on her residual feelings of depression. By this time, the feeling of depression had decreased significantly. Jennifer was encouraged to tap on the back of her hand between the little finger and ring finger (BH) while continuing to focus on the feelings of depression, which she described as being centered "in my heart." As her feelings of depression decreased, she was asked to tap under the collarbone (UCB) a few times and then return to tapping on the BH. Within a few minutes Jennifer was not experiencing any depression at all. Throughout the treatment, she frequently exclaimed, "This is crazy. It's weird, but it's good."

When Jennifer was seen the following week she indicated that she had not felt depressed for three days after the initial treatment. In all, only a few visits were needed to help Jennifer improve her mood tremendously. She found it much easier to concentrate, she slept and ate better, and her interest in life and teenage activities returned. Her full-blown depression never returned. She became involved in social activities with friends and eventually started dating again. In consultation with our treatment of Jennifer's depression, her physician tapered her off the antidepressant medication that had been prescribed for her.

Switching

As previously mentioned, sometimes treatment sequences will not work to alleviate depression due to an even more pervasive energy disruption referred to as neurologic disorganization or *switching*. If you find that the treatment sequences below do not alleviate your depression or low mood, or if they are inefficient, correcting possible switching may be just what you need. See chapter 2 for more information on switching and an exercise to treat it.

BASIC TREATMENT FOR DEPRESSION

1. Think about your feelings of depression. Rate your level of depression on a scale of 0 to 10, with 10 representing the highest level of distress and 0 indicating no stress.

2. Treat for the possibility of reversal by tapping repeatedly on the Side of Hand (SH) or rubbing the Sore Spot (SS) while thinking or saying three times, "I deeply accept myself even though I'm depressed." It also may be helpful to tap the SH or rub the SS while saying, "I accept myself with all my problems and limitations."

3. Look at diagram 17 and the basic treatment sequence for depression under the diagram to identify the locations for the meridian points for Back of Hand (BH) and Under Collarbone (UCB). While thinking about your depression (don't get into it so much that you experience any major discomfort during the process), tap on BH fifty times or more until you notice a decrease in depression, and then tap on the UCB five times. Tap them in the following order 1 → 2. Tap only hard enough to feel it. The tapping shouldn't cause any pain.

4. Again, rate your depression on a 0 to 10 scale (a number should just pop into your mind). If there is no decrease, go back to step 2 and cycle through the sequence again. If there is not a decrease after three attempts, this is probably not an appropriate sequence for this event, or else there is another sabotaging belief (reversal) that needs correction. (See step 8.)

5. Next, do the Brain Balancer (BB) by tapping repeatedly at the Back of Hand (BH) while rotating your eyes clockwise, rotating your eyes counter-clockwise, then humming a tune, counting to five, and humming again.

6. Repeat the tapping sequence 1 → 2.

7. Again, rate your level of depression from 0 to 10. It should be lower yet. When the depression is within the 0 to 2 range, go to step 9. Sometimes you'll need to repeat the treatment several times—while you are thinking about your depression—before you feel complete relief from the depression symptoms.

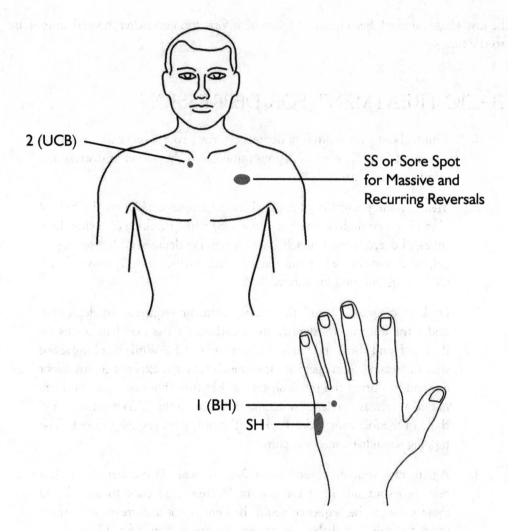

2 (UCB)

SS or Sore Spot for Massive and Recurring Reversals

1 (BH)

SH

Diagram Seventeen: Basic Depression

Basic Treatment Sequence for Depression

Meridian		Location
Back of Hand (BH)	1	Back of hand between little and ring fingers
Under Collarbone (UCB)	2	One inch under collarbone near throat

8. As long as there is a decrease in the level of depression, continue with the sequence until there is very little or no depression remaining. If the treatment stalls at any point, this indicates a mini-reversal. Treat this by tapping on the little finger Side of Hand (SH) while saying three times, "I deeply accept myself, even though I still have some of this depression."

9. When the depression level is 0 to 2, do the Eye Roll (ER) to lower the distress further or to complete the treatment effects. To do this, tap on the Back of Hand (BH), hold your head straight, and, moving only your eyes, look at the floor and then slowly raise your eyes toward the ceiling.

If the feelings of depression should return at a later time, repeat these treatments. In time, recurrence of depression symptoms will become less and less frequent. For many people, it will be unlikely for depression to recur at all.

COMPLEX TREATMENT FOR DEPRESSION

When the Basic Treatment Sequence for depression does not alleviate your symptoms, it is likely that your depression is more complex. In some instances, this is due to another level of psychological reversal that must be corrected before the depression treatment will be effective (see chapter 6). For example, it may be necessary to tap at the Under Nose (UN) treatment point, while saying, "I deeply accept myself if I never get over this depression." (Alternative reversals may also be involved.) In other instances, it is not a matter of a reversal, but rather that your energy system is more pervasively in a state of disruption, requiring more treatment points. Essentially, the Complex Depression Treatment Sequence involves combining additional treatment points with the Basic Depression Treatment Sequence. A detailed description of this process follows:

1. Think about your feelings of depression. Rate your level of depression on a scale from 0 to 10, with 10 representing the highest level of distress and 0 indicating no stress.

2. Treat for the possibility of reversal by tapping repeatedly on the Side of Hand (SH) or rubbing the Sore Spot (SS) while thinking or saying three times, "I deeply accept myself even though I'm depressed." It also may be helpful to tap the SH or rub the SS while saying, "I accept myself with all my problems and limitations."

3. Look at diagram 18 and the complex treatment sequence for depression under the diagram to identify the locations for the meridian points for Eyebrow (EB), Side of Eye (SE), Under Eye (UE), Under Nose (UN), Under Bottom Lip (UBL), Under Arm (UA), Under Collarbone (UCB),

Little Finger (LF), and Index Finger (IF). While thinking about your depression (don't get into it so much that you experience any major discomfort during the process), tap five times at each of these meridian points. Tap them in the following order: 1 → 2 → 3 → 4 → 5 → 6 → 7 → 8 → 9. Tap only hard enough to feel it. The tapping shouldn't cause any pain.

4. After completing the sequence above, identify the location for the meridian points for Back of Hand (BH) and Under Collarbone (UCB). While thinking about your depression, tap on BH fifty times or more until you notice a decrease in depression, and then tap on the UCB five times (see basic depression treatment sequence chart above).

5. Again, rate your depression on a 0 to 10 scale (a number should just pop into your mind). If there is no decrease, go back to step 2 and cycle through the sequence again. If there is not a decrease after three attempts, this is probably not an appropriate sequence for your depression, or else there is another sabotaging belief (reversal) that needs correction. (See step 9.)

6. Next, do the Brain Balancer (BB) by tapping repeatedly at the Back of Hand (BH) while rotating your eyes clockwise, rotating your eyes counterclockwise, then humming a tune, counting to five, and humming again.

7. Repeat the tapping sequence 1 → 2 → 3 → 4 → 5 → 6 → 7 → 8 → 9, followed by the BH → UCB sequence.

8. Again, rate your level of depression from 0 to 10. It should be lower yet. When the depression is within the 0 to 2 range, go to step 10. Sometimes, you'll need to repeat the treatment several times—while you are thinking about your depression—before you feel complete relief from the depression symptoms.

9. As long as there is a decrease in the level of depression, continue with the sequence until there is very little or no depression remaining. If the treatment stalls at any point, this indicates a mini-reversal. Treat this by tapping on the little finger Side of Hand (SH) while saying three times, "I deeply accept myself, even though I still have some of this depression."

10. When the depression level is 0 to 2, do the Eye Roll (ER) to lower the distress further or to complete the treatment effects. To do this, tap on the Back of Hand (BH), hold your head straight and, moving only your eyes, look at the floor and then slowly raise your eyes toward the ceiling.

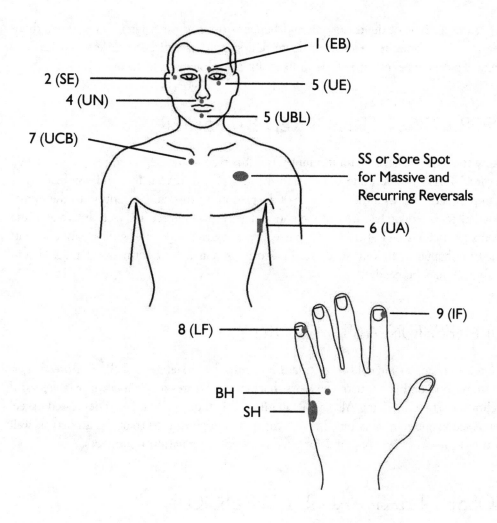

Diagram Eighteen: Complex Depression

Complex Treatment Sequence for Depression

Meridian		Location
Eyebrow (EB)	1	Beginning of eyebrow at bridge of nose
Side of Eye (SE)	2	Side of eye on bony orbit near temple
Under Eye (UE)	3	Under the center of eye on tip of bone
Under Nose (UN)	4	Above upper lip and below the center of nose
Under Bottom Lip (UBL)	5	Under bottom lip in cleft of chin
Under Arm (UA)	6	Six inches under armpit
Under Collarbone (UCB)	7	One inch under collarbone near throat
Little Finger (LF)	8	Inside tip of little fingernail on the side
Index Finger (IF)	9	Inside tip of index fingernail on the side

If the feelings of depression should happen to return at a later time, repeat these treatments. In time, recurrence of depression symptoms will become less and less frequent. For many people, it will be unlikely for the depression to recur.

DEPRESSION TRIGGERED BY ANGER

Many therapists believe—and in many cases it is true—that depression is "anger turned inward." That is, some undesirable event has happened in your life, and you beat yourself up by suffering an unhealthy dose of depression. In this case, attention to the events that led to the depression is important. Referring to chapter 10, you can treat these events as traumas and also forgive yourself by using the anger and guilt treatments outlined in chapter 8. If your anger at yourself is extreme, the treatment for rage, also in chapter 8, may be needed.

DEPRESSION AND ANXIETY

Quite often depression and anxiety are intermixed. Anxiety is a feeling of dread, nervousness, and perhaps fear of the worst happening. Depression is a *down* or a *depressed* feeling and state of affairs. Also, you can often feel anxious about being depressed or feel depressed about being anxious. In such cases, it is important to treat the anxiety as well as the depression. See chapter 7 for effective anxiety reduction treatments.

LOSSES THAT CAUSE DEPRESSION

Frequently, significant losses are involved in depression. If this is the case, it may be important for you to specifically target the loss as a trauma and neutralize it with one of the trauma treatment sequences. (See chapter 10 for more information.)

MASSIVE PSYCHOLOGICAL REVERSALS

Massive reversal is commonly involved in depression (see chapter 6). Often, it is important to repeat the massive reversal treatment frequently throughout the day during the time when you are treating yourself for depression. The following more intricate treatment for massive reversal may prove beneficial if the standard treatment for massive reversal proves insufficient. You should repeat this treatment at least five times throughout the day:

1. Briskly massage the Sore Spot (SS) on the left side of your chest while saying or thinking three times, "I deeply and profoundly accept myself with all my problems and limitations, even though I'm depressed."

2. Then tap at the Under Nose (UN) point while saying or thinking three times, "I deeply and profoundly accept myself with all my problems and limitations, even if I never get over this depression."

3. Tap at the Under Bottom Lip (UBL) point while saying or thinking three times, "I deeply and profoundly accept myself with all my problems and limitations, even if I don't deserve to get over this depression."

QUIT THINKING SO MUCH

As noted previously, there are many causes of depression, although the energy imbalance cause is the most fundamental. Nonetheless, your thinking is very much interrelated with your energy and you may have developed some "bad thinking" habits over the years. Even though you may have balanced your energy, it is advisable to observe the connection between your thoughts and your feelings. Recognizing when you are entertaining thoughts that in the past promoted and supported your depression is an important step. You need alternative solutions so you can readily dismiss such thoughts. For example, if depressive thoughts reoccur when you are alone too often, then you must take the time to develop a more active social life. This can be as simple as taking classes after work or learning new hobbies or skills. This will help you to remain in a more balanced state of mind and energy, aiding the specific energetic treatments provided in this book.

It also is important to note that dismissing depressive thoughts doesn't mean suppressing them. When you suppress, you're just trying to push the thought out of your mind, but you still essentially believe that what you are thinking is true. Instead, you need to make a shift in your understanding of depressive thoughts. That is, you need to recognize that the real cause of the depression is the connection between your thoughts and energy. As you allow such thoughts to evaporate, you will see that they were not the truth at all, but rather were a distorted way of thinking about your life and yourself. The thought only appeared to be true because your energy system was disrupted. In essence, the depressive thought is a mirage or an illusion, and you need to become *disillusioned* about it. Once you are able to see through it, your energy will be balanced.

SUMMARY

In this chapter we have provided information about clinical depression and its treatment. Although we've offered detailed energy psychology treatments that have proved effective in the treatment of depression and related aspects of this disease, self-help is not always sufficient. If you find that you have been able to use these suggestions to alleviate depression, wonderful—keep it up. If the treatments did not prove sufficient for your needs, however, you are strongly advised against seeing this as an indication that effective help is not available. Depression is eminently treatable. We strongly encourage you to contact a qualified mental health professional for assistance in general and to assist you specifically with regard to the energy approach described in this book.

10

Resolving Trauma and Painful Memories Rapidly

We must rid ourselves of yesterday's negative thoughts to receive today's new and positive feelings.

–Sydney Banks

Painful memories are the result of experiencing traumatic events. Unfortunately, traumatic events are far too common in today's society and are the cause of many psychological problems and much unhappiness. Many health care professionals also believe that trauma is a major contributing cause to many physical disorders, such as cancer and heart disease. When the distressing emotions attached to the memories of these traumas are eliminated, their negative effects dissipate as well. For example, relationships and emotional and physical health improve. The treatment sequences in this chapter will help you to eliminate the impact of the various kinds of trauma you've experienced in your life.

Have you ever wondered why you consciously remember so little about your past? Whether you remember it or not, all that information is nonetheless stored within you, affecting the way you think, feel, and behave. This not only applies to your memories of traumatic events, but also to those memories that you remember as positive or neutral. Your *conscious* mind has a limited capacity for storing information. The majority of your life is stored as memories filed away in your unconscious mind. Current events or thinking about a specific time frame in your life may trigger these memories. If a memory pops up in certain situations or at certain times, it probably has meaning to you. You must evaluate the memory and determine if the event you remember had a traumatic impact on you. In most cases, the answer is self-evident.

Although this chapter primarily addresses the treatment of major traumas, you don't want to overlook other negative events that may have altered and shaped your life. These events, however, are usually not classified clinically as traumas. They can be events that occurred when you were much younger and now, as an adult, you believe that they should be viewed as trivial. At the time that the incident occurred, however, you did not have the coping resources now available to you. Therefore, the event may have left an emotional mark on you. That is, it may have lowered your sense of self or contributed to your not accepting a part of yourself. This is frequently how energy imbalances and reversals are created.

It is amazing how a cruel remark made by an acquaintance or even a stranger can have a significant, long-lasting effect on you. One woman, for example, said that a remark made by a shoe salesman twenty years ago continued to affect the way she felt about herself today. It can be that simple. Of course, this doesn't mean that all negative events that happened when you were younger will have a lasting impact on you. But if an incident hurt your feelings or affected the way you feel about yourself, it's time to treat that memory with the techniques covered in this chapter.

There is no shortage of major traumas. Generally, the death of a child is the most traumatic. In 1997, in the United States alone, there were 28,000 infant deaths and an additional 46,000 deaths of children and young adults ages one to twenty-four (National Center for Health Statistics 1997). Additionally, crime victims have been traumatized, and the judicial process often retraumatizes them. Each year there are millions of reported crimes involving rape, robbery, and assault. Furthermore, there are countless families traumatized by the 20,000 homicides and 30,000 suicides each year in the United States alone (National Center for Health Statistics 1997). Other traumatic events include sexual abuse, incest, natural disasters like floods or hurricanes, car accidents, and more. If you were traumatized by any events like these, you can use the treatments in this chapter to put these painful memories to rest.

Traumas and lingering painful memories can lead to secondary problems, such as an "unwillingness" to psychologically let go of the event. After some traumatic events, psychological reversal can set in and block your ability to see the situation from any perspective other than a distressing one. For example, if you were to lose a child, you might believe that if you allowed yourself to let go of your pain, it would mean that you had not cared about your child. Nothing, however, could be further from the truth. No matter what you do, you will always care about your child and you will continue to feel sadness and loss. Once your energy system is balanced about the event, however, the memory no longer will continue to overwhelm you or prevent you from moving on with your life.

Being assaulted also can provoke an "unwillingness-to-let-go-of . . ." response. If you were mugged or beaten, for example, you might feel that letting go of the trauma would either jeopardize your safety or be equivalent to absolving the perpetrator of wrongdoing. Again, these types of thoughts are not accurate. Getting over a trauma such as assault does not invariably set you up to be assaulted again. Although resolving the trauma helps you to feel and function better, it doesn't cause you to forget what happened or to forget any useful information you gained from the experience. That is, if a specific person assaulted you, you would still know to avoid that person in the future. Also, as far as exoneration is concerned, what's right is right, and what's wrong is wrong. How you currently react to your memory of the event does not affect the fact that the perpetrator was nothing short of evil in his actions. When you resolve your painful memories, however, you become stronger and better able to deal with the traumatic memory.

Trauma also can lead to other problems, such as shame, self-blame, belittlement, powerlessness, and resignation. By reviewing the information in chapter 1, you can gauge the trauma's impact on your energy level. If you are feeling one of these strong emotions, it is possible that a psychological reversal has occurred, causing you to sabotage some area of your life. If such is the case, you will also have to treat the secondary problems, along with the painful memories, in order to resolve the problem. The treatments in this chapter will make this task easier.

THE TREATMENT PROCESS

Traumatic events are divided into three groups: simple trauma, complex trauma, and highly complex trauma. At times, resolution of traumatic issues may require the assistance of a qualified psychotherapist who is trained in energy therapy. In many cases, however, self-administering the treatment sequences in this chapter will yield positive healing results.

Self-Treatment

There are some instances when a traumatic memory will continue to bother you even after you have tried to treat it. In these cases, simply assume that the trauma has not been completely treated and then cycle through the appropriate treatment sequence again. Be optimistic. Once the pain associated with the memory has been completely treated, it should never bother you again. There are instances in which severe psychological stress or energy toxins cause a thoroughly treated problem to return. This is rare, however, and your persistence in treating the traumatic memories with the sequences in this chapter will pay off in time.

Treatment for Simple Trauma

As was noted earlier in this chapter, simple traumas can be any event in your life that you feel is holding you back. They can involve cruel remarks, embarrassing situations, times when you were bullied, or perceived mistakes you've made in your life for which you continue to punish yourself. Often, a single isolated event can be treated with this sequence. If there is more than one part involved, however, each aspect should be treated individually, one at a time. For example, let's say that the event was an argument with a friend and that the friend said something insulting and then, later in the argument, did something else that was hurtful. The argument, that is, the traumatic event, would involve two distinct aspects, and each would be treated separately.

As always, the first step in the treatment sequence is to remember the event. It's not necessary to experience any discomfort, except for a brief moment when the memory of the event is recalled. The purpose of recalling the event is twofold: to get a distress rating, and to make sure that the problem memory is tuned in so that it can be successfully treated. Concerning the latter, to simply go through energy psychology treatments without tuning in to the event possibly could result in a pleasant feeling of relaxation, but it would do nothing to resolve a specific problem. The problem must be brought to your awareness, although it need be only at the subtlest level.

1. Think about a traumatic or painful memory. It should be a single, specific event. Rate your level of distress on a scale of 0 to 10, with 10 representing the highest level of distress and 0 indicating no stress.

2. Treat for the possibility of reversal by tapping repeatedly on the Side of Hand (SH) or rubbing the Sore Spot (SS) while thinking or saying three times, "I deeply accept myself even though I'm upset." It also may be helpful to tap the SH or rub the SS while saying, "I accept myself with all my problems and limitations." You can be specific about the event.

3. Look at diagram 19 and the treatment sequence for simple trauma under the diagram to identify the locations for the meridian points for Eyebrow (EB) and Under Collarbone (UCB). While vaguely thinking about the event (don't get into it so much that you experience any major discomfort during the process), tap five times at each of these meridian points. Tap them in the following order 1 → 2. Tap only hard enough to feel it. It shouldn't cause any pain.

4. Again, rate your distress on a 0 to 10 scale (a number should just pop into your mind). If there is no decrease, go back to step 2 and cycle through the sequence again. If there is not a decrease after three attempts, this is probably not an appropriate sequence for this event, or else there is another sabotaging belief (reversal) that needs correction. Consider using the Complex Trauma Sequence (in this chapter).

5. Next, do the Brain Balancer (BB) by tapping repeatedly at the Back of Hand (BH) while rotating your eyes clockwise, rotating your eyes counterclockwise, then humming a tune, counting to five, and humming again.

6. Repeat the tapping sequence 1 → 2.

7. Again, rate your level of distress from 0 to 10. It should be lower yet. When the distress is within the 0 to 2 range, go to step 9. Sometimes,

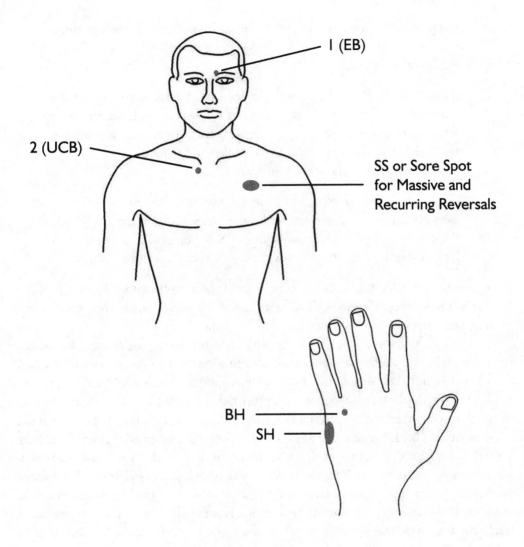

Diagram Nineteen: Simple Trauma

Treatment Sequence for Simple Trauma

Meridian		Location
Eyebrow (EB)	1	Beginning of eyebrow near bridge of nose
Under Collarbone (UCB)	2	One inch under collarbone near throat

you'll need to repeat the treatment several times—while you are thinking about your trauma—before you feel complete relief from the distressing situation.

8. As long as there is a decrease in the level of distress, continue with the sequence until there is very little or no stress remaining. If the treatment stalls at any point, this indicates a mini-reversal. Treat this by tapping on the little finger Side of Hand (SH) while saying three times, "I deeply accept myself, even though I'm still upset."

9. When the distress level is 0 to 2, do the Eye Roll (ER) to lower the distress further or to complete the treatment effects. To do this, tap on the Back of Hand (BH), hold your head straight and, moving only your eyes, look at the floor and then slowly raise your eyes toward the ceiling.

In most cases, once a trauma has been treated successfully with this sequence, the distress will not return. If distress should return at a later time, repeat these treatments. In time, the distress will become less and less frequent.

It should be noted that the trauma treatment sequences do not change the memories themselves. Rather, they eliminate the upsetting emotional elements of the memory. So, when you have successfully treated a trauma, notice that you will still be able to recall the event in detail, although you may feel rather detached from it. Also, you may notice that you can actually recall the event more vividly than you could before you did the treatment. This is because you are no longer distracted by emotional upset, making it possible for you to look unwaveringly at the event and think about what happened. It's as though a memory has different tracks: visual, sound, emotional, and belief. Energy psychology treatments serve to erase the negative emotional track, not the visual or sound tracks. Moreover, because the belief track is generally attached to the emotional track, the treatment may affect your beliefs about the trauma, usually moving them in a more positive direction.

In some cases, however, people report that although the memory no longer bothers them, they are no longer able to recall it clearly. The image might be described as vague, unclear, disjointed, fragmented, and so forth. If this happens to you, it is not cause for concern. You might like to repeat the treatment, however, because the difficulty seeing and/or hearing the event is sometimes, although not always, an indication that the trauma has not been thoroughly treated. Repeating the treatment may result in an ability to clearly see and hear what happened in a calm, relaxed manner.

Complex Trauma

Generally, complex traumas involve traumatic or other painful memories that have many aspects and greater complexity in terms of emotional distress than do single-event focused simple traumas. The following two case studies will help you to understand the types of complex traumas that can be resolved by using energy psychology.

WAR TRAUMA: A CASE STUDY

Bill was a Vietnam vet who had been decorated with honors for his valor in combat. However, he bore the scars of the war: an amputated left leg above the knee, a respiratory condition caused by Agent Orange, alcohol and drug dependence, and a whole host of traumatic memories that found their way into his dreams at night, and often surfaced during his waking hours as well. He suffered frequent flashbacks about fellow soldiers who had been blown up in the war and the people he had had to kill. He also maintained the belief that the world is a hopeless place and that he had been guilty of committing atrocities. Although he had only defended himself in battles, he nonetheless suffered guilt, including survivor's guilt.

Bill had been in psychotherapy before. He had tried group work, emotional reliving, numerous medications, alcohol and drug rehabilitation, and so on. He was barely getting by in life. When Bill's sister heard about energy psychology, she made a consultation appointment for him to see if it would be of any help. On the day of the initial session, Bill was exceptionally nervous. He expected therapy to proceed in the same way that he had previously experienced. He didn't want to take trips back into his painful memories, or to relive scenes that he would have preferred had never happened in the first place. In fact, he would have liked to forget about them altogether, although that was not possible at the time.

Most people receive optimal treatment if they are in a more secure mood. After becoming more relaxed, Bill described one scene that had haunted him since his tour in Vietnam. He had been engaged in hand-to-hand combat and that scene continued to exist in his memory as a source of distress. When Bill talked briefly about the event, he turned white and started to shake. He was told to tap on several specific meridian points. He repeated this and some other treatments several times and, within the course of approximately five minutes, the memory of that incident no longer bothered him. He could remember what happened clearly, but he no longer turned white, nor did he shake. Actually, he was quite calm. With some bewilderment in his voice, he stated: "It doesn't bother me. I can see what happened, but it doesn't bother me!"

After the treatment, Bill no longer felt guilty about the event. He could see clearly that he had had no alternative other than to defend himself and his fellow soldiers in the war. Bill was seen many times over the next few years and at no time did that particular memory bother him again. He has remained calm about it ever since. It should be noted, however, that resolving that particular combat memory was not sufficient to resolve all of Bill's problems. Treatment for many other traumatic memories and other issues was needed. However, he never experienced nightmares, flashbacks, or emotional distress about that specific memory again. Furthermore, as his energy psychology treatments progressed, he experienced improvement in many other areas of his life as well.

RAPE TRAUMA: A CASE STUDY

When Barbara was thirteen years old, her eighteen-year-old boyfriend raped her. This trauma devastated her well into her early thirties. She had an extensive drug and alcohol problem and, in most respects, lived a notably anxious and depressive lifestyle. Over the years, she had received treatment at a number of inpatient and outpatient psychiatric facilities. When she began energy psychology treatments, she was taking a regimen of psychiatric medications, including Lithium, Prozac, and Desyrel. Even so, she was not doing well. During her first energy treatment session, Barbara discussed her rape incident; it was evident that she was still traumatized. She cried deeply and, in many respects, seemed to be reliving the event in memory. She said that she had been to blame, that she should have known better, that she had never listened to her mother. As she spoke, it was as though she were that thirteen-year-old girl once again.

Although not all of her psychological problems could necessarily be traced back to the rape, there was no question that the event was a significantly painful memory that had set her on a path of great misery. The energy trauma treatment took less than ten minutes and it completely resolved Barbara's painful memory. Not only did Barbara no longer feel painful emotions while reviewing the memory, but her belief about the situation and herself changed dramatically as well. Immediately after the treatment was completed, she was able to tell me with obvious conviction that the rape was "just something that happened" in her past and that she was "not to blame."

Both of these situations are examples of a complex trauma. Remember, when treating this type of trauma, each aspect involved in the traumatic event should be treated individually, one at a time.

TREATMENT SEQUENCE FOR COMPLEX TRAUMA

1. Think about the traumatic event. It should be a single, specific event. Rate your level of distress on a scale from 0 to 10, with 10 representing the highest level of distress and 0 indicating no stress.

2. Treat for the possibility of reversal by tapping repeatedly on the Side of Hand (SH) or rubbing the Sore Spot (SS) while thinking or saying three times, "I deeply accept myself even though I'm upset about what happened." You can be specific about the event. It also may be helpful to tap the SH or rub the SS while saying, "I accept myself with all my problems and limitations."

3. Look at diagram 20 and the treatment sequence for complex trauma under the diagram to identify the location for the meridian points for Eyebrow (EB), Under Eye (UE), Under Arm (UA), and Under Collarbone (UCB). While thinking about the event (don't get into it so much that you experience any major discomfort during the process), tap five times at each of these meridian points. Tap them in the following

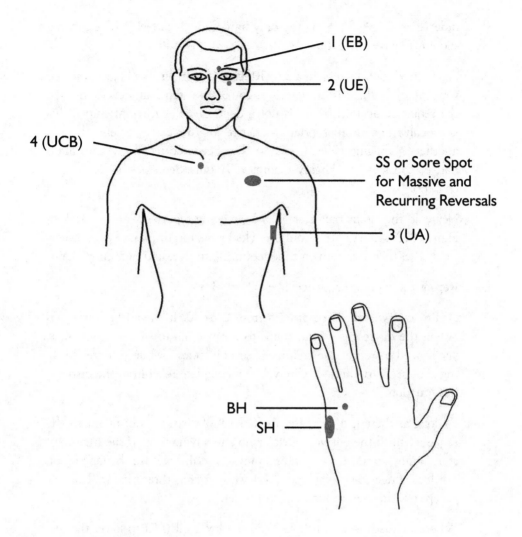

Diagram Twenty: Complex Trauma

Treatment Sequence for Complex Trauma

Meridian		Location
Eyebrow (EB)	1	Beginning of eyebrow near bridge of nose
Under Eye (UE)	2	Under the center of the eye on tip of bone
Under Arm (UA)	3	Six inches under armpit
Under Collarbone (UCB)	4	One inch under collarbone near throat

order 1 → 2 → 3 → 4. Tap only hard enough to feel it. The tapping shouldn't cause any pain.

4.   Again, rate your distress on a 0 to 10 scale (a number should just pop into your mind). If there is no decrease, go back to step 2 and cycle through the sequence again. If there is not a decrease after three attempts, this is probably not an appropriate sequence for this event, or else there is another sabotaging belief (reversal) that needs correction. As an alternative, consider the Highly Complex Trauma Sequence (later in this chapter).

5.   Next, do the Brain Balancer (BB) by tapping repeatedly at the Back of Hand (BH) while rotating your eyes clockwise, rotating your eyes counterclockwise, then humming a tune, counting to five, and humming again.

6.   Repeat the tapping sequence 1 → 2 → 3 → 4.

7.   Again, rate your level of distress from 0 to 10. It should be lower yet. When the distress is within the 0 to 2 range, go to step 9. Sometimes, you'll need to repeat the treatment several times—while you are thinking about your trauma—before you feel complete relief from the distressing situation.

8.   As long as there is a decrease in the level of distress, continue with the sequence until there is very little or no stress remaining. If the treatment stalls at any point, this indicates a mini-reversal. Treat this by tapping on the little finger Side of Hand (SH) while saying three times, "I deeply accept myself, even though I'm still upset."

9.   When the distress level is 0 to 2, do the Eye Roll (ER) to lower the distress further or to complete the treatment effects. To do this, tap on the Back of Hand (BH), hold your head straight, and, moving only your eyes, look at the floor and then slowly raise your eyes toward the ceiling.

In most cases, once a trauma has been successfully treated with this sequence, the distress will not return. If distress should return at a later time, however, repeat these treatments. In time, the distress will become less and less frequent.

Highly Complex Trauma

One analogy or image for highly complex traumas is that of a cafeteria tray dispenser. As soon as you remove one tray, another pops into place. If the objective was to remove all of the trays, you would continue to remove trays, one after another, until the last tray had been removed. The same line of reasoning applies to many psychological and emotional problems. That is, after you treat one problem, another appears. Problems are often not just singular events, but are composed of many aspects. They can even be layered, one on top of another.

Arthur Koestler (1967) coined the term "holon" to describe this concept. A *holon* indicates a whole that is part of an even greater whole. If a trauma is composed of many holons, for instance, each element of the trauma both encompasses and goes beyond the one that came before it. Consequently, each individual holon, that is, element of the trauma, must be treated before the trauma as a whole can be resolved.

One exception to this theory occurs when the trauma being treated is the earliest one in a series. Often, resolving the earliest trauma will also alleviate all of the later ones. In this case, each of the traumas is a holon to the network or series of interrelated traumas. One patient, for example, had been physically abused by her father repeatedly when she was a child. The first incident of her trauma was when, at age seven, she incurred her father's physical wrath after she accidentally dropped her baby brother, who cried, but was not seriously injured. She reported that after that particular trauma had been resolved with energy psychology treatments, all the later incidents in which her father had abused her no longer caused her any distress. She expressed the view that perhaps this was because the various events had been so similar.

Please note: Even though simultaneous collapsing of related traumas frequently happens, this does not always occur. Therefore, when treating a disturbing memory, it is important to think about the event sequentially, from beginning to end, treating each aspect as you go along. In this way, you can be assured that the trauma as a whole has been successfully and thoroughly treated.

In some cases, the complex trauma treatments will totally eliminate the distress associated with the painful event, and repeating the treatment with each component of the problem will not be necessary. However, an untreated aspect may continue to stir up negative emotions, making it appear as if the treatment is not working. This is why it is important to break down the trauma into sequenced events and be prepared to treat each one. For example, one woman's husband had committed suicide shortly after an argument with her. Her memory of the event had the following sequential aspects:

1. An embarrassing scene at a party

2. An ensuing argument upon returning home

3. Her husband threatening her with a gun

4. Her husband shooting himself

5. Calling her sister on the phone for help

6. Calling 911

7. The police arriving and accusing her of shooting her husband

8. Events related to the funeral, having to move, and so forth

Each of the scenes in the woman's memory carried with it specific negative emotions, including embarrassment, anger, fear, and then panic. In treating this trauma, all of these negative aspects had to be treated thoroughly. That is, it was not enough to treat an aspect that was at a high level of distress and reduce it to a 4 or 5; it had to get down to a 0 (no distress at all). Also, if an important aspect was not addressed at all, the patient would continue to experience distress. The following case study illustrates the procedure and benefits of treating highly complex traumas.

THE DEATH OF A CHILD: A CASE STUDY

Debbie had been suffering from trauma and depression ever since her infant son had died in the hospital a couple days after birth. This had happened more than two years before our initial session. The trauma was taking its toll on Debbie emotionally as well as on her relationship with Harold, her husband. They couldn't talk about their child's death, and Harold's silence and seeming nonchalance suggested to her that he didn't care about what had happened or about her. They were on the verge of divorce.

Debbie and Harold entered treatment because of their frequent arguments. After the arguments took place, Harold often would withdraw for days, frequently not coming home after work. Their entire relationship was on a downward spiral. It was apparent that neither of them had resolved the trauma concerning the baby's death. Debbie's way of coping was to talk about it, whereas Harold's approach was to leave it alone.

Their first energy psychology session was taken up gathering details about their relationship and their problems. During the second session, however, it was explained to them that a significant aspect of their relationship difficulties might be the fact that they had continued feeling distressed about the loss of their infant. Although obviously nothing could be done to bring their child back, energy psychology treatments could relieve the trauma and thus increase their chances of regaining a healthy relationship.

They were both treated in the office on the same day. Debbie was first. When she thought about the death she immediately began to cry. Within a few minutes of providing energy psychology treatments, she was able to think about the event in a much calmer manner. Although there was still great sadness attached to the memory, the extreme distress had dissipated. It was explained to Debbie that this treatment might need to be repeated until all of the traumatic aspects were resolved.

Next, Harold was taken through the same type of treatment. At first he claimed that he felt no distress. While the energy psychology treatments were being provided, however, he started to cry. We discussed his emotions and he indicated that he had not realized that there was so much distress under his surface calm. Debbie had an opportunity to witness that he did care. With his permission, the treatments were administered again and he felt much better.

A follow-up visit the next week revealed a significant shift in both Harold and Debbie's distress levels regarding their infant son's death. Although there was still sadness concerning the child's death, they were finally able to lay the baby to rest. They were now in a better position to deal with their relationship as a whole.

HIGHLY COMPLEX TRAUMA TREATMENT

A treatment sequence for highly complex trauma follows. Generally, this treatment works with traumatic or other painful memories that have many aspects and greater complexity in terms of emotional distress than can be resolved adequately by the previous treatment sequences. If there are a number of aspects involved in the traumatic event, each aspect should be treated individually, one at a time.

1. Think about the traumatic event. It should be a single, specific event. Rate your level of distress on a scale of 0 to 10, with 10 representing the highest level of distress and 0 indicating no stress.

2. Treat for the possibility of reversal by tapping repeatedly on the Side of Hand (SH) or rubbing the Sore Spot (SS) while thinking or saying three times, "I deeply accept myself even though I'm upset." You can be specific about the event. It also may be helpful to tap the SH or rub the SS while saying, "I accept myself with all my problems and limitations."

3. Look at diagram 21 and the treatment sequence for highly complex trauma under the diagram to identify the locations for the meridian points for Eyebrow (EB), Under Eye (UE), Under Arm (UA), Under Collarbone (UCB), Little Finger (LF), and Index Finger (IF). While thinking about the event (don't get into it so much that you experience any major discomfort during the process), tap five times at each of these meridian points. Tap them in the following order 1 → 2 → 3 → 4 → 5 → 4 → 6 → 4. **Note:** The UCB appears three times in the sequence. Tap only hard enough to feel it. The tapping shouldn't cause any pain.

4. Again, rate your distress on a 0 to 10 scale (a number should just pop into your mind). If there is no decrease, go back to step 2 and cycle through the sequence again. If there is not a decrease after three attempts, this is probably not an appropriate sequence for this event, or else there is another sabotaging belief (reversal) that needs correction. Also there may be an earlier trauma that needs to be addressed.

5. Next, do the Brain Balancer (BB) by tapping repeatedly at the Back of Hand (BH) while rotating your eyes clockwise, rotating your eyes counterclockwise, then humming a tune, counting to five, and humming again.

6. Repeat the tapping sequence 1 → 2 → 3 → 4 → 5 → 4 → 6 → 4.

7. Again, rate your level of distress from 0 to 10. It should be lower yet. When the distress is within the 0 to 2 range, go to step 9. Sometimes, you'll need to repeat the treatment several times while thinking about your trauma before you feel complete relief from the distressing situation.

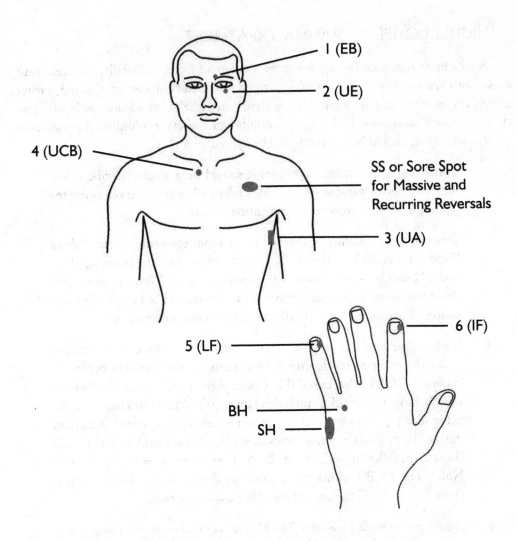

Diagram Twenty-One: Highly Complex Trauma

Treatment Sequence for Highly Complex Trauma

Meridian		Location
Eyebrow (EB)	1	Beginning of eyebrow near bridge of nose
Under Eye (UE)	2	Under the center of the eye on tip of bone
Under Arm (UA)	3	Six inches under armpit
Under Collarbone (UCB)	4	One inch under collarbone near throat
Little Finger (LF)	5	Inside tip of little fingernail on the side
Index Finger (IF)	6	Inside tip of index fingernail on the outside

8. As long as there is a decrease in the level of distress, continue with the sequence until there is very little or no stress remaining. If the treatment stalls at any point, this indicates a mini-reversal. Treat this by tapping on the little finger Side of Hand (SH) while saying three times, "I deeply accept myself, even though I'm still upset."

9. When the distress level is 0 to 2, do the Eye Roll (ER) to lower the distress further or to complete the treatment effects. To do this, tap on the Back of Hand (BH), hold your head straight and, moving only your eyes, look at the floor and then slowly raise your eyes toward the ceiling.

In most cases, once a trauma has successfully been treated with this sequence, the distress will not return. However, if distress should return at a later time, repeat these treatments. In time, distress will become less and less frequent.

SUMMARY

This chapter has covered how to resolve traumatic and other painful memories rapidly. Many other conditions covered in this book, such as phobias, panic, depression, rage, and even negative beliefs about who you are and what you are capable of doing originate from experiences that can be effectively treated with these sequences. Weeding out the traumas of our lives is an important step toward becoming psychologically, emotionally, and physically healthy. Perhaps if these treatments were to be used on a widespread basis (for example, as the psychological equivalent of the Heimlich maneuver), many of the problems that we experience in society would quickly dissolve.

11

Improving Your Sports Performance

The game of golf is 90 percent mental.

—Jack Nicklaus

The goal in an athletic event is to play to the best of your ability; that is, to maintain an energy level that allows your natural ability to come through without hesitation or doubt. This doesn't mean that you'll win—it means that you are giving yourself every opportunity to win. The key to doing this is to eliminate the self-defeating beliefs and anxiety that can cause mistakes and result in you playing at less than your ability.

Energy work will not compensate for a lack of ability or the practice required to excel at any sport. It can, however, help you to eliminate any self-sabotaging thoughts and excessive anxiety that prevent you from playing at your best, especially in crucial situations. When using energy psychology to improve your sports performance, you must factor in your skill level and mental attitude when evaluating your success. Additionally, you must be realistic about what you are trying to accomplish. For instance, a golfer who shoots in the 90s isn't going to make the pro tour just by using energy psychology methods, but that player can eliminate a lot of needless mistakes and probably shoot consistently in the 80s.

Athletes often lose their mental focus when playing a sport, especially if they have unrealistic expectations or feel that they are playing poorly. Energy work can help you to regain your focus, but you still need realistic expectations about your playing ability that day. For example, if you know from experience that you normally hit 70 percent of your free throws in basketball, then that is what you should expect to do in crucial situations. That means that even if you are focused and at your best, you can miss the shot. If the miss results in you becoming angry or losing your focus, this is a self-defeating behavior. When used regularly, energy psychology is a tool that can help you to improve your game. You will be less anxious in crucial situations and will remain focused and positive while you are playing.

> Energy psychology will not improve your natural athletic ability, but it certainly can help you to play consistently at your best.

The energy psychology techniques in this chapter can easily be applied to any athletic situation. If you play competitive sports, you know that some mistakes are created purely by anxiety. Most likely, you know the feeling as it occurs. It is obvious that an athlete is anxious, for example, when he or she cannot perform a task that is within their ability level. What really occurs when a professional basketball player shoots an air ball from the free-throw line or a golfer repeatedly misses short putts? If flubs happen often or in crucial situations, anxiety, fear, and self-sabotaging beliefs are probably involved.

MANAGING PERFORMANCE ANXIETY AND FEARS

Choking in the sports world refers to an inability to manage anxiety and fears at crucial times during athletic events. Although anxiety is usually the central cause of choking, negative beliefs can also fuel this feeling. When you are too tense, for instance, your muscles tighten up and can cause you to lose the keen sense of touch and feel that is crucial in any athletic event. Once that subtle feeling is lost, you may try to compensate by doing something harder or faster, which is generally an ineffective solution.

When using energy psychology to improve your athletic performance, it is important to identify crucial situations in which you know that you have the skill to play better, and yet you regularly err. For example, golfers most likely have an energy problem if 80 percent of the time they are on the driving range they can hit the ball high and 140 yards with their seven iron, but when they are in front of a pond, they consistently slice the ball or hit it into the water. In this situation, the golfers' belief that they can't hit the ball over the water sabotages their game; they become so anxious in front of the water that it prevents them from completing their normal swing.

Focus

The most difficult task in many sports is maintaining focus. Many professional athletes have reported that energy psychology helps them to improve their focus significantly. There are two types of focus: mechanical and mental. Although they overlap, energy work primarily affects the latter. You need to work on your mechanical focus with a qualified instructor or coach. Mechanical considerations include physical skills, such as how you stand and set up to hit or putt a ball. If, during a game, you become too concerned about your mechanics, it is difficult for you to focus mentally. This, in turn, limits your ability to relax and play at your best.

Energy psychology indirectly helps the mechanical part of your game. As you use energy work to decrease your anxiety and eliminate sabotaging thoughts, you will find it much easier to identify and correct your mechanical skills. For example, continually missing short- and medium-length putts will lead you to feel anxious and to lack confidence in your game. Once you balance your energy and lower your anxiety, however, you will be better able to detect and resolve real performance issues that may, in part, be mechanical.

You must also have faith in yourself and not lose your focus because of any one particular performance. No athlete can perform at the same level every day. The goal is to stay focused no matter what happens and continue playing to your best ability. If you lack confidence or have unrealistic expectations, you will start to focus on your mistakes or bad breaks and apply less focus to the task at hand.

Events that are not within your control can also alter the game. The key is to determine how you respond to a situation that's out of your control. Again, if you worry about what happened or dwell on bad outcomes, you will lose focus and diminish your chances for success. If you use energy work to accept these situations, you will stay focused. Your opponents may eventually encounter similar situations and lose their focus. You never know, even professional athletes "fumble the ball," so to speak. So, don't ever give up. Keep in mind that it is impossible to perform at your best skill level when you become angry or frustrated or blame outside situations.

In the treatment section that follows, we will examine the beliefs that create self-sabotage and provide treatment sequences that will eliminate sabotage and any accompanying anxiety. We will also help you to identify a single treatment point that will help to reduce anxiety and keep you focused while you are playing your sport of choice.

CREATING PEAK PERFORMANCE IN SPORTS

Self-acceptance is always a crucial element of success in sports. If you can't accept yourself or the situation when you make a mistake, you are less likely to succeed. This doesn't mean that you are not trying to improve or work harder. There is a big difference between players who think they can play better and those who become angry or blame others for their own poor performance.

Three Common Beliefs

There are three common beliefs that affect your sporting performance: a fear of success, overcompetitiveness, and outside influences.

FEAR OF SUCCESS

Fear of success centers around the fact that you don't think you are good enough to succeed. We're not talking about your athletic skills, but your overall sense of who you are. What would change if you became a great (at your level) athlete? People might think about you differently or treat you differently. Perhaps by self-sabotaging your skill, it helps you to maintain a certain belief you have about yourself, such as you don't deserve to win, or that you aren't worthy of the situation.

OVERCOMPETITIVENESS

Winning is an outcome, not a process. Those who are winners never lose the composure or focus that allows them to play at their best. If your focus becomes one of beating your opponent, rather than the strategy or activity that you must employ, you have a self-defeating behavior. There is a very fine line between being a winner and wanting to win too much, but once you cross it, you are no longer focused on playing at the best of your ability.

OUTSIDE INFLUENCES, AKA "I'M NOT GETTING ANY BREAKS"

Here the athlete believes that he or she is not lucky or that other athletes are lucky. Although this may be true to some extent, luck in sports usually derives from the athlete not making any crucial mistakes or not trying to accomplish goals that are beyond his or her ability level. If an athlete blames his game on outside influences, he usually loses focus and becomes angry or frustrated with the situation. Then he may believe that only something special will make the difference and therefore attempt a low percentage play or shot. Perhaps his belief is that it's his "turn to get lucky." In this case, the athlete has moved away from the central point of all athletic events: to stay focused and execute your role to the best of your ability. You may be aware of other beliefs that limit your success in sports, and you can easily include them in the following treatment plan. Look for emotions or beliefs that make you lose your focus or prevent you from regaining it. Examples include emotions such as anger, frustration, and anxiety; or beliefs such as, "I can't win," "I don't care anymore," "I'm unlucky," or "I'm not good enough." While deep-seated beliefs such as "I don't deserve to win" may sound strange, they are very real and limit many athletes.

> No matter what happens when you play, your ability to accept it and stay focused is the only way to play to the best of your ability each day.

TREATMENT PLAN FOR SPORTS ISSUES

All energy treatments to some degree revolve around self-acceptance. When you are angry or lose trust in yourself, you are thinking that the situation should not happen. You can be so concerned about the outcome that you lose your focus. This, in turn, blocks your ability to reach your peak performance. On the other hand, once you accept yourself—even if you do not succeed—you have opened the door to change, enabling yourself to get back on track and regain your focus.

Although the examples in the following treatment focus on golf, the same concepts can be used in any athletic or performance situation.

1. Clearly define the problem that you want to resolve. It must be specific and within your current level of ability to achieve. For example, "When I become anxious I miss short putts that I easily make during practice." Remember to be specific and not to generalize, such as "I stink at golf." You can, however, experiment with some generalizations, such as "I always make mistakes at crucial times." The more specific your statement, the better the outcome. Now rate your nervousness or level of tension on a scale of 0 to 10, with 10 representing the highest level of tension and 0 indicating no tension.

2. Identify any sabotaging beliefs or feelings that you think are affecting your performance. Don't be hesitant. If you think it might be a problem, treat it. It takes only a minute. In time, you will come to know which beliefs are most typical of you and need to be treated regularly. Treat each reversal by tapping on the Side of Hand (SH) or rubbing the Sore Spot (SS) while thinking or saying to yourself the sabotaging belief. Below are some examples of affirmations used to correct for various reversals and beliefs:

   - I accept myself even though I am too competitive in sports.

   - I accept myself even though my anger makes me lose my focus.

   - I accept myself even though I think I'm not good enough to shoot in the 80s.

   - I accept myself even though I am too nervous when I putt.

   If you think your problem is a deep-level reversal (see chapter 6) and that you can *never* get over your problem, then tap under your nose (UN) while saying three times, "I accept myself even if I can never get over (the situation)."

3. Now look at diagram 22 and the treatment sequence for sports performance under the diagram to identify the locations for the meridian

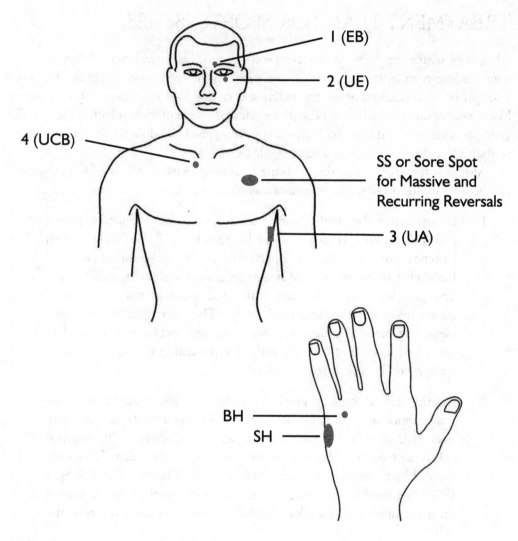

Diagram Twenty-Two: Sports Performance

Treatment Sequence for Sports Performance

Meridian		Location
Eyebrow (EB)	1	Beginning of eyebrow near bridge of nose
Under Eye (UE)	2	Under the center of the eye on tip of bone
Under Arm (UA)	3	Six inches below armpit
Under Collarbone (UCB)	4	One inch below the collarbone near throat

points for Eyebrow (EB), Under Eye (UE), Under Arm (UA), and Under Collarbone (UCB). While thinking about the situation and/or feeling, tap five times at each of these meridian points. Tap them in the following order 1 → 2 → 3 → 4. Tap only hard enough to feel it. The tapping shouldn't cause any pain.

4. Again, rate your level of distress on a 0 to 10 scale (a number should just pop into your mind). If there is no decrease, go back to step 2 and cycle though the sequence again. If there is no decrease after three attempts, this is possibly not the appropriate sequence for this situation, or else there is another sabotaging belief (reversal) that needs correction. (See step 8.)

5. Next, do the Brain Balancer (BB) by tapping repeatedly at the Back of Hand (BH) while rotating your eyes clockwise, rotating your eyes counterclockwise, then humming a tune, counting to five, and humming again.

6. Repeat the tapping sequence 1 → 2 → 3 → 4.

7. Again, rate your level of distress from 0 to 10. It should be lower yet. When the distress is within the 0 to 2 range, go to step 9. Sometimes you'll need to repeat the treatment several times while you are imagining your fear—or even while you are in the actual situation—before you feel complete relief from the distressful situation.

8. As long as there is a decrease in your level of distress, continue with the sequence until there is very little or no tension remaining. If the treatment stalls at any point, this indicates a mini-reversal. Treat this by tapping on the little finger Side of Hand (SH), while saying three times, "I deeply accept myself, even though I still have some of this problem."

9. When the distress level is 0 to 2, consider doing the Eye Roll (ER) to lower the distress further or to complete the treatment effects. To do this, tap on the Back of Hand (BH), hold your head straight and, moving only your eyes, look at the floor and then slowly raise your eyes toward the ceiling.

Note: Results sometimes do not happen instantly. In fact, it may be five or ten minutes before you are focused and playing better.

Visualization Practice

Visualization is usually a beneficial means of improving your performance in sports, as well as a number of other areas. The more confidently you can visualize accomplishing your goal, the greater your chances are of actually achieving it.

Some people have difficulty visualizing, however. One strategy that helps to enhance your visualization ability is to tap on the EB and the UA meridian points (see diagram 22) five times each, while thinking about your desired goal. Now visualize achieving your goal in as much detail as possible. You may need to repeat this process several times before you see results.

You can also attach to your visualization any positive feelings that could be associated with your goal, such as sensations of confidence or pride in your hard work. Imagine, for example, that you need a five-foot putt to put you ahead in a golf match or to break a score of 90 for the first time. Now, imagine that you are feeling a little anxious in this situation, but also confident and focused. See yourself putt the ball and watch the ball go into the cup. Smile! Although each person differs in her ability to visualize, your mind/body knows what you are doing and even a vague image may be all that is required for you.

Golf is used again as the example in the treatment sequence below. So, be sure to substitute appropriate phrases and mental images to match the sport of your choice.

1. Imagine yourself on the putting green attempting a difficult putt. Now, imagine that you have putted the ball, and you see your ball rolling toward the hole. Did it go in? If yes, then continue to pick new situations. If you did not see the ball drop in the hole, then what do you think the problem is? Do you have doubts about your ability or are you feeling too anxious?

2. If you did not see the ball roll into the hole, tap on the Side of Hand (SH) or rub the Sore Spot (SS) while thinking or saying three times, "I accept myself even if my anxiety prevents me from sinking this putt."

3. Again, think about the problem and repeat tapping on the following meridian points: 1 → 2 → 3 → 4 (see diagram 22). Now imagine the situation again. In most instances, you will be able to see the ball roll into the hole. If the putt still doesn't go in, repeat steps 2 and 3. Then tap under your nose (UN) while saying three times, "I accept myself even if I never sink this putt." Next, repeat the tapping sequence: 1 → 2 → 3 → 4. In most instances, you should now be able to see the ball go into the hole. If not, another type of reversal may be interfering with your success (see chapter 6).

You can also use this exercise to learn to cope with other anxiety-provoking situations, such as achieving a hit in baseball when the bases are loaded, hitting a good first serve in tennis, or hitting a ball over water in golf.

Key Meridian Points During the Game

The strategy at this point is to identify a *key meridian point* that helps you to focus at any point in your game when beliefs or anxieties are blocking your success. In most instances, when you tap on one of the four meridian points listed below, you will regain significant focus in a short period of time, assuming that you are not reversed. (See chapter 6 for more on reversals and self-sabotage.) You should experiment to determine which meridian points work best for you.

- Under Eye (UE)

- Under Collarbone (UCB)

- Under Arm (UA)

- Under Nose (UN)

ELIMINATE SELF-SABOTAGING THOUGHTS

Although this chapter has given you some effective treatments for anxiety, your performance in any sport is a complex and interactive activity. This means that reversals and self-sabotage can frequently occur. If you are reversed, your original problem can reoccur over and over. It is very common to experience reversals in crucial situations or when you are nearing a breakthrough goal. Therefore, significantly reducing instances of reversal will most likely require numerous treatments over an extended period of time. The good news is that if you are persistent, you will eliminate those sabotaging beliefs and reach your peak performance. (See chapter 6 for more information on reversals and self-sabotage.)

As we pointed out in the beginning of this chapter, people tend to quit when they don't receive immediate and long-lasting success with the mental element of their sport. A strong mental component takes a lot of practice, work, and time to develop; it is a complex skill, but once you learn to stay focused for long periods of time, you will be able to play more consistently at your highest skill level. The good news is that the more clearly you can identify your particular beliefs or issues, the easier it is to correct them.

Be aware of flashing thoughts when you are in the middle of your game. If you have a negative thought or visualize hitting the ball poorly, you have a self-sabotaging thought or reversal that needs to be corrected.

When you sense that you are reversed, there are two common types of reversals. For the first type, simply tap on the Side of Hand (SH) or rub the Sore Spot (SS) while thinking or saying three times to yourself, "I accept myself even though (name problem)." If that isn't effective, perhaps you believe that you can *never* eliminate the problem. To treat this second type of reversal, tap under your nose (UN) while thinking or saying several times to yourself, "I accept myself even if I never get over (name the problem)."

Then, tap on your *key point* (the key meridian point that works best for you that you explored earlier in this chapter) to regain focus and be ready to play more consistently at your best ability. After doing the following exercises, you should be more relaxed and that should be reflected in your game and by your ability to improve it.

TOUCH AND BREATHE

The Touch and Breathe method (Diepold 1999) should be used only after you first learn the treatment sequences by tapping on your meridian points. Once you've achieved success by tapping, you are ready to try the Touch and Breathe technique. It is very simple: You use the same methods to treat your problem, but instead of tapping, you use two fingers to place mild pressure on the specific meridian point while taking in a deep breath, holding it, and releasing it. For example, if you feel that you are too nervous to sink your putt on the golf course or to successfully shoot a free throw, touch the Side of Hand (SH), while thinking or saying to yourself, "I accept myself even if I miss this putt (free throw)." Then touch your key point and, if you feel the need, touch the Under Nose (UN) while thinking, "I can make this putt (free throw)." (Also see chapter 2, just above the summary, to learn about Imaginary Tapping.

SPECIFIC SPORTS

Energy psychology can be used to deal with many sports-related issues. Following are some specific suggestions for basketball, baseball, tennis, and golf. It is best to start with a situation over which you have the most control, for example, free-throw shooting in basketball, as your performance in these sports can depend on the ability and skill of your opponents over which you have the least control.

Basketball

In basketball, improving your performance at the free-throw line is the most effective place to begin using energy psychology to improve your game because your opponent cannot affect your performance, and you know your free-throw shooting percentage. The question to ask yourself is this: Does your anxiety affect your free throw? Nothing can create more tension in a game than when your free throw will determine the final outcome. Your anxiety level can skyrocket or your sabotaging beliefs can quickly surface. Other basketball-related situations that respond well to energy psychology include the occasions when you feel you cannot guard your opponent and when shots that you normally make are not going into the basket.

1. Think about a specific situation or belief that you have had while playing basketball that made you feel anxious and/or tense. Rate your level of distress on a scale of 0 to 10, with 10 representing the highest level of distress and 0 indicating no distress.

2. Treat for any sabotaging beliefs (reversals) by tapping on Side of Hand (SH) or rubbing the Sore Spot (SS) while thinking or saying to yourself three times something like, "I deeply accept myself, even though I miss free throws at the end of the game." It is best to phrase the sentence in your own words. It also may be helpful to tap the SH or rub the SS while saying, "I accept myself with all of my problems and limitations."

3. Now look at the Treatment Sequence for Basketball Performance below and at diagram 22 to identify the locations for the meridian points Eyebrow (EB), Under Eye (UE), Under Arm (UA), and Under Collarbone (UCB). While thinking about the situation or feeling, tap five times at each of these meridian points. Tap them in the following order: 1 → 2 → 3 → 4. Tap only hard enough to feel it. The tapping shouldn't cause any pain.

Treatment Sequence for Basketball Performance

Meridian		Location
Eyebrow (EB)	1	Beginning of eyebrow near bridge of nose
Under Eye (UE)	2	Under the center of the eye on tip of bone
Under Arm (UA)	3	Six inches below armpit
Under Collarbone (UCB)	4	One inch below the collarbone near throat

4. Again, rate your distress on a 0 to 10 scale (a number should just pop into your mind). If there is no decrease, go back to step 2 and cycle through the sequence again. If there is not a decrease after three attempts, this is probably not the appropriate sequence for this event, or else there is another sabotaging belief (reversal) that needs correction. (See step 8.)

5. Next, do the Brain Balancer (BB) by tapping repeatedly on the Back of Hand (BH) while rotating your eyes clockwise, rotating your eyes counterclockwise, then humming a tune, counting to five, and humming again.

6. Repeat the tapping sequence of 1 → 2 → 3 → 4.

7. Again, rate your distress from 0 to 10. It should be lower yet. When the distress is within the 0 to 2 range, go to step 9. Sometimes, you'll need to repeat the treatment several times while you are imagining your fear—or even while you are in the actual situation—before you feel complete relief from the distressful situation.

8. As long as there is a decrease in the level of distress, continue with the sequence until there is very little or no tension remaining. If the treatment stalls at any point, this indicates a mini-reversal. Treat this by tapping on the little finger Side of Hand (SH) while saying three times, "I deeply accept myself, even though I still have some of this problem."

9. When the distress level is 0 to 2, consider doing the Eye Roll to lower the distress further or to complete the treatment effects. To do this, tap on the Back of Hand (BH), hold your head straight and, moving only your eyes, look at the floor and then slowly raise your eyes toward the ceiling.

Repeat this treatment until you have little or no anxiety and then use the visualization exercises explored previously in this chapter. In a game situation, you can quickly treat your key point by using the Touch and Breathe technique to help you stay focused.

The goal of energy work is to help you to regain focus, play smart, and perform to the best of your ability that day. The result is that you stop making the same mistake repeatedly. That is, you eliminate any psychological reversals. No one plays at the same level in every game; you may need to adjust your game to compensate by passing more or requesting that your team help you more on defense. Once you are thinking clearly and are not too tense, you will understand what is wrong and you will know how to correct it.

Baseball

In baseball, pitching and hitting are the two dominant components of the game. The pitcher is under pressure each time an opposing team member is batting. If you are pitching and you have flashing thoughts, such as the batter hitting a home run, this is a strong signal to treat yourself and reevaluate what you intend to do. After you treat any distress, you should be able to visualize your pitch to the plate and a successful outcome. Because the batter's skill is going to affect the outcome, even good pitches will be hit. The goal, as in basketball, is to play smart and not make crucial mistakes. Energy psychology will help you to achieve this.

Hitting is another situation that can be successfully addressed with energy psychology. As always, defining a situation is very important. For example, there are hitters who have a great batting average when no one is on base, but whose batting average drops significantly in situations with players on second or third base. Clearly, there is more anxiety and pressure when other players are in scoring positions. Once you identify the specific situations and beliefs that are creating your anxiety, you can use the following treatment to address your fears. Then, when you are going to bat, touch your key point, take a deep breath, let it out, visualize what you want to do, and step up to the plate ready for success.

1.   Think about a specific situation or belief that you have had while playing baseball that made you feel anxious and/or tense. Rate your level of distress on a scale of 0 to 10, with 10 representing the highest level of distress and 0 indicating no distress.

2.   Treat for any sabotaging beliefs (reversals) by tapping on the Side of Hand (SH) or rubbing the Sore Spot (SS) and while thinking or saying three times something like, "I deeply accept myself even though I rarely get hits with the bases loaded." It is best to phrase the sentence in your own words. It also may be helpful to tap the SH or rub the SS while saying, "I accept myself with all my problems and limitations."

3.   Now look at the Treatment Sequence for Baseball Performance below and at diagram 22 to identify the locations for the meridian points for Eyebrow (EB), Under Eye (UE), Under Arm (UA), and Under Collarbone (UCB). While thinking about the situation or feeling, tap five times at each of these meridian points. Tap them in the following order: 1 → 2 → 3 → 4. Tap only hard enough to feel it. The tapping shouldn't cause any pain.

Treatment Sequence for Baseball Performance

Meridian		Location
Eyebrow (EB)	1	Beginning of eyebrow near bridge of nose
Under Eye (UE)	2	Under the center of the eye on tip of bone
Under Arm (UA)	3	Six inches below armpit
Under Collarbone (UCB)	4	One inch below the collarbone near throat

4.   Again, rate your distress on a 0 to 10 scale (a number should just pop into your mind). If there is no decrease, go back to step 2 and cycle through the sequence again. If there is not a decrease after three attempts, this is probably not an appropriate sequence for this situation, or else there is another sabotaging belief (reversal) that needs correction. (See step 8.)

5.   Next, do the Brain Balancer (BB) by tapping repeatedly at the Back of Hand (BH) while rotating your eyes clockwise, rotating your eyes counterclockwise, then humming a tune, counting to five, and humming again.

6. Repeat the tapping sequence of 1 → 2 → 3 → 4.

7. Again, rate your level of distress from 0 to 10. It should be lower yet. When the distress is within the 0 to 2 range, go to step 9. Sometimes, you'll need to repeat the treatment several times while you are imagining your fear—or even while you are in the actual situation—before you feel complete relief from the distressful situation.

8. As long as there is a decrease in your level of distress, continue with the sequence until there is very little or no tension remaining. If the treatment stalls at any point, this indicates a mini-reversal. Treat this by tapping on the little finger Side of Hand (SH) while saying three times, "I deeply accept myself, even though I still have some of this problem."

9. When the distress level is 0 to 2, consider doing the Eye Roll (ER) to lower the distress further or to complete the treatment effects. To do this, tap on the Back of Hand (BH), hold your head straight and, moving only your eyes, look at the floor and then slowly raise your eyes toward the ceiling.

Tennis

Energy psychology can be quite effective in improving your tennis game. When you want to enhance your ability to receive a serve or to volley, you should use the same procedure as a baseball player at the plate (see sequence above). The more you do before the match, the easier an actual game should be for you. You should treat any anxious feelings or doubts and be able to successfully visualize how you want to serve and receive the ball. When it is your turn to play, the treatments and exercises that you did before the game will allow you more time and control. Then, just before serving or receiving the ball, touch your key point, take a deep breath, and let it out. You should now be focused.

Golfing

At the beginning of this chapter, Jack Nicklaus was quoted as saying "The game of golf is 90 percent mental." One reason the game is "90 percent mental" is the difficulty of staying focused over a long duration. When you play golf, you are on the course for four hours, but you actually play golf for less than thirty minutes. You walk a lot, talk to other players, and then you must stop, focus, and hit your ball. You have to do this again and again. Once it is your turn to hit the ball, many elements can affect your game negatively. The treatment sequences in this chapter all apply to the game of golf. What follows, however, are golf-specific sequences and suggestions that may help you to further improve your game.

PRACTICE RANGE SITUATIONS

1. Set up golf balls in reasonable locations where you are least comfortable for a par or a birdie. Now imagine a situation that would make you nervous. Rate your level of nervousness on a scale of 0 to 10, with 10 indicating extreme nervousness and 0 indicating calmness.

2. Treat for the possibility of reversal by tapping the Side of Hand (SH) or rubbing the Sore Spot (SS) while thinking or saying to yourself three times, "I accept myself even if I (state the problem in your own words)." It also may be helpful to tap the SH or rub the SS while saying, "I accept myself with all my problems and limitations."

3. Look at the Treatment Sequence for Practice Range Situations below and at diagram 22 to identify the locations for the meridian points for Under Eye (UE), Under Arm (UA), and Under Collarbone (UCB). While thinking about the situation and/or feeling, tap five times at each of these meridian points. Tap them in the following order: 1 → 2 → 3. Tap only hard enough to feel it. The tapping shouldn't cause any pain.

Treatment Sequence for Practice Range Situations

Meridian		**Location**
Under Eye (UE)	1	Under the center of the eye on tip of bone
Under Arm (UA)	2	Six inches below armpit
Under Collarbone (UCB)	3	One inch below the collarbone near throat

4. Again, rate your level of distress on a 0 to 10 scale (a number should just pop into your mind). If there is no decrease, go back to step 2 and cycle through the sequence again. If there is not a decrease after three attempts, this is probably not an appropriate sequence for this situation, or else there is another sabotaging belief (reversal) that needs correction. (See step 8.)

5. Next, do the Brain Balancer (BB) by tapping repeatedly on the Back of Hand (BH) while rotating your eyes clockwise, rotating your eyes counterclockwise, then humming a tune, counting to five, and humming again.

6. Repeat the tapping sequence 1 → 2 → 3.

7. Again, rate your level of distress from 0 to 10. It should be lower yet. When the distress is within the 0 to 2 range, go to step 9. Sometimes, you'll need to repeat the treatment several times while you are imagining your fear—or even while you are in the actual situation—before you feel complete relief from the distressful situation.

8. As long as there is a decrease in your level of distress, continue with the sequence until there is very little or no tension remaining. If the treatment stalls at any point, this indicates a mini-reversal. Treat this by tapping on the little finger Side of Hand (SH), while saying three times, "I deeply accept myself, even though I still have some of this problem."

9. When the distress level is 0 to 2, consider doing the Eye Roll (ER) to lower the distress further or to complete the treatment effects. To do this, tap on the Back of Hand (BH), hold your head straight, and, moving only your eyes, look at the floor and then slowly raise your eyes toward the ceiling.

PRACTICING LONG PUTTS

Practicing long putts (more than fifteen feet) is a good test to determine the strength of your mind-body connection. First, putt several balls until you start to feel the speed of the green. Then, go to a different hole, do your normal setup, and line up your putt. Once you have your line, take some practice swings beside your ball. Don't look down. Instead, look at the pin or the cup and let your arms swing back and forth in a putting motion. What should happen is that as you focus on the cup, your eyes should send signals back to your brain-body about how hard you should be swinging. Once you feel this, trust yourself. Set up as you normally would for a putt, and you should putt the ball with the correct pace. If you cannot do this, then you may still be too anxious and need to repeat the treatment sequence or treat for reversal.

SUMMARY

As we have pointed out throughout this chapter, you will need to work on your mechanical skills as well as your mental game. Energy psychology will help you to be more focused and confident when you are playing your sport of choice. As a result, you most likely will become more aware of the mechanical flaws in your game that need improvement. You also should have less need to blame outside situations. As you eliminate self-sabotaging beliefs and anxious feelings, you may feel an increase in the amount of enjoyment that you receive from playing your sport.

12

Developing an Effective Weight-Loss Strategy

One way to get thin is to reestablish a purpose in life.

—Cyril Connolly

During his morning commute, a middle-aged man was telling his friends about a book he was reading that was helping him to change his diet. Later, he mentioned that he had not yet eaten breakfast, so they stopped at a food store. He saw a sign for fruit and picked up a banana, an apple, and a bottle of water. On the way to the cashier, he saw a section full of cakes and doughnuts, and he proceeded to share his expertise on this subject. He picked out a box of chocolate-covered doughnuts and said to his companion, "Always get the ones with devil's food cake inside. They are much tastier than the white cake." Then he said he had read that combining the fructose from the fruit with foods high in carbohydrates (and fat) like chocolate doughnuts was not a good idea. So, he put the fruit back and bought a cup of coffee to go with his doughnuts. Clearly, that was not what the authors of the book he was reading had in mind.

STRIVING TO LOSE WEIGHT

Have you ever made a decision to go on a diet, and then watched that decision crumble the moment you encountered foods that you love? The healthier foods that are helpful to your weight-reduction plan are forgotten just as soon as your cravings start up. If you haven't dealt with your food cravings, you will find a reason to eat that food—and you'll even find a way to make it seem rational. You may say to yourself, "I have to cheat sometimes; no one can be strict all the time!" Or "It won't hurt just this once!" Or "I feel bad, so I deserve this!" Or "I'll start my diet tomorrow." The information in this chapter will teach you how to decrease your cravings for certain foods.

Not surprisingly, some of the foods you crave are energy-toxic and can create self-sabotage in many areas of your life. Along with a growing number of writers on diet, nutrition, and weight loss, we also believe that the focus for losing weight must be on dealing with the emotional issues that sabotage the dieter's weight-loss goals. Overeating or an inability to diet is often a symptom of another problem that must also be treated. Once these issues have been addressed, you will be able to create the changes that will help you to maintain a diet, lose weight, and get into shape.

If you are trying to lose weight, you aren't alone. The United States represents one of the most overweight societies in the world. In 2005, The National Health and Nutrition Examination Survey reported that 66 percent of all Americans are overweight (NHANES 2005). The Centers for Disease Control (CDC) recently reported that more than one-third of American adults are obese. In the age group forty to fifty-nine, the percentage increases to 40 percent for men and 41 percent for women. The CDC has made the prevention of obesity a top health priority (Ogden et al. 2007). To complicate matters even further, people are becoming overweight at an increasingly younger age (NHANES 2005). These data support our belief that the main reason people cannot lose weight is an energy-related problem. It is unlikely that the problem is due to a lack of knowledge about dieting, because at least one new book on weight-loss strategies appears on the best-seller list every year.

American society perpetuates a myriad of contradictions about health and lifestyles. Fast-food restaurants have been a huge growth industry, yet in many polls the citizens of the United States claim to be very health-conscious. The result is that diet books, magazines, health and diet foods, exercise programs, and health spas are flooding the market. Yet these products and all of the media attention to the need for weight loss have had a minimal effect on the majority of the population's commitment or ability to lose weight.

If you are one of the 140 million overweight adult Americans, then you are at a higher risk of developing high blood pressure, gallbladder disease, and even certain types of cancer (Ogden et al. 2007). The correlation between heart disease—a major cause of premature death—and obesity is often ignored. It has also been suggested that the increase in American adults' consumption of sugar is related to the rise in the onset of adult diabetes.

Nonetheless, the correlation between health problems and weight has had little impact on people losing their unwanted and unhealthy pounds or, if they do manage to lose weight, on their ability to maintain their weight loss. It seems that every time our society takes a healthy step forward with more emphasis on diet and exercise, it takes two steps backward as our consumption of fast food continues to grow.

Another discouraging fact is that most dieters gain even more weight after each diet attempt. And, for those who do lose weight, only a small percentage are able to maintain the weight loss for more than two years. For many Americans, especially women, it seems that they are forever going on and off diets (thus creating the "yo-yo diet effect"), and never succeed at achieving their goal of substantial permanent weight loss.

There are three main reasons why you can't lose weight or keep the weight off permanently. They are as follows:

1. You have a physical reason that keeps you from losing weight, and medical assistance is required.

2. You have insufficient knowledge about how to design an effective diet to lose weight.

3. You have an energy-related problem that triggers cravings and sabotages your efforts to implement any diet program. This means that you have an energy imbalance, possibly due to a prior trauma, and that self-sabotaging beliefs undermine your motivation and your ability to diet successfully.

Any combination of the concerns listed above may apply in your individual case. The treatment sequences in this chapter, however, will focus on correcting energy-related problems, including frustration and impatience, food cravings, urge reduction, and more.

Physical Issues

If you have any health concerns or if you need to lose a significant amount of weight, you should definitely consult a health care professional to assist you in designing a diet that best suits your individual circumstances. You may have hormonal problems or other ailments that necessitate medications or a specialized program to help you lose weight safely. Energy psychology will help you to identify and treat the emotional problems that block you from successfully carrying out the lifestyle changes you want to accomplish.

Having Sufficient Knowledge and Information

Having sufficient knowledge as to how to lose weight is your first priority. Although most people do know how to lose weight, there is a growing body of research and information that can assist you. There are dozens of diet plans; you can select one or combine aspects of several different plans. Once you understand the basic strategies that are involved in dieting, you can design an eating plan that best fits you. If you don't know how to diet, and even if you do, we recommend that you review a few diet programs that can serve as a guide while you develop your plan.

The New Sugar Busters (Steward et al. 2003) identifies foods that may be fattening, even though they are not generally thought of as such. *Making the Connection: Ten Steps to a Better Body and a Better Life* (Greene and Winfrey 1999) offers an overall approach that involves exercise, eating more fiber and less fat, and drinking more water daily.

There are dozens of more recent books that you might wish to explore, and now many focus on the psychological reasons why you can't lose weight. We should add that a recent research study found energy psychology to be an effective way to maintain weight loss (Elder et al. 2007).

The more you know, the better equipped you'll be to design an appropriate nutrition program for yourself. It takes planning to change your approach to eating and to lose weight. With all the fast-food options available, it will be much harder for you to stick to a healthy diet and achieve your goals if you haven't prepared yourself with a plan. Remember, once you understand the basics, you can design a unique eating plan that meets your unique set of personal needs.

CHANGING YOUR MIND-SET

For most people, losing weight is challenging. However, if you have a good plan and you put forth the effort, without too much cheating, you will lose weight. When designing your plan, it's important to understand that Americans are bombarded daily with information about how hard it is to lose weight, which can undermine the desire to even try.

Frustration and Impatience

If you believe that it takes longer to lose weight than it did to gain it, you can become frustrated and/or impatient with the process of dieting. But there is no evidence to support that belief. The fact is, it's just not as much fun losing weight as it is putting it on, especially when you are eating delicious foods. The amount you deviated from your normal food intake to gain weight is exactly what will be required to lose it. This requires a change in your mind-set from one direction (overeating) to another (eating in moderation). Also, you may have forgotten that you didn't gain all of your weight in two weeks. So don't focus on crash diets and try to lose it all in two weeks. In fact, if you try crash diets, it is likely that your body will fight to prevent you from losing weight by slowing down your metabolism (Jibrin 1998). And, as we all know, if you keep overeating, eventually you'll gain those excess pounds.

Think back to all those times that you ate large amounts of fattening foods day after day, engaged in late-night eating, or consumed lots of alcohol. Just because it is more enjoyable to put on weight than it is to take it off doesn't change the fact that weight maintenance is still a fair deal. With sufficient exercise and a proper change of diet, it is inevitable that you will lose weight.

Effective weight-loss programs require a change in lifestyle. It is not a one-time-only event that you complete and then abandon, only to return to your old habits that created the problem in the first place. Once you view your diet and nutrition as a continuing lifestyle process, your plan will change as you learn which foods create problems for you, and what is required for you to achieve your goals. We recommend and hope that you will keep this in mind when you determine your timetable for changing your diet so that you can lose weight.

The timetable will not determine how long you have been overweight, but rather the time it took for you to gain the excess weight. If you can accept that losing weight is a fair deal, it will help you to minimize the frustration that occurs when you don't lose weight as quickly as you would like. Once you develop a plan, with the proper foods readily available, you will find it easier to maintain your nutrition program.

TREATMENT SEQUENCE FOR FRUSTRATION AND IMPATIENCE

Although the commonsense tips discussed above can help you to plan and better maintain your diet, they cannot help you deal with the emotional issues that often undermine your program. This is especially true in regard to frustration and impatience. These two emotions often cause critical problems in losing weight because when people are frustrated or impatient, they give up; they think that their diet isn't working, so they tell themselves, "Why even bother?" If frustration and impatience are problems for you, then the following treatment will prove beneficial.

1. Identify the problem with a phrase such as: "I'm not losing weight as fast as I want." Or say "I have cut back on my eating and I still don't lose weight." It is always best to put it in your own words. Think about the problem and rate your level of frustration or impatience on a scale of 0 to 10, with 10 meaning that you are completely impatient and frustrated to the point of giving up, and 0 meaning that you experience no impatience and frustration (and you understand that if you stick to your diet, you will lose weight).

2. Treat for the possibility of reversals by tapping repeatedly on the Side of Hand (SH) or rubbing the Sore Spot (SS) while thinking or saying to yourself three times, "I accept myself even though I'm impatient and frustrated about not losing weight as fast as I want to." Again, it is always best to say it in your own words. For example, you may prefer the words "upset" or "distressed" to "impatient" or "frustrated." It also may be helpful to tap the SH or rub the SS while saying, "I accept myself with all my problems and limitations."

3. Look at diagram 23 and the treatment sequence for frustration and impatience under the diagram to identify the locations for the meridian points for Eyebrow (EB), Under Eye (UE), Under Arm (UA), Under Collarbone (UCB), and Little Finger (LF). While thinking about your feelings of impatience and frustration about dieting, tap five times at each of these meridian points. Tap them in the following order: 1 → 2 → 3 → 4 → 5 → 4. **Note:** The UCB is repeated twice in

the sequence. Tap only hard enough to feel it. The tapping shouldn't cause any pain.

4. Again, rate your distress on a 0 to 10 scale (a number should just pop into your mind). If there is no decrease, go back to step 2 and cycle through the sequence again. If there is not a decrease after three attempts, this is probably not an appropriate sequence for this situation, or else there is another sabotaging belief (reversal) that needs correction. (See step 8.)

5. Next, do the Brain Balancer (BB) by tapping repeatedly on the Back of Hand (BH) while rotating your eyes clockwise, rotating your eyes counter-clockwise, then humming a tune, counting to five, and humming again.

6. Repeat the tapping sequence 1 → 2 → 3 → 4 → 5 → 4.

7. Again, rate your impatience and frustration from 0 to 10. It should be lower yet. When the distress is within the 0 to 2 range, go to step 9. Sometimes, you'll need to repeat the treatment several times while you are imagining your frustration or impatience—or even while you are in the actual situation—before you feel complete relief from the frustrating situation.

8. As long as there is a decrease in your level of frustration or impatience, continue with the treatment sequence until there is very little or no tension remaining. If the treatment stalls at any point, this indicates a mini-reversal. Treat this by tapping on the little finger Side of Hand (SH) while saying three times, "I deeply accept myself, even though I still have some of this problem."

9. When the distress level is 0 to 2, consider doing the Eye Roll (ER) to lower the distress further or to complete the treatment effects. To do this, tap on the Back of Hand (BH), hold your head straight and, moving only your eyes, look at the floor and then slowly raise your eyes toward the ceiling.

Although this treatment effectively relieves frustration and impatience, you must be realistic. If you are easily frustrated, it will be necessary to treat this problem regularly before it becomes just an occasional occurrence. Although you will still experience moments of impatience and frustration, this approach will significantly reduce this tendency during certain situations in which you would rather feel more patient, such as with your eating plan.

When trying to lose weight, it is important to consider all potential reversals including massive or deep-level reversals.

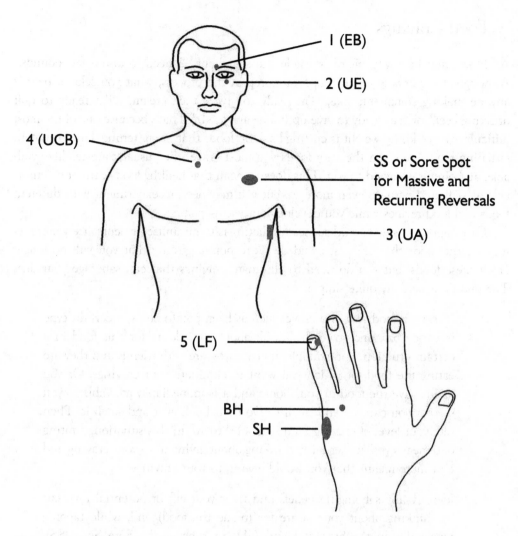

Diagram Twenty-Three: Frustration and Impatience

Treatment Sequence for Frustration and Impatience

Meridian		Location
Eyebrow (EB)	1	Beginning of eyebrow near bridge of nose
Under Eye (UE)	2	Under the center of the eye on tip of bone
Under Arm (UA)	3	Six inches under armpit
Under Collarbone (UCB)	4	Once inch below collarbone near throat
Little Finger (LF)	5	Inside tip of little fingernail on the side

Food Cravings

How often have you heard or made the statement, "I need to lose a few pounds." Although this admission is an important step in the process, what you seldom hear is anyone making statements like, "I'm ready to give up ice cream," "I'm ready to quit drinking beer," or "I'm ready to give up (name any food)." That's because one of the most difficult parts of losing weight is cutting back on foods that are fattening. Unfortunately, fattening foods are often the very foods you most crave, they usually are readily available, and often taste good to you. This doesn't mean that healthy foods cannot be enjoyable as well, and perhaps even more so, but you may need to experiment with different foods and food recipes while you develop your eating plan.

One important step toward successful dieting is to minimize or neutralize your cravings for the foods that are best avoided. We're not suggesting that you will no longer enjoy these foods, but you do need to eliminate cravings that can sabotage your diet. The process is actually quite simple.

1. Identify a food that you crave, such as beer, potato chips, a certain type of candy bar, and so forth. Think about your desire for this food in a certain situation. For example, imagine you are with friends and they are eating the food for which you want to eliminate your cravings. Or you might have the food in your home and it is immediately available to you so that you can see and smell it. Do that. Look at it and smell it. Then rate your level of craving on a scale of 0 to 10. In this situation, a rating of 6 means you are seriously thinking about giving in to your craving and 8 or more means that you would give in to your cravings.

2. Identify any sabotaging beliefs and treat yourself for potential reversals by thinking about your desire for (name the food) and, while tapping repeatedly on the Side of Hand (SH) or rubbing the Sore Spot (SS), think or say three times, "I deeply accept myself even though I cannot control my craving for (name the food)." If you don't think you can ever get over your cravings, tap under your nose (UN) for a deep-level reversal while saying, "I deeply accept myself even if I never get over my food cravings." It also may be helpful to tap the SH or rub the SS while saying, "I accept myself with all my problems and limitations."

3. Look at diagram 24 and the treatment sequence for food cravings under the diagram to identify the locations for the meridian points for Under Eye (UE), Under Collarbone (UCB), Under Arm (UA), and Little Finger (LF). While thinking about your craving, tap five times at each of these meridian points. Tap them in the following order: 1 → 2 → 3 → 4 → 3 → 2 → 1. Note that the UE, UCB, and UA are repeated twice in the sequence. Tap only hard enough to feel it. The tapping shouldn't cause any pain.

4. Again, rate your craving on a 0 to 10 scale (a number should just pop into your mind). If there is no decrease, go back to step 2 and cycle through the sequence again. If there is not a decrease after three attempts, this is probably not an appropriate sequence for this situation, or else there is a sabotaging belief (reversal) that needs correction. (See step 8.)

5. Next, do the Brain Balancer (BB) by tapping repeatedly on the Back of Hand (BH) while rotating your eyes clockwise, rotating your eyes counter-clockwise, then humming a tune, counting to five, and humming again.

6. Repeat the tapping sequence 1 → 2 → 3 → 4 → 3 → 2 → 1.

7. Again, rate your craving from 0 to 10. It should be lower yet. When the distress is within the 0 to 2 range, go to step 9. Sometimes, you'll need to repeat the treatment several times while you are imagining your craving—or even while you are in the actual situation—before you feel complete relief from the situation.

8. As long as there is a decrease in your level of cravings, continue with the treatment sequence until there is very little or no feeling of cravings remaining. If the treatment stalls at any point, this indicates a mini-reversal. Treat this by tapping on the little finger Side of Hand (SH), while saying three times, "I deeply accept myself, even though I still have some of this problem."

9. When the distress level is 0 to 2, consider doing the Eye Roll (ER) to lower the distress further or to complete the treatment effects. To do this, tap on the Back of Hand (BH), hold your head straight and, moving only your eyes, look at the floor and then slowly raise your eyes toward the ceiling.

ALTERNATE SEQUENCE FOR FOOD CRAVINGS

If you have treated for any potential reversals and the sequence above was not effective, repeat the treatment and tap on the meridian points using the alternate sequence order of 3 → 1 → 2 → 4 → 2 → 1 → 3. In most instances this treatment will at least temporarily eliminate your craving for the "forbidden" food. Realistically, however, you may need to repeat this treatment several times before the craving is significantly reduced on an ongoing basis.

Also, to substantially alleviate your "addiction," it is important to treat your craving for the targeted food in a variety of situations. For example, you may tend to eat candy bars when you are bored, feeling tired, or watching television. Thinking about each of these situations or contexts while doing the treatment will go a long way toward effectively alleviating your craving for candy bars.

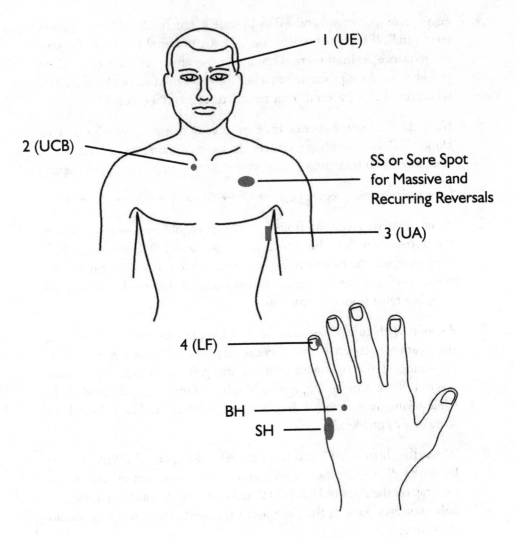

Diagram Twenty-Four: Food Cravings

Treatment Sequence for Food Cravings

Meridian		Location
Under Eye (UE)	1	Under the center of the eye on tip of bone
Under Collarbone (UCB)	2	Once inch below collarbone near throat
Under Arm (UA)	3	Six inches below armpit
Little Finger (LF)	4	Inside tip of little fingernail on the side

Preparation is an important part of dealing with food cravings. For example, many people want to have a snack in the evening. Although it is best to cut down on late-night eating if you are going to reduce your weight, you may find it hard to eliminate the late-night snack. The problem is that although a bowl of ice cream is very fattening, it is also very easy to prepare. Once the craving starts, you could have ice cream in your mouth in a matter of minutes. What can you substitute that would taste good to you and keep you on your eating plan? It has to be your own choice.

The point is that you need to have healthy substitutes close at hand to satisfy your cravings. If you continue to have a problem with the targeted food, read further and work through the problems examined in the personal problems and belief systems sections of this chapter. Once you eliminate any underlying problems, you will be able to control your cravings more effectively by using the treatment sequences provided.

PERSONAL PROBLEMS

Throughout previous chapters, we've identified and provided treatments for problems such as anger, rejection, fear, shame, and depression. If you feel that any of those problems still exist in your life, they should be treated as part of your weight-loss program. Most psychologists believe that these underlying problems must be resolved before you can create and implement an effective weight-loss program. We also find that as you treat emotional issues, it becomes easier for you to change your environment and lifestyle. Although we cannot explore every issue related to being overweight, if you honestly examine your life, you can most likely identify the issues that are blocking you from achieving your desired goal. Examples of these types of issues are discussed below.

Sexual Abuse

Some people who were sexually abused as children develop obesity. On a subconscious level they may view their obesity as a shield that protects them by making them less sexually desirable. Of course, not everyone who is obese was sexually abused. If you do have a history of sexual abuse, however, you should utilize the treatments from chapter 10 on resolving painful memories and trauma. Once you have obtained relief from those early traumatic events, you should feel much stronger and be better able to deal with other issues in your life, including obesity. You may also have a reversal that deals with feelings of shame. The sequence used to treat shame is in chapter 8.

Rejection

If you live in fear of being rejected or if you have been significantly rejected in the past, you may be inclined to withdraw from social situations and blame yourself or past events for your problems. This only serves to lower your self-esteem and, in many cases, results in you spending more time alone engaged in sedentary activities, like watching television. Although television may help to occupy your time, it cannot help you to feel better, and the reduced physical activity can lead to weight gain.

Simultaneously, while you are watching TV or are otherwise withdrawing, you may gravitate toward food in an effort to help you feel better. For that reason, you need to treat your feelings and fears of rejection so that you can change your lifestyle and prevent situations from arising that encourage overeating. One approach to alleviating this problem is to use the Midline Energy Technique described in chapter 8.

Depression

Feeling depressed about a situation or an event in your life can alter your lifestyle radically. For instance, you may go to bars and drink to feel better temporarily, which also sabotages your diet plans because alcohol is fattening. Also, because alcohol blocks your ability to notice when you are full, it may cause you to overeat as well. Your depression may include feelings of anger and the desire to withdraw from social situations. Clearly, if you don't treat your feelings of depression, it is unlikely that you will be able to diet effectively. Your depression can have many sources; see chapter 9 to understand the symptoms of depression and to employ a treatment.

Shame

If you feel ashamed of yourself for any reason, you may use food as a means of making yourself feel better. Shame can be the result of an event over which you had no control or one that happened when you were very young and lacked the resources to help yourself. To break the emotional cycle that may now revolve around food, the issue you feel ashamed about must first be treated. You can find the treatment sequence for shame in chapter 8.

Anger and Guilt

There is no question that certain foods, due to their pleasurable taste, are used to help soothe a variety of feelings, including anger and guilt. Often, food becomes a way to comfort yourself when you've had a bad day. If you are trying to lose weight, however, this approach doesn't support your goal of a slimmer, healthier body. Violating your dietary goals can even produce additional feelings of frustration and guilt, as you realize that you weren't able to stick to your diet. Such emotional reactions can serve to further sabotage your weight-loss efforts. You can find the treatment for anger and guilt in chapter 8.

FRUSTRATION, LONELINESS, AND WEIGHT LOSS: A CASE STUDY

At age thirty-six, Sally was attractive yet overweight. She often became angry with herself because she could not lose weight and look her best. Her weak spot was a craving for sweets. When she went on a diet, she would get frustrated and then go on a binge and overeat, usually with very fattening foods like ice cream. It didn't matter if she was hungry or not. She would keep on eating until she ran out of that food or until she was so stuffed that she needed to go to sleep immediately.

Sally's sense of loneliness was a related problem. When she was alone at night, she was more likely to give in to her cravings. The first step for Sally was to use the Midline Energy Treatment described in chapter 8 to help her to cope with her fears of rejection in social situations. This allowed her to feel better about herself and to feel more self-confident.

After one week of doing energy treatments for her problems, Sally was ready to change her social life to lose weight. Because she liked to read, she decided to spend more time at her favorite bookstore and coffee shop in the evenings. There, she was able to meet friends and socialize. At the same time, Sally was working on her goal to lose twenty-five pounds during a three-month period.

She picked a diet plan that worked best for her lifestyle. She chose to drink her breakfast and lunch, using a popular health-food powdered supplement that she blended with skim milk and fruit. Although she had to pay more for the best supplements, they were lower in sugar and had more nutrients. She experimented until she found some flavor combinations that satisfied her tastes. She chose a peach-vanilla blended shake in the morning and a banana-chocolate shake for lunch, but she also mixed in other fruits, such as strawberries. This was a great strategy for Sally because, historically, lunch had been a high fat and calorie disaster for her, often made up entirely of fast foods.

It took Sally the entire three months to lose the twenty-five pounds. During the first month, she frequently used the energy treatments for frustration and impatience to deal with not losing weight as quickly as she would have preferred. She also used the treatment for food cravings to reduce her desire for some of her favorite fattening foods.

When she went off her weight-loss program, she still drank one meal a day and then identified new lunch and breakfast meals that were not as fattening as those she had previously eaten. Whenever old habits started to return, she treated herself for being reversed and used the appropriate treatments to get her energy balanced again. In this way, she was able to maintain her desired weight.

BELIEF SYSTEMS

There are many beliefs that could block you from successfully making a lifestyle change. These beliefs may fall into the category of deep-level reversals if your particular belief creates a feeling that you can never lose weight. To treat a deep-level reversal, tap under your nose (UN) while saying three times, "I accept myself even if I never lose weight because I (state your belief)." The following section discusses some of the beliefs that can greatly affect your ability to lose weight.

I'm Too Old

There are some realities—such as advancing age—that must be faced about your physical abilities and the way your body responds to diet and exercise. Age, however, is also a state of mind. If you simply accept the fact that you are growing older, and let go of struggling and being upset about this reality, you also will realize that aging has nothing to do with your ability to lose weight. Whatever your situation, once you accept it, you are in a much better mental state to achieve your goals.

Another age-related issue is the tendency to think that being more shapely shouldn't matter, "because I'm older." Your weight, however, can affect your ability to participate happily in the events of other family members' lives. And, of course, your health always affects the quality of your own life. Today, many people are living active lives well into their nineties. As a matter of fact, in some communities a large number of healthy people live to be more than one hundred years old.

I'm Too Fat

When someone believes she is "too fat to lose weight," usually, she cannot visualize how she could ever reach her desired weight. She has a short-term focus and thinks only about which foods she must give up, rather than the wonderful lifestyle she could have if she lost the excess weight. If you fall into this category, you may be massively and deep-level reversed. It is advisable to regularly treat both of these reversals (see chapter 6). After treating the reversals, you can use the visualization exercises in this chapter to realize your thinner, healthier body.

I Can't Change My Diet

Believing that you can't change your diet also may indicate a deep-level reversal. Once this reversal is corrected (sometimes this must be done on a regular basis), you should be able to use the other treatments in this book to implement and maintain your new eating plan.

I Have No Time

Believing that you have no time to plan and implement a diet can be a complex problem with multiple issues. Time is always a problem, but there are solutions. The fruit shakes that were referred to in the previous case study are a quick way to have a nutritious meal. Once you treat the time-related, deep-level reversal, other issues may appear that need to be treated as well.

For example, although you care about your appearance, it may have become of secondary importance to you, and this may frustrate you. After reviewing any emotional issues that may contribute to the cause of your overeating, treat each one. You may have to do this continually, as unforeseen situations can regularly create reversals, alter your emotional feelings, and make you more susceptible to food cravings. If you continue using the energy treatments, however, you will be able to stick to your diet.

It Takes Too Much Effort

If you believe losing weight takes too much effort, you have a deep-level reversal or a motivation-related reversal. To treat this, tap the Side of Hand (SH) while thinking or saying three times, "I accept myself even though I am not motivated to lose weight." By treating the reversal and using the sequences for frustration and food cravings (found earlier in this chapter), you should be able to generate the energy to lose weight.

I Can't Stop Overeating

If you believe you can't stop overeating, then treat yourself for a deep-level reversal. Another reversal to consider is your resistance to the possibility of losing weight. In this case, tap on Side of Hand (SH) while thinking or saying three times, "I accept myself even though it is not possible for me to stop overeating." Situations or bad habits in your life can also lead to chronic overeating. Once you identify the situations that you feel contribute to your overeating, try to avoid those situations or use the visualizing treatment that follows to help you deal with that problem.

VISUALIZING LIFE SITUATIONS

You can use visualization to help you determine and become aware of whether you are going to have an eating problem during certain situations, such as birthdays, work-related events, and when you're feeding your children. Visualization will help to minimize the self-sabotage that occurs at those times. In each case, the object is to visualize a potential problem situation and decide whether you need to use energetic treatments to stay on your diet.

Begin with an overall visualization: See yourself at your desired goal weight. If you're having trouble doing this, tap ten times on the Under Arm (UA) and ten times on the Eyebrow (EB) meridian points. You may need to repeat this treatment several times before it works to your satisfaction. It doesn't have to be a clear vision—just an image.

Can you visualize yourself at this new weight? How would people respond to you? What other events could happen?

These mental visualizations should feel good and help you to reinforce your desire to lose weight. If there were any negative feelings or you could see yourself only as overweight, then you are reversed on being able to lose weight. We suggest you use the treatment for a massive reversal (see chapter 6 for details on the Sore Spot (SS), and then use the treatment for frustration and impatience described earlier in this chapter).

Next, identify situations that might present eating challenges. Once you review a few of the following examples, you may imagine the situations that would most likely happen to you. In each example, visualize yourself in that situation and then rate your desire or cravings for the foods or beverages. Using the same process, rate yourself on a scale of 0 to 10, with 6 indicating that you are seriously thinking about giving in to your desires and 8 or more indicating that you will give in to your desires.

If one of the situations is a particular problem for you, treat yourself for food cravings and repeat the visualization until the feeling is eliminated. Here are some examples:

- You are at work and a colleague brings in several boxes of your favorite doughnuts, more than the staff can eat. The doughnuts are just sitting on the table going to waste. What do you see yourself doing?

- You are at a social club and your friends at the bar are encouraging you to drink. Can you see yourself having only one alcoholic beverage and then ordering low-calorie drinks the rest of the evening?

- You cook large quantities of one of your favorite foods. Can you see yourself eating a moderate amount of that food?

- Your children or your spouse loves to have tasty, but high-fat, foods in the house. What do you see yourself doing?

- One of the ways you have fun with your children is to eat delicious desserts with them. Can you see yourself having just a bite and then eating a low-calorie food as a substitute?

The goal is to prepare yourself for the life situations that can sabotage your dieting efforts if you aren't prepared for them. Although treating emotional problems is the key to losing weight, you may also have created many bad habits that must be eliminated.

Self-Destructive Behavior and Weight Loss: A Case Study

Carlos was a classic example of massive reversal. He had numerous problems, and his gluttony was only one among many. He drank excessively and used other drugs. Generally, he behaved in a reckless manner. He had trouble keeping his job, but because he was well liked; people protected him. His 300-pound body, however, was becoming a problem. His knees and back were a source of continual pain and because of that, he couldn't do any exercise. His eating strategy was to go to a local bar for happy hour for drinks and a large quantity of high-fat foods, and to eat his dinner late at night. Usually, he went to bed stuffed with food. His doctor warned him that because he was forty-five years old, his lifestyle could create major health issues, such as a heart attack or diabetes.

Carlos is an example of someone who almost has to literally crash and burn before he is ready to change. Carlos went bankrupt, lost his longtime girlfriend, and had a car accident that put him in the hospital for a week. At that time, he came to see us and we taught him the energy treatments that he needed to balance his system. It was an off-and-on process for two months. He would follow the treatment suggestions, experience some results, and then go back to drinking excessively.

This behavior sabotaged the whole process and soon he was overeating again. We encouraged him to join support groups to help him to cope with his many problems. The biggest problem was that his massive reversal kept coming back and re-creating his sabotaging and self-defeating thoughts and behaviors. Finally, we were able to convince Carlos to treat his massive reversal regularly and to apply several other treatments for food cravings, addictions, and anger.

After a few weeks, Carlos finally went to and enjoyed attending an Alcoholics Anonymous meeting. He developed a new group of friends who were not into his old addictive lifestyle. His continual use of the energy treatments and his change in lifestyle helped him to develop the focus he needed to design a diet and to stick to it. Although there were some relapses during the following year, Carlos was able to lose almost one hundred pounds. The key was to stop the drinking and drugs that were sabotaging his life. To do that, he had to change his social life and some of his friends.

Carlos provides a good example of how changing one part of your life can lead to changes in other areas. Energy treatments done on a regular basis can help you to develop the willpower and strength to overcome many limitations in your life.

TONING YOUR BODY

Toning your body is a very important part of the weight-loss process, especially as you become older and inclined to reduce your physical activity. If you are going to lose a lot of weight, you need to tone your body as part of the process. If you don't tone it, you won't like the flabby way you look after you lose the excess weight. The good news is that if you do tone your body, it will start to regain its shape much faster, and you will look better even before you get down to your desired weight.

Too often, people think that if they don't do an extensive exercise program, a less rigorous program won't help. Although it is true that the more calories you burn exercising, the faster and easier it is to lose weight, it is also true that aerobic exercise is not a substitute for a toning program.

To tone your body, you should do exercises for your arms, back, and chest by using light dumbbells. You should also do stomach crunches and leg extensions to firm up your abdomen, hips, and buttocks. There are many good books that describe and discuss how to exercise each part of your body properly. The goal is to do high numbers of repetitions for each exercise, without hurting yourself. If you can't do fifteen to twenty repetitions of an exercise with a dumbbell, then you are using too much weight. If you have an injury or any other health concern, always seek the assistance of a health care professional before beginning an exercise program.

The two common problems that interfere with maintaining any exercise program are time and motivation. As far as time is concerned, the program we recommend should take no more than fifteen to thirty minutes daily to complete, and it can be done while you are watching television. If you are having trouble motivating yourself to do a simple exercise program, do the following treatment to enhance your efforts:

Enhancing Your Motivation to Exercise

1. Imagine a situation when you come home after work and you have absolutely no motivation to exercise, even though it will take just fifteen minutes. Rate your level of motivation on a scale of 0 to 10, with 10 representing the fact that you are highly unmotivated to do the exercises and 0 indicating that you are highly motivated to exercise.

2. Treat for the possibility of reversal by tapping repeatedly on the Side of Hand (SH) or rubbing the Sore Spot (SS) while thinking or saying three times, "I deeply accept myself even though I have little or no motivation to exercise." It also may be helpful to tap the SH or rub the SS while saying, "I accept myself with all my problems and limitations."

3. Now look at diagram 25 and the treatment sequence for enhancing your motivation under the diagram to identify the locations for the meridians for Under Eye (UE), Under Collarbone (UCB), and Eyebrow (EB). While thinking about your lack of motivation to exercise, tap five times at each of these meridian points. Tap them in the following order: 1 → 2 → 3 → 2. **Note:** The UCB is listed twice. Tap only hard enough to feel it. The tapping shouldn't cause any pain.

4. Again, rate your motivation on a 0 to 10 scale (a number should just pop into your mind). If there is no decrease, go back to step 2 and cycle through the sequence again. If there is not a decrease after three attempts, this is probably not the appropriate sequence for this situation, or else there is another sabotaging belief (reversal) that needs correction. (See step 8.)

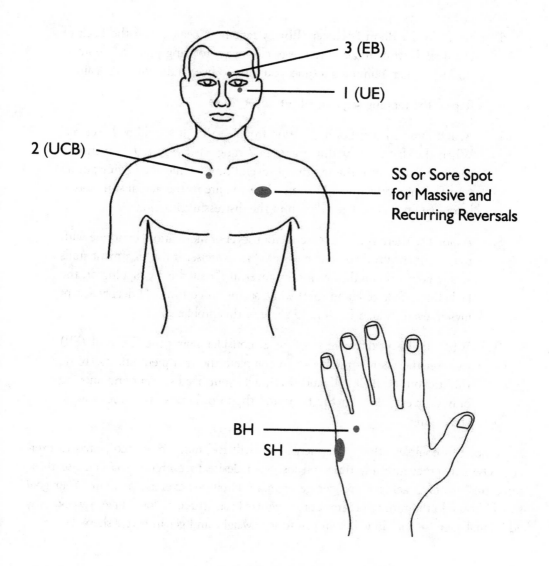

Diagram Twenty-Five: Motivation

Treatment Sequence for Enhancing Your Motivation

Meridian		Location
Under Eye (UE)	1	Under the center of the eye on tip of bone
Under Collarbone (UCB)	2	One inch below collarbone near throat
Eyebrow (EB)	3	Beginning of eyebrow near bridge of nose

5. Next, do the Brain Balancer (BB) by tapping repeatedly on the Back of Hand (BH) while rotating your eyes clockwise, rotating your eyes counterclockwise, then humming a tune, counting to five, and humming again.

6. Repeat the tapping sequence 1 → 2 → 3 → 2.

7. Again, rate your level of motivation from 0 to 10. It should be lower yet. When the distress is within the 0 to 2 range, go to step 9. Sometimes, you'll need to repeat the treatment several times while you are imagining your lack of motivation—or even while you are in the actual situation—before you feel complete relief from the distressful situation.

8. As long as there is an increase in your level of motivation, continue with the treatment until you feel motivated to exercise. If the treatment stalls at any point, this indicates a mini-reversal. Treat this by tapping on the little finger Side of Hand (SH) while saying three times, "I deeply accept myself, even though I still have some of this problem."

9. When the level of distress is 0 to 2, consider doing the Eye Roll (ER) to lower the distress further or to complete the treatment effects. To do this, tap on the Back of Hand (BH), hold your head straight and, moving only your eyes, look at the floor and then slowly raise your eyes toward the ceiling.

Once you complete these treatments, you will feel much more motivated to exercise. Use this procedure any time you lose your desire to exercise. You can use these same treatments to achieve an average or more ambitious exercise program. Your goal should be to do the toning program on a regular basis, three or four times a week. Any additional exercise you do will help you to lose weight and get in better shape faster.

SUMMARY

Sabotaging thoughts or unhealthy behaviors can destroy the best diet plans by preventing you from staying on your diet. Although knowledge about dieting is important, it is the underlying emotional issues that must be corrected to help you maintain your program. Losing weight is not going to be done for you, but there is no reason for you to believe that you are unable to stick to a diet or an exercise program. You must understand why you are overweight. Yes, a sedentary lifestyle and too many fattening foods in your diet are problems, but why do you have that lifestyle? Is your appearance really secondary to you or do you have certain beliefs or situations that make it secondary? You need to resolve what causes overeating in your life, and the best way to start is to use the personal profile in chapter 5.

Weight loss is a complex and interactive problem, which may require a variety of energy treatments to balance your system and to help you to change your lifestyle. If you continue using the energy treatments, you will eventually rid yourself of the sabotaging tendencies that undermine your ability to achieve your goals in life. And, in the end, it is inevitable that you will lose weight.

13

Eliminating Addictive Behaviors: Smoking, Alcohol, Drugs, Sex, and Gambling

Seek without seeking, for what you hope to attain is already within you.
Look for common sense; plain old-fashioned common sense.

—Sidney Banks

It is common knowledge that alcohol, drug, gambling, and sex addictions are a major problem in the United States and throughout the world. They account for untold consequences in terms of money, productivity, health, and happiness. In addition, addiction can wreak havoc in the lives of the addicted person's loved ones. Furthermore, although it's true that tobacco addiction is not as destructive psychologically as alcohol and drugs are, it continues to represent a major health problem, as do most addictions.

Addiction is a dependence on a mind-altering substance or activity. When you are addicted, you and your body associate alcohol, drugs, gambling, or tobacco with the alleviation of anxiety and other uncomfortable emotional states. In essence, addiction is dependence on a "tranquilizer." The fundamental goal of the behavior that leads to addiction is the elimination of uncomfortable feelings.

Why do people become addicted in the first place? The fact is that many people use emotion-altering substances and engage in dangerous activities without becoming addicted to them. Addiction, however, can become a problem due to hereditary causes (as is the case with alcohol addiction), as well as when an addictive activity or substance is paired with the reduction of discomfort.

Some people have an immediate family history or genealogy that sets them up to develop an addiction, due to both genetic and environmental causes. If many people in your extended family have had problems with addiction, this can result in you being predisposed to develop an addiction. Notice that we said *predisposed*, not *inevitable*. Even if many people in your immediate family and ancestry were or are addicted, this doesn't mean that you will become addicted too. There's plenty of room for choice. And with energy psychology, there's also plenty of room for hope.

From a behavioral perspective, the development of an addiction involves *pairing*. That is, if you are stressed, depressed, bored, or uncomfortable in other ways, and you resort to an emotion-altering distraction, such as alcohol, drugs, sex, or gambling to alleviate these feelings, you will increasingly turn to that substance or activity to cope with those emotional states. This is what is referred to as a *stimulus-response bond.* The *stimulus* of emotional discomfort, which may be triggered by all sorts of internal and external cues or triggers, is paired with a substance or activity, which is the *response*. This response is reinforced because it is accompanied by the alleviation of the uncomfortable feelings. In time, you may develop an addiction. Keep in mind, however, that the development of addiction is far more complex than just the simple stimulus-response.

If we back up a little, it becomes obvious that the addiction itself is not the primary problem. True enough, once you are addicted, all sorts of problems enter your life, and, of course, these need to be dealt with too. But the most fundamental problem is the way you cope with those original and continuing uncomfortable feelings of stress, anxiety, depression, and so forth. To a large extent, these feelings are the result of what may be referred to as *perturbed thought*; that is, a thought that causes a disruption in your body's energy system.

For example, you may have the thought that your life is stagnating. To simply hold this thought in your mind, without believing it is true, cannot cause a disturbance in and of itself. However, if for whatever reasons you believe the thought is valid, it may result in a feeling of anxiety or despair. Those feelings, of course, can significantly add to your difficulties, possibly making it even more unlikely that your life will be productive. Generally, chronic uncomfortable feelings do not help you to move in a positive direction. Most often, such feelings interfere with your ability to get in touch with your inner resources, such as your hope and courage, and they affect your ability to plan an effective course of action.

As noted, perturbed thoughts result in a disruption in your body's energy system that, in turn, causes chemical, neurological, and behavioral disturbances that further contribute to the problem. Removing the disruption resulting from these core thoughts that trigger the addiction process is a primary key to recovery. This is where energy psychology techniques can help you overcome your addiction.

COMPREHENSIVE TREATMENT

Although energy treatments are helpful to recovery, chronic addictions require a comprehensive treatment approach. Besides involvement in intensive individual and family therapy, we highly recommend 12-step programs, such as Alcoholics Anonymous,

Narcotics Anonymous, Overeaters Anonymous, and Gamblers Anonymous. These programs provide a wonderful support system, a fellowship that assists the addicted person in the many steps to recovery, including recognizing his or her need for abstinence, teaching the person to make amends for past wrongdoings, developing a relapse-prevention plan, contributing to the welfare and sobriety of others, and focusing on spiritual development.

For those who have a difficult time with the spiritual component of programs like Alcoholics Anonymous, perhaps seeing it as a religious denomination of sorts, there is the Secular Organizations for Sobriety (SOS), which enlists many principles similar to the 12-step organizations, but also focuses on scientific approaches to overcoming addiction.

It is imperative that the addicted person practice abstinence. There is no good scientific evidence that a person can become a social drinker or drug user once she or he has experienced extreme alcohol or drug dependence. In fact, there is considerable clinical evidence to the contrary. This also seems to hold true for people who have been addicted to gambling and even tobacco. Therefore, we highly recommend that if you have had a problem with addiction, you not become seduced by any claims that it is possible to drink, use drugs, gamble, or smoke occasionally. If you start to believe that you can occasionally engage in these activities, remember, this is a sneaky aspect of addiction that leads only to relapse.

In Alcoholics Anonymous and Narcotics Anonymous they talk about "Slick," who is the addictive component of the addict's personality. Slick is very good at deceiving you into believing that you can *have just one,* that you *deserve* to drink or use, that *no one will ever know,* and other similar manipulations. Such thoughts are all an aspect of addictive thinking that leads to relapse. It is also consistent with what we refer to as psychological reversal.

Furthermore, it is crucial for the addicted person to use the personal profile to identify and treat the specific beliefs and behaviors that may be the source of his or her energy imbalance (see chapter 5). This process, used in combination with the urge reduction treatments and psychological reversal treatments that follow, will help to break up the addictive pattern.

In this chapter, we provide energy psychology and related techniques that can be used to augment other therapeutic approaches. These techniques will help you to eliminate addictive urges and support your recovery process. If you start to have relapse-related thoughts, it is important that you repeat the treatment process you will find in this chapter.

PSYCHOLOGICAL REVERSALS

As we have noted throughout this book, psychological reversals are frequently the primary obstacles to getting over any problem. When you are psychologically reversed, regardless of the substance or activity—smoking, alcohol, drugs, overeating, sex, or gambling—you continue to use at an addictive level, even though you know that what you are doing is bad for you. In a sense, when you are reversed, you treat something that is bad as though it is good or as though it were helping you. This type of faulty thought process draws you back to addictive use even after you have abstained for a period of time. Being psychologically reversed prevents otherwise effective treatments from working.

It is essential to avoid becoming psychologically reversed if you are going to remain on the road to recovery from addiction. To achieve this, it is important to treat yourself for reversals on a regular basis. During the initial phase of recovery, it is important to correct reversals frequently throughout the day, even as often as once an hour. This can easily be prompted by setting a wrist alarm to sound every hour, or by whatever other means you prefer.

The importance of regularly treating psychological reversal is well illustrated by the experience of one woman who had been addicted to pain medication. This patient did not have a pain problem, but narcotics were her drug of choice. After she went through the energy treatment described below, her urges were reliably alleviated both in sessions and independently on her own. Unfortunately, she had a psychological reversal that caused her to refuse to use the treatment every time an urge occurred.

When she was asked why she chose to take pain pills rather than implement the urge reduction treatment, she said, "I don't use that all the time. It works!" Obviously, when this woman was in a state of psychological reversal, she preferred doing what was bad for her (the drugs) to doing something that could support her recovery (the treatment). However, as she became aware of her tendency to be psychologically reversed, she became able to correct for the reversal consistently, and then she was well on her way to recovery.

There are certain types of reversals that appear most frequently with addiction. In addition to the reversals covered in chapter 6, the reversals discussed below commonly affect addicted individuals.

Deprivation Reversal

With *deprivation reversal*, you feel terribly deprived when you are not engaged in your addiction. It's as though your unconscious is whining. To treat this reversal, tap on the Side of Hand (SH) or rub the Sore Spot (SS) while saying or thinking three times, "I deeply accept myself even though I'll feel deprived if I get over my addiction to (name your addiction; for example, alcohol, drugs, gambling, sex, or overeating)."

Identity Reversal

With *identity reversal*, the addiction has become a part of your personality. To treat this reversal, tap on the Side of Hand (SH) or rub on the Sore Spot (SS) while saying or thinking three times, "I deeply accept myself even though this addiction is a part of my identity."

Self-Acceptance

When doing these corrections, some people have a difficult time making the statement, "I deeply accept myself," because they realize that they really don't accept themselves. This is all the more reason why this phrase should be used. In time, it helps to instill a deeper sense of self-acceptance, which is an important aspect of being able to recover from any problem.

DEVELOPING EMOTIONAL COMMITMENT

Some time ago, one of the authors of *Energy Tapping* was highly addicted to nicotine. He smoked two to three packs of cigarettes daily. Every time he would muster up enough disgust to enable himself to quit the repulsive habit of smoking, he would eventually relapse. Immediately preceding his relapse, all of his reasons for quitting smoking became less significant, more foggy, even forgotten. Only after he was once again smoking at an addictive level did his original reasons for quitting become, yet once again, all too apparent. His motto could have been, to paraphrase Mark Twain: "It ain't hard to quit smoking; I've done it a hundred times."

Certainly, with any addiction, it is not easy to remain substance-free. Eventually, the author realized that he had started smoking again because he continually forgot the reasons he had quit in the first place. So, just before his next attempt at quitting, he wrote down a list of his reasons, which included the following: clothing smelling like cigarettes, bad taste in his mouth every morning, fear of a heart attack, wasted money, considerable tension at the end of a day of smoking excessively, being controlled by cigarettes, family complaints and concerns, tendency to plan his day around the time he can have his next cigarette, and so forth.

When he quit again, he carried this list with him at all times, realizing that at some point his motivation would fade and hoping that reviewing these reasons would help him to reactivate his emotional commitment not to smoke. That emotional commitment was what finally allowed him to succeed. To simply think it would be a good idea to quit smoking (or to alleviate any other addiction in your life) is one thing; to have a strong emotional commitment to quitting is quite another.

Ongoing emotional commitment really yields results. In this way, the author was able to maintain his course any time his resolve began to waver. His last attempt to quit smoking was more than seventeen years ago, and he has remained a comfortable non-smoker ever since. If energy psychology had been around at that time, quitting would have been a much easier task for him. Now, he uses the energy treatments for those very rare periods when his thoughts and urges to smoke return. These techniques are described in the next section.

URGE REDUCTION TREATMENTS

The urge reduction treatments described below can be used to treat any addictive urge, including those for tobacco, alcohol, drugs, gambling, sex, and so forth. The treatment generally will eliminate the urge, sometimes briefly and sometimes for extended periods. Once the urge has been eliminated and you find that you cannot resurrect it, it is time to focus on developing new and more positive directions in your life. This is a very important part of the treatment process, and if you cannot do it on your own, you should seek the assistance of qualified professionals and support groups. As you continue using the treatment sequences on a regular basis, the period of time that you remain urge-free will continue to increase.

Complex Urge Reduction Treatment

1. If you are currently experiencing an addictive urge/craving, rate it on a 0 to 10 scale, with 10 representing the highest level of urge and 0 indicating no urge. If you are not currently experiencing addictive craving, think about a situation that tends to trigger urges for you and then rate the level of that urge.

2. Treat for the possibility of reversal by tapping repeatedly on the Side of Hand (SH) or rubbing the Sore Spot (SS) while saying or thinking three times, "I deeply accept myself even though I have this urge." It also may be helpful to tap the SH or rub the SS while saying, "I accept myself with all my problems and limitations."

3. Look at diagram 26 and the treatment sequence for complex urge reduction under the diagram to identify the locations for the meridian points Under Eye (UE), Under Collarbone (UCB), Under Arm (UA), and Little Finger (LF). While thinking about the urge, tap five times at each of these meridian points. Tap them in the following order: 1 → 2 → 3 → 4 → 3 → 2 → 1. **Note:** The UE, UCB, and UA are repeated twice in the sequence. Tap only hard enough to feel it. The tapping shouldn't cause any pain.

4. Again, rate your addictive urge on a 0 to 10 scale (a number should just pop into your mind). If there is no decrease, go back to step 2 and cycle through the sequence again. If you do not experience decrease

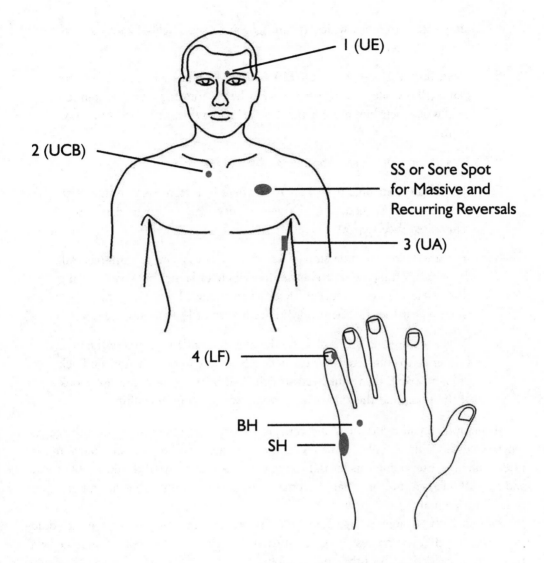

Diagram Twenty-Six: Complex Urge Reduction

Treatment Sequence for Complex Urge Reduction

Meridian		Location
Under Eye (UE)	1	Under center of eye on tip of bone
Under Collarbone (UCB)	2	One inch under collarbone near throat
Under Arm (UA)	3	Six inches under armpit
Little Finger (LF)	4	Inside tip of little fingernail on the side

after three attempts, which is rare, go on to the Highly Complex Urge Reduction Treatment.

5. Next, do the Brain Balancer (BB) by tapping repeatedly at the Back of Hand (BH) while rotating your eyes clockwise, rotating your eyes counter-clockwise, then humming a tune, counting to five, and then humming again.

6. Repeat the tapping sequence 1 → 2 → 3 → 4 → 3 → 2 → 1.

7. Again, rate your urge from 0 to 10. If there is a decrease, continue with the treatment sequence until there is very little or no addictive urge remaining. (See step 9.)

8. If at any point the urge stops decreasing, this indicates a mini-reversal. Treat this by tapping on the little finger Side of Hand (SH) while saying three times, "I deeply accept myself even though I still have this urge." Then repeat the treatment until there is very little or no urge left.

9. When the urge level is 0 to 2, do the Eye Roll (ER) to decrease the urge further or to complete the treatment effects. To do this, tap on the Back of Hand (BH), hold your head straight and, moving only your eyes, look at the floor, and then slowly raise your eyes toward the ceiling.

If the urge should return at a later time, repeat these treatments. In time, the recurrence of addictive urges will become less and less frequent. When you are unable to resurrect the urge after doing this overall treatment, it is best to avoid thinking about your addiction. Once you are urge-free, become involved in activities that are far removed from the addiction.

Although the Complex Urge Reduction Treatment effectively reduces most addictive urges, at times it proves to be insufficient. In this case, a more comprehensive treatment is needed, such as the one that follows.

Highly Complex Urge Reduction Treatment

1. If you are currently experiencing an addictive urge/craving, rate it on a scale of 0 to 10, with 10 representing the highest level of urge and 0 indicating no urge. Otherwise, think about a situation that tends to trigger urges for you, *really think about it*, and rate the level of that urge.

2. Treat for the possibility of reversal by tapping repeatedly on the Side of Hand (SH) or rubbing the Sore Spot (SS) while thinking or saying three times, "I deeply accept myself even though I have this urge." It also may be helpful to tap the SH or rub the SS while saying, "I accept myself with all my problems and limitations."

3. Look at diagram 27 and the treatment sequence for highly complex urge reduction under the diagram to identify the locations of the meridian points for Eyebrow (EB), Side of Eye (SE), Under Eye (UE), Under Nose (UN), Under Bottom Lip (UBL), Under Collarbone (UCB), Under Arm (UA), Under Breast (UB), Little Finger (LF), Middle Finger (MF), Index Finger (IF), and Thumb (T). While thinking about your urge/craving, tap five times at each of these meridian points. Tap them in the following order: 1 → 2 → 3 → 4 → → 5 → 6 → 7 → 8 → 9 → 10 → 11 → 12. Tap only hard enough to feel it. The tapping shouldn't cause any pain.

4. Again, rate your urge or craving on a 0 to 10 scale (a number should just pop into your mind). If there is no decrease, go back to step 2 and cycle through the sequence again. If three rounds of this treatment do not alleviate the addictive urge, you should consider other possible reversals, that is, the Midline Energy Treatment in chapter 8 and the Over-Energy Correction Method in chapter 2.

5. If there is a decrease of two or more points, do the Brain Balancer (BB) by tapping repeatedly at the Back of Hand (BH) while rotating your eyes clockwise, rotating your eyes counterclockwise, then humming a tune, counting to five, and humming again.

6. Repeat the tapping sequence 1 → 2 → 3 → 4 → 5 → 6 → 7 → 8 → 9 → 10 → 11 → 12.

7. Again, rate your urge/craving from 0 to 10. It should be lower by at least two points. If it is lower, continue with this treatment until there are very few or no signs of urge remaining.

8. If the progress of urge reduction stalls at any time, this indicates a mini-reversal. Treat this by tapping on the little finger Side of Hand (SH) while saying three times, "I deeply accept myself, even though I still have some of this urge." Then resume the treatment sequence, alternating with the Brain Balancer (BB), until the urge is gone.

9. When the urge/craving is 0 to 2, consider doing the Eye Roll (ER) to lower the urge/craving further or to complete the treatment effects. To do this, tap on the Back of Hand (BH), hold your head straight and, moving only your eyes, look at the floor and then slowly raise your eyes toward the ceiling. Then rate your urge level again. This technique generally results in a feeling of calmness and relaxation, eliminating any remaining urge.

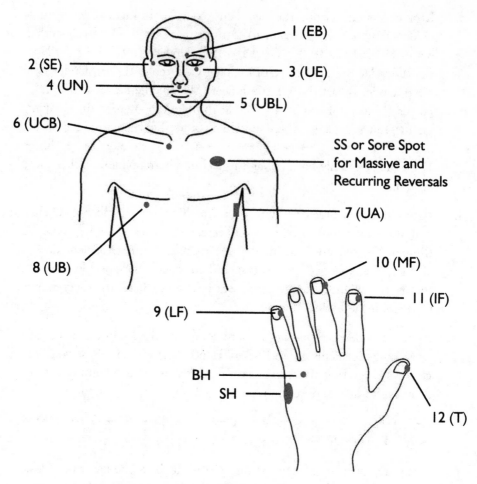

Diagram Twenty-Seven: Highly Complex Urge Reduction

Treatment Sequence for Highly Complex Urge Reduction

Meridian		Location
Eyebrow (EB)	1	Beginning of eyebrow near bridge of nose
Side of Eye (SE)	2	Side of eye on bony orbit near temple
Under Eye (UE)	3	Under the center of eye on tip of bone
Under Nose (UN)	4	Under nose and above upper lip
Under Bottom Lip (UBL)	5	Under bottom lip in cleft of chin
Under Collarbone (UCB)	6	Under collarbone next to chest bone
Under Arm (UA)	7	Six inches under armpit
Under Breast (UB)	8	Directly under breast on rib
Little Finger (LF)	9	Inside tip of little fingernail on the side
Middle Finger (MF)	10	Inside tip of middle fingernail
Index Finger (IF)	11	Tip of index fingernail on the side nearest the thumb
Thumb (T)	12	Outside tip of thumbnail

As noted earlier, when you are unable to resurrect the urge after doing this treatment, it is best to avoid thinking about your addiction. Now is the time to become involved in positive activities far removed from the addiction.

The two treatment sequences described above are methods to alleviate addictive urges. These techniques can be used whenever an urge arises, for whatever reasons. However, there are numerous internal and environmental triggers for these urges and to be thorough, as many triggers as possible need to be neutralized with this method. Internal triggers may include feeling stressed, tired, hungry, nervous, lonely, angry, depressed, and so forth. Environmental triggers, depending on the addiction, may include a cup of coffee, passing a bar, being at a specific location in your city, encountering certain people, and so on.

Any time these triggers occur, using an addictive urge reduction treatment will help to neutralize the impact of the trigger. However, urge reduction treatments may not prove sufficient to alleviate depression, guilt, or anger. In this regard, other treatment sequences in this book will be useful to help you stay on the road to recovery. When necessary, freely refer to those sections of the book.

For example, one patient was having excellent results relieving the desire for alcohol by using the urge reduction treatment. At times, however, he experienced a deep feeling of "emptiness" that caused him to consider drinking again just to make the "pain go away." He said that although he knew that drinking would settle the feeling of emptiness, he also knew that the feeling would return once he was sober again. Although this man's feeling certainly had a great deal to do with the events of his life, his first step involved implementing the energy treatments for depression, which worked rapidly to eliminate his feeling of "emptiness." Then, he began to fill his life with positive elements, such as becoming involved in Alcoholics Anonymous, satisfying work, and healthy, loving relationships. Of course, this took some time. With dedication and the help of energy psychology, however, his life improved dramatically.

SUMMARY

In this chapter, we have covered treatment for addictive urges and psychological reversals that interfere with a commitment to recovery. Using these treatments on a regular basis can go a long way toward eliminating addictive urges. Addiction, however, is often related to other emotional issues, such as social anxiety, depression, anger, trauma, guilt feelings, and energy toxins. These areas are covered in other chapters of this book. If you have an addiction problem, we recommend that you address it in a comprehensive way. In addition to utilizing the techniques covered in this book, you must make other positive, healthy life decisions. Your life and happiness, as well as the lives and happiness of those you love, are at stake.

Lowering Your Blood Pressure

There is an old Hindu saying that no matter whether the knife falls on the
melon or the melon falls on the knife, it is the melon that suffers.

—Merle Shain

It seems that whether you use anger to challenge life situations or passively allow life's events to overwhelm you, it is your body that suffers. The impact of certain situations may result in feelings of chronic stress or behavioral responses like excessive eating, but another problem occurs when your blood pressure elevates past a certain level—you then have hypertension and the facts about this health problem are frightening. Every year one in eight people worldwide die from the effects of hypertension (Kottke, Strobel, and Hoffman 2004).

Yet hypertension is often a silent killer with no symptoms—that is until there is a major problem, such as a heart attack or stroke. In the United States, 65 million adults have elevated systolic (top number) or diastolic (bottom number) blood pressure, and these numbers represent a 30 percent increase over the last two decades (Fields et al. 2004). It is also a growing global problem; a study by the International Collaborative Study of Cardiovascular Disease in Asia found that cardiovascular disease is a leading cause of death in Asian countries (Inter-Asia 2003).

UNDERSTANDING HYPERTENSION

Hypertension, or high blood pressure, is a medical condition in which constricted blood vessels make it harder for the heart to pump blood, which creates an increase in pressure against the walls of the arteries. In the majority of cases, no clear medical reason can be identified as the cause of high blood pressure. If undetected, over time, this increases the risk for stroke, heart attack, and kidney failure, as well as for many other medical problems. Increased pressure on the inner walls of your blood vessels makes them less flexible, which increases the buildup of fatty deposits and the risk of heart attack. Increased blood pressure also can create weak spots in the blood vessels, which can then "balloon" and rupture, leading to a stroke. Hypertension also forces the heart to work harder and this can cause the heart muscle to enlarge, which may lead to heart failure (AMA 2004).

According to the Joint National Committee on prevention, detection, evaluation, and treatment of high blood pressure, hypertension occurs when your systolic blood pressure (the top number) is over 139 and/or your diastolic blood pressure (the bottom number) is over 89 (Chobanian et al. 2003). However, recent research has found that people who have *high normal* blood pressure, that is, their systolic blood pressure is at 120 to 139 mm Hg or their diastolic blood pressure is at 80 to 89 mm Hg also have an increased risk of cardiovascular disease and this has led to a new category of risk, called *pre-hypertension* (Chobanian et al. 2003).

This new category is especially important for women, because estrogen helps women to maintain lower blood pressure, so they may not think of high blood pressure as a problem that has much relevance for them. However, after menopause, women quickly catch up to male rates for high blood pressure. In fact, the 2007 guidelines for preventing cardiovascular disease in women point out that heart disease accounts for one-third of all female deaths. The authors of the guidelines believe that 40 percent of postmenopausal women have pre-hypertension and thus have a 58 percent higher chance of a cardiovascular death (Hsia et al. 2007).

Nonetheless, men are still the primary target group because they develop these problems much earlier in life than women do. One study found that 77 percent of men with pre-hypertension will develop hypertension (*Hypertension Week* 2004). And in a 2006 article, Chobanian reported that 40 percent of pre-hypertensive individuals developed hypertension within two years after being diagnosed as pre-hypertensive.

Simply put, you want your systolic blood pressure to be at or below 120 and your diastolic blood pressure to be at or below 80. If you don't know your blood pressure, then it's important for you to see your physician to obtain an accurate reading, especially because one in three people who are hypertensive are unaware of their condition (Hajjar and Kotchen 2003).

A national survey found that only 27 percent of those who had been diagnosed as hypertensive had reduced their blood pressure to acceptable levels (Lloyd-Jones et al. 2002). One concern is that psychosocial problems such as chronic stress lead to unhealthy lifestyles and self-sabotaging behaviors. Often, these behaviors are used to temporarily cope with stressful feelings. The problems are compounded because guidelines for managing psychosocial problems in cardiac practice are lacking (Rozanski et al. 2005).

There is no cookbook strategy for successfully lowering high blood pressure; the actions that lead to the control of hypertension must be the criterion for success (Rumsfield and Ho 2005). One goal of behavioral cardiology is to identify the psychosocial and behavioral problems that help to create or maintain hypertension, so that strategies for treatment can be developed. For example, several studies have linked depression, stress, and trauma to both hypertension and cardiovascular disease (Curtis and O'Keefe 2002; Esler and Kaye 2000).

One theory that is gaining support holds that chronic emotional problems can weaken the immune system through excessive sympathetic nervous system stimulation and reduced parasympathetic nervous system input (Marano 2004; Bleil et al. 2004). The *sympathetic nervous system* is like the gas pedal in a car. It provides the energy to tackle life's challenges, as opposed to the parasympathetic nervous system, which acts like a brake, slowing you down and helping your body to heal.

Normally, there is a balance between these two systems, providing you with the needed energy to cope with life and calming your body down to reenergize. Chronic emotional turmoil, however, does result in excessive sympathetic nervous system stimulation. It also suppresses the parasympathetic system, which then upsets the balance between the two systems. When that occurs, a pathway is created for behavioral/addictive problems like smoking, overeating, and alcoholism to take root and take their toll (Curtis and O'Keefe 2002).

When you are undergoing stress, your body energizes by releasing hormones and neurotransmitters that will help you deal with the stressful situation. But if you are experiencing stress day after day, your body is constantly gearing up to deal with it, and over time it will wear down. Stress also interferes with your parasympathetic system, which helps your body heal and rejuvenate. This leads to a weakening of your immune system that, eventually, may allow the natural weaknesses in your family's genetic makeup, such as a predilection for cancer or heart disease, to develop.

For example, depression activates blood platelets increasing the propensity to form clots (Marano 2004), not a good situation for anyone, but especially for those with a family history of heart attack or stroke. Stress and/or depression can increase inflammatory markers such as C-reactive protein that can lead to insulin resistance, diabetes, and cardiovascular problems. Stress automatically increases the level of the hormones, adrenaline and cortisol, in your body. In fact, they are sometimes called the "stress hormones." Elevated adrenaline and cortisol levels constrict your blood vessels. This increases your blood pressure by causing your heart to beat faster (AMA 2004).

The situation becomes even more complex when your coping strategies include behavioral concerns such as excessive alcohol consumption, overeating, smoking, or lack of exercise, all of which have also been associated with hypertension (Rozanski et al. 2005; Kottke, Strobel, and Hoffman 2004).

UNDERSTANDING YOUR RISK FACTORS

Your goal is to identify a strategy that will help you reduce your blood pressure; to do this effectively, you need to understand your risk factors. For example, if your parents have or had hypertension, you are more likely to become hypertensive and will have to work harder than others to keep your blood pressure in check. If you have a disease, this may be a cause of high blood pressure, and your treatment for hypertension would also focus on treating the disease. However, for most people there is a list of common problems they must deal with in everyday life, and we believe that most people are sufficiently intuitive to know which problems are most likely to be involved in their hypertension, but we will also try to guide you.

Problems highly correlated with hypertension include chronic stress, depression, trauma, obesity, smoking, and alcoholism (AMA 2004; Rozanski et al. 2005) and each of these topics is addressed in various chapters throughout this book. We encourage you to read those sections to obtain more information about any particular health problem and the strategies you can use to resolve it.

Obesity

Your weight can be a primary contributor to hypertension, and the U.S. Department of Health and Human Services offers the following guidelines concerning body weight. If you are female and have a waist measurement of 35 inches or 40 inches for a male, you are considered obese and in need of weight loss. Another indicator is your body mass index (BMI). In this formula your height and weight are used to calculate your BMI index. For example, for both genders, if your height is 5'4," you are considered overweight at 150 pounds and obese at a weight of 175 pounds. Or if you are 5'10," you are considered overweight at 190 pounds and obese at a weight of 210 pounds. You can search the Internet using "body mass index" as the keyword to find a chart that exactly matches your height and weight.

If you are overweight according to these measures, your weight is considered a source of risk for high blood pressure; however, these formulas are not perfect and your bone structure may determine the right weight for you. Again, most people know if they are overweight, and perhaps equally important, why they are overweight. If you are overweight or obese, we encourage you to review chapter 12 on weight loss to develop an intervention strategy.

DIET AND LIFESTYLE

Fast-food restaurants continue to expand all over the world and, although efforts are currently being made to control trans fats, these fast foods are still very high in calories and the size of the portions often leads to overeating. Also, fast foods usually contain much more sodium (salt) than is needed daily, and this, too, can be a source of hypertension. Lifestyle is also a concern. Too many people appear to be rushed, which leads them to eat foods that are not good for them. We bring these points up because changing your diet is difficult, even though there may be many reasons to do so. Along with dealing with the underlying emotional issues, you must search to find a diet that you can stick with and, more importantly, you must make a healthy lifelong change in your eating habits that will work with your lifestyle.

Substance Abuse

Under the heading of "substance abuse," we include daily smoking and excessive consumption of alcohol or drugs—including the misuse of prescription medication, a fast-growing problem. Any form of substance abuse indicates that something is missing in your life and that you are using the substance as a way to cope. The degree of abuse differs from person to person, but it is important for you to examine this concept and to start developing what is missing from your life as a part of your treatment process.

Sleep

Another problematic lifestyle issue concerns sleep, the time when our bodies are at rest and can heal. Gangwisch et al. (2006) reports that lack of sleep, that is, less than six hours of sleep per night makes the risk of developing hypertension twice as likely as it is for those who get enough sleep. Furthermore, too little sleep time increases the risk for diabetes and obesity. The study also found that this problem affects more men than women and that up to 18 percent of the population is affected in the northeastern part of the United States. There are many reasons someone may experience a lack of sleep, or what many people call "poor sleep," because they wake up feeling tired rather than refreshed. For example, chronic stress is often involved in sleep problems, but the point is to include this issue while you are examining possible reasons for your high blood pressure.

Anger

Chronic anger has also been associated with developing hypertension and can be a function of problems such as depression or lack of sleep. The inability to cope with problems or deal with situations in which you are not in control can often provoke anger. It can even become an automatic response to such situations and lead to inappropriate behaviors. In effect, being angry can become a very bad habit. You may even start to manufacture reasons to become angry because when you lash out at those who have offended you, you get positive feelings of being in control. Nonetheless, you must understand that when you are angry, you are telling your body to prepare for a fight.

That preparation sets off the physiological responses known collectively as the "fight-or-flight syndrome," which, when activated too often, can wear down your immune system over time. Even worse, by being frequently angry, you train yourself to respond with anger in conflict situations, rather than deal with the problems in a healthier way.

What follows are strategies to help reduce your blood pressure if you are pre-hypertensive. They have been designed specifically for individuals who are pre-hypertensive or high normal. If you have Stage I or Stage II hypertension (systolic blood pressure: 140 or higher or diastolic blood pressure: 90 or higher), you need to work with your physician. However, you can still use these strategies to help yourself make lifestyle changes in conjunction with appropriate medical consultation.

Furthermore, it is important that you make such changes because a major study on drug treatment found that, although medication did significantly reduce the percentage of those with pre-hypertension who developed full-blown hypertension, once the medication had been stopped, that group of pre-hypertensives quickly developed hypertension (Chobanian 2006). Hypertension drugs are also very costly, have unpleasant side effects, and their long-term effects on organs like the liver as still not well understood (Chobanian et al. 2003). Our goal is to provide you with an approach that will allow you to maintain normal blood pressure and not require long-term medication.

DEVELOPING YOUR STRATEGY

In chapter 5, Identifying Problems That You Want to Resolve, we talked about how you "do" a problem. The goal is to understand how you help to create or maintain problems in your life. It's hard to change if you don't understand that the process and the way problems manifest themselves in your life are unique to you and are most likely fairly complex. This means that there are likely to be multiple problems and that they interact.

It is much easier to change if you have a satisfying life with relatively few stresses, and you are overweight or obese just because you love to eat. Compare that situation to someone who is struggling at work, stressed at home with family problems, and who has chosen drinking as a way to help cope with the stress, along with overeating. Then this person finds out that she has high blood pressure and her doctor advises her to lose weight. Where to begin?

The bad news is that if you try to lose weight without addressing your other problems, you will most likely fail. Try to connect the dots to understand how you do this problem. What behaviors and beliefs have led you to being overweight and thus to high blood pressure? The good news is that you don't have to have an exact answer. Once you start working on a problem, the issues will become clearer to you and you can change your focus or add another problem to address. Usually, there is a core problem that you are aware of and that you need some help to resolve.

Try sketching a diagram of the troublesome situations in your life. It will be like making a flow chart. In the far right draw a circle and write high blood pressure in it. Then starting at the far left, list all the life situations you believe are contributing to your high blood pressure. Try to put them in an order that you think leads to your high blood pressure.

For example, stress at work makes you feel tired and angry at work, as well as when you think about certain situations at home. When you are home, you don't have the motivation to do anything relevant or necessary to move toward your life goals. Instead, you watch television throughout the evenings. Although the tube keeps you entertained, it doesn't make you feel better, so you use eating—or drinking and eating—to help sedate your uncomfortable feelings. Then you gain weight, and that can increase your blood pressure.

So, begin to create a picture of your situation and think about how to address your problems. In the sample flow chart, the problem begins with work-related stress leading to feelings of anger.

This can elevate cortisol levels and lead to overeating to soothe your emotional stress. Both the elevated cortisol level and the overeating can lead to elevated blood pressure. In this series of causal events, what you have the most control over is your response to the stress at work. That means that your anger at work would be the best place to start making changes.

Now, use the strategies in this book to change how you respond to stress situations and, in turn, to reduce your anger. Once you've done this, other issues may appear that will need to be resolved, but you will have begun the process of changing your mind-body connections. In time, you will be better able to implement a change in your diet, as well as in how your body responds to stressful situations.

Be realistic; many people experience excessive stress in their jobs or relationships and they can't just walk away. Accept that small steps are needed as you focus on changing specific situations. When you successfully address one piece of a problem, you can try to make other life changes where possible. Dealing with complex problems takes a

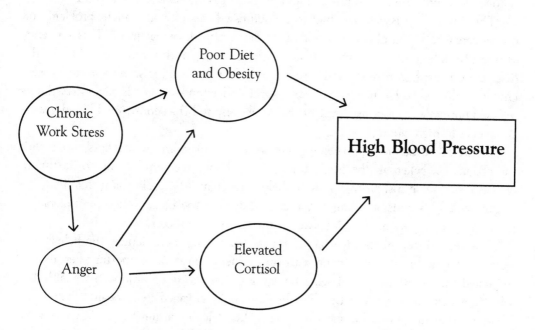

Flow Chart of One Possible Path
to Develop High Blood Pressure

lot of work and it takes time to change. However, as you use the strategies you will find here to balance your energy, new solutions will appear.

Be aware that your initial goal of losing weight may be possible only after you have resolved several other concerns in your life. Lowering your blood pressure is a long-term process and you will be developing strategies that you will be able to use for the rest of your life.

LEO'S STORY: A CASE STUDY

Leo is a fifty-one-year-old man who holds a managerial position in a large company. One of his problems is that he is a perfectionist. Although this trait had helped him to succeed at work, it has also fueled his inability to accept certain situations that led to his feelings of chronic stress. He often got angry, but rarely showed it. To cope with his stress, he overate. He was sixty pounds overweight and struggled with obesity. Although he was a likable person, he was divorced and lived alone.

As the years took their toll on him, he began to feel stuck. He no longer liked his job. He was in good shape financially, but needed to work at least seven more years before he could afford to retire. He came to see us to help him cope with his chronic stress. His physician had recently warned him about his blood pressure and told him that soon he would have to take medications to lower it. Leo was pre-hypertensive with systolic blood pressure at 138 mm Hg and diastolic blood pressure at 87 mm Hg.

There were two issues that had to be addressed: his obvious weight problem and his tendency to brood about situations that did not work out at work. This tendency caused Leo to become angry and frustrated with the people who work with him. So, the first step was for him to understand the impact that his chronic stress and anger were having on his body. He needed to learn—and understand—that his high stress levels released hormones that constricted his blood vessels; and that constricted blood vessels contribute to high blood pressure.

So, we asked Leo to read the chapters on stress, anger, and weight loss, along with the chapter on beliefs in the first edition of this book. We wanted him to do this in order to gain some insight into how he helped to create the problems in his life. This reading aided his understanding of the complexities of the issue. When he understood that, he became more actively involved in the treatment process.

The second step in the treatment process was to help Leo identify the beliefs that were sabotaging his ability to cope with his problems. This was important because we suspected that Leo had several self-sabotaging beliefs revolving around his health and self-acceptance. So we asked Leo why he knowingly engaged in unhealthy behaviors. We knew that in spite of his success at work, Leo felt like a failure. We knew that he was depressed and that he used food to make himself feel better and to cope with his negative thoughts and feelings. But his blood pressure was sending a clear signal that his health was being affected by his lifestyle.

Leo's problems were quite complex. His first step had to be to treat his belief about it being okay to use food for coping with negative feelings and frustrations when events didn't turn out as he hoped they would. So, before beginning the hypertension treatment described in the next section, Leo focused on his self-sabotaging beliefs by doing the following:

1. He found the Sore Spot (SS) on the left side of his chest and rubbed that spot while saying to himself three times, "I accept myself with all my problems and limitations."

2. Then he tapped the Under Bottom Lip (UBL) spot three times, while saying, "Even if a part of me believes that I don't deserve to be healthy and I don't value my success in life, I deeply accept myself."

He then used the treatment recipe below at least three times a week over a twelve-week period.

The results were excellent. Although Leo still got angry, he stopped brooding about whatever had angered him. He got angry only in the moment, and he learned how to let his anger go without dwelling on it. Instead, he focused on the parts of his life that were important to him and made him feel better about himself and his actions. When he stopped being obsessed with work-related problems, he then found the desire to explore his food cravings. He used the treatments in chapter 12, Developing an Effective Weight-Loss Strategy, to help him gain control over his cravings.

Over the twelve-week time frame, he lost fifteen pounds. When he had his blood pressure checked again, it had dropped; his systolic pressure was 130 mm Hg and his diastolic pressure was 83 mm Hg. He continued using the energy tapping strategies and experienced further weight loss and even lower numbers. His blood pressure was normal, he was no longer pre-hypertensive.

Leo's multitargeted approach is often required for dealing with complex problems effectively. If your issues are as complex as Leo's were, you may wish to consult with a psychologist who has some expertise in using these strategies.

TREATMENT STRATEGY FOR HYPERTENSION

Up to this point, our goal has been to inform you about the many problems that can be the source of your high blood pressure. We've also discussed how complex high blood pressure can be, and said that dealing with it may mean there are several problems that must be resolved. We encourage you to review the chapters dealing with your specific issues so that you can better understand how to resolve them.

A Twelve-Week Treatment

In the following approach, a twelve-week time frame is recommended because you are unlikely to experience any physical changes that will result in significantly lowered blood pressure in a shorter amount of time.

Step 1. Identify the Problems That You Wish to Change

You should work on identifying the problems you want to change before you get your blood pressure reading. We've found that along with their obvious problems, most people intuitively recognize the emotional situations that are likely to be responsible for creating their high blood pressure. Your focus should be on the chronic problems in your life, such as a traumatic event that you continue to dwell on years after the event, or on an ongoing behavioral problem like overeating. Again, we encourage you to read the appropriate chapters that address your particular issues.

Step 2. Get an Accurate Reading of Your Blood Pressure Taken in the Morning

If your blood pressure is taken in the morning, this means that your body is in a normal state and you didn't run to answer the doorbell a few minutes before the reading was taken. It also means that you didn't drink a caffeinated beverage or smoke tobacco before the reading. Caffeine and tobacco increase your heart rate and may give you an artificially high reading. Whether you choose to buy a blood pressure monitor and take the reading yourself or you choose to have it taken by medical personnel, have the reading done twice within one fifteen-minute interval.

The systolic and diastolic readings should not be more than 5 mm Hg apart. If they are, then a third reading is required; but, in either case, an average of the readings should be used as your baseline. Keep a record of your readings. Write down your numbers and the date.

Step 3. Treatment Sequence for Hypertension

Use the following hypertension treatment at least three times a week over a period of twelve weeks

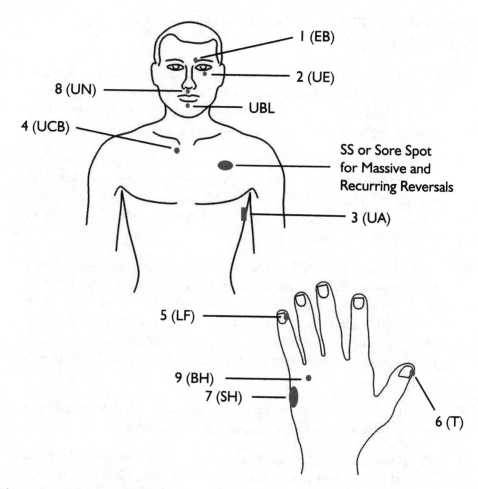

Diagram Twenty-Eight: High Blood Pressure

Treatment Sequence

Meridian		Location
Eyebrow (EB)	1	Beginning of eyebrow near bridge of nose
Under Eye (UE)	2	Under the center of the eye on tip of bone
Under Arm (UA)	3	Six inches under armpit
Under Collarbone (UCB)	4	One inch under collarbone near throat
Little Finger (LF)	5	Inside tip of little fingernail on the side
Thumb (T)	6	Outside tip of thumbnail on the side
Side of Hand (SH)	7	On palm crease on the side of hand when a fist is made
Under Nose (UN)	8	Above upper lip and below the center of nose
Back of Hand (BH)	9	Back of hand between little and ring fingers

TREATMENT SEQUENCE FOR LOWERING YOUR BLOOD PRESSURE

1. Think about the problem you want to change; for example, you can imagine a specific situation that causes you to become angry or to experience a food craving. Then rate your distress on a 0 to 10 scale, with 0 representing no distress and 10 representing the highest level of distress.

2. Locate and rub the Sore Spot (SS) on the left side of your chest while saying to yourself three times, "I accept myself with all my problems and limitations." Then tap Under Nose (UN) point three times while saying, "I deserve to be healthy and to value my successes in life." Then focus on the problem you wish to address.

3. Look at diagram 28 and at the treatment sequence for lowering your blood pressure directly under the diagram. Now tap seven to ten times on the Eyebrow (EB), Under Eye (UE), Under Arm (UA), Under Collarbone (UCB), Little Finger (LF), Thumb (T), Side of Hand (SH), Under Nose (UN), and Back of Hand (BH). The sequence is numbered, so just follow the sequence in this diagram $1 \rightarrow 2 \rightarrow 3 \rightarrow 4 \rightarrow 5 \rightarrow 6 \rightarrow 7 \rightarrow 8 \rightarrow 9$.

4. Now, briefly check how you feel. If the distress level has decreased by at least two points, continue. If not, repeat steps 2 and 3.

5. The Brain Balancer (BB) can be done next by tapping repeatedly at the Back of Hand (BH) point while rotating your eyes clockwise, rotating your eyes counterclockwise, humming a tune, counting to five, and then humming again. (Note that this step is not needed, if your distress level keeps improving.)

6. Now tap seven to ten times on the Eyebrow (EB), Under Eye (UE), Under Arm (UA), Under Collarbone (UCB), Little Finger (LF), Thumb (T), Side of Hand (SH), Under Nose (UN), and Back of Hand (BH) points. The algorithm or recipe is numbered, so just follow the sequence in the diagram $1 \rightarrow 2 \rightarrow 3 \rightarrow 4 \rightarrow 5 \rightarrow 6 \rightarrow 7 \rightarrow 8 \rightarrow 9$.

7. If the discomfort has not decreased even further, tap on the little finger Side of Hand (SH) while saying three times, "I deeply accept myself, even though I still have some of this problem." Then repeat steps 3 through 6.

8. Once your level of distress is within the 0 to 2 range, do the Eye Roll (ER) to complete the treatment effects. To do this, tap on the Back of

Hand (BH), hold your head straight and, moving only your eyes, look at the floor, and then slowly raise your eyes toward the ceiling.

Step 4. Make an Evaluation Every Four Weeks

The fact that you are indirectly treating your hypertension by addressing the issues causing it is very important. At the end of a four-week period, you should have achieved some degree of change in your beliefs and behaviors. At that point, you need to evaluate the effectiveness of the treatment on the concerns you have addressed. For example, have you observed an obvious behavior change or do you no longer become upset over a specific problem?

Examine any other issues that may have surfaced in the past four weeks. You can use the treatment to address them as well. Most importantly, if you feel that the treatments are not helping, our experience is that a self-sabotaging belief is undermining your success. We recommend that you review chapter 4 on Beliefs That Hold You Back and use your intuition to identify your problem beliefs.

Step 5. Have Your Blood Pressure Checked Again

After twelve weeks of treatment, have your blood pressure checked again. It should have gone down. Moreover, equally as important as lowered blood pressure, you should now feel that you have more control over the way you respond to the situations in your life. Remember, you are indirectly going to lower your blood pressure by changing the behaviors and beliefs that were adversely affecting your body.

SUMMARY

Hypertension is a serious and growing problem worldwide. The dual purpose of this chapter is to help you understand hypertension and to recognize how your behaviors contribute to this problem. You know what needs to be done to keep yourself healthy. You can use the strategies in this book to eliminate the self-sabotaging beliefs and behaviors that weaken your motivation. Your body is very resilient, but over time, chronic emotional turmoil creates a pathway for problems like hypertension to develop. The treatments offered in this chapter and throughout the book can be used to help you cope with these problems and prevent or lower high blood pressure. Nonetheless, we must again warn you that hypertension is a serious problem and if you are Stage I or Stage II hypertensive, you should seek the advice of your physician in conjunction with using the strategies in this book.

Allergies and Your Immune System

Don't go out with wet hair; you'll catch a cold.

—Your Mom

Although it is unlikely that wet hair will directly lead to a cold, there is research supporting the fact that being cold saps your body's resources and can weaken your body's immune system. In fact, it may tap into the same mind-body system that leads to cold symptoms (Azar 2001). Recently, many news media personnel including those from Bloomburg and CNN have been discussing the effects of global warming on disease. Researchers are concerned that the warmer climate, as well as more rainfall in some parts of the planet, will increase the number of disease carriers, such as mosquitoes. They are also concerned about the outbreak of new diseases. These emerging problems make it all the more important to have a strong immune system.

This chapter focuses on the new field of psychoneuroimmunology (PNI), which examines how the brain, central nervous system (CNS), and neuroendocrine system interact to affect and alter our immune system. Three topics are addressed: allergies, heart rate variability, and the autoimmune system.

ALLERGIES

You may have first become aware of your immune system when you started sneezing repeatedly during "hay fever season," even though you knew you were not sick. Or perhaps you heard a story about two healthy teenagers walking through a park on a spring day. Both were stung by bees. For the first teenager, the bee sting was merely a painful annoyance; however, because of freshly blooming flowers and abundant new leaf growth she was mostly bothered by her runny nose and watery eyes. For the second teenager, however, the bee sting was a potentially deadly event. She had to be hospitalized.

Both girls' very different responses are examples of allergic reactions; the first to pollen and the second to the toxin injected by the bee sting. *Allergies* are abnormal responses of the immune system. People who have allergies have immune systems that react poorly to a substance in the environment that is usually harmless. The substance, *pollen*, for example, is called an *allergen* and it adversely affects about 20 percent of the total population (WebMD.com 2007). Once your body becomes sensitive to pollen (or any other substance), it treats that substance as a dangerous intruder, which results in the release of histamines that cause most of the symptoms of an allergy, including itchiness and a runny nose.

If the allergen is in the air, the allergic reaction will likely occur in the eyes, nose, and lungs. If the allergen is ingested, the allergic reaction often takes place in the mouth, throat, stomach, and intestines. Sometimes enough chemicals (including histamines) are released to cause a reaction throughout the body, such as hives, decreased blood pressure, shock, or loss of consciousness.

The symptoms of allergies can be divided into three groups:

1.   Mild reactions include symptoms that affect a specific area of the body such as a rash, sneezing, or congestion.

2.   Moderate reactions include symptoms that spread to other parts of the body and may be accompanied by difficulty breathing.

3.   A severe reaction is called *anaphylaxis*, a life-threatening emergency. Although rare, the response to the allergen intensely affects the whole body. This may include dizziness, vomiting, and swelling, which can make breathing and swallowing difficult.

It is not understood yet why the body responds with such reactions to one particular harmless substance and not to another. Nor is it clear why some individuals are allergic to many substances and others to none or only one. There are a number of theories, many involving a mind-body connection. For example, excessive stress, a traumatic event or prolonged depression produces adrenaline-related hormones, and your body must draw on its oxygen reserves for their production and eventual oxidation. In the process, this weakens your immune system (Rakel and Faass 2005).

There is also research indicating that certain allergic disorders, such as hay fever, are affected by the adrenaline and other hormones released into the body when you are stressed (Wright et al. 2005). If this becomes a chronic pattern, it can result in disruption of the normal balance of hormones and neurotransmitters and have an impact on your immune system's ability to respond to certain substances.

Studies have shown that psychological interventions may influence the allergic response by lowering cortisol levels (cortisol is a stress hormone) and strengthening the immune system (Rakel and Faass 2005). Although you may still need medication to cope with allergic reactions, you can lessen your dependency and strengthen your immune system. In addition to the following treatment, it is also recommended that you identify other negative emotional patterns in your life and use the strategies in this book to treat them.

To learn more about allergies, visit Internet sites such as WebMD or the National Institutes of Health.

How to Treat Allergies

Please note that there are many considerations when dealing with allergies and that these energy-tapping treatments are recommended for "minor allergies," not for the kind of allergy that can lead to life-threatening anaphylactic shock. We assume that your allergy happens only in very specific situations or that you have sought medical assistance to understand which substances are creating your allergic reaction.

INHALANT ALLERGIES

Use the following treatment and after several treatments, you should feel no stress when you think about the substance. Then stay away from the substance for at least a week before testing the result by exposing yourself to the substance.

1. Once you have identified a substance to which you are allergic, think about the substance and rate your distress. Again, rate your distress on a 0 to 10 scale, with 0 representing no distress and 10 representing the highest level of distress. A number should just pop into your mind.

2. Look at diagram 29 and the treatment sequence for inhalant allergies under the diagram to identify the locations for the meridian points Middle Finger (MF), Under Arm (UA), Under Collarbone (UCB), and Under Nose (UN). While thinking about the substance, tap at each of these meridian points five to ten times. Tap them in the following order: 1 → 2 → 3 → 4 → 3. Only tap hard enough to feel it. The tapping itself should not cause any pain.

3. Again, rate your distress on a 0 to 10 scale. If there is no decrease, go back to step 2 and cycle through the sequence again. If there is not a decrease after three attempts, this is probably not an appropriate sequence or there is another reversal that needs correction. Review the chapter on reversals for further instruction.

4. Next, do the Brain Balancer (BB) by tapping repeatedly at Back of Hand (BH) while rotating your eyes clockwise, rotating your eyes counterclockwise, then humming a tune, counting to five, and then humming again.

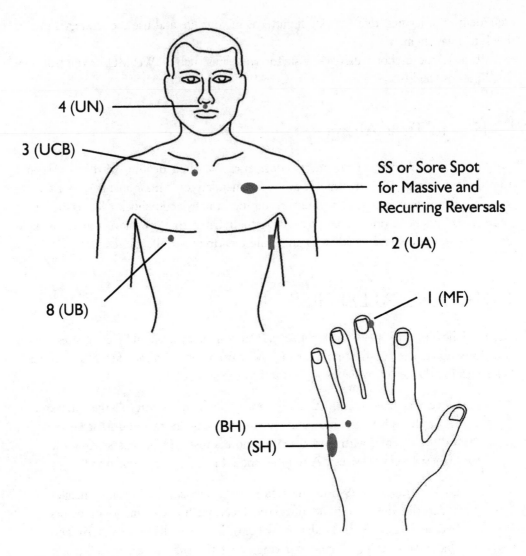

Diagram Twenty-Nine: Inhalant Allergy

Treatment Sequence for Inhalant Allergies

Meridian		Location
Middle Finger (MF)	1	Inside tip of fingernail on the side
Under Arm (UA)	2	Six inches under armpit
Under Collarbone (UCB)	3	One inch under collarbone near throat
Under Nose (UN)	4	Above upper lip and below the center of nose

5. Repeat the tapping sequence. Tap in the following order: 1 → 2 → 3 → 4 → 3.

6. Again, rate your level of distress from 0 to 10. It should be lower yet.

7. When the distress is 0 to 2, do the Eye Roll (ER) to lower the distress further or to complete the treatment effects. Tap on Back of Hand (BH) while holding your head straight and, only with your eyes, look at the floor and then slowly raise your eyes toward the ceiling.

FOOD ALLERGIES

Have you ever eaten a particular food and felt tired or ill afterward? Food allergies can release histamines to cause a rash, but they can also have a much stronger effect. Again, if it is minor and very specific, you can identify your allergens, but if you feel ill, you should seek medical assistance to help identify and treat the problem. The eight foods most often responsible for allergic reactions are: milk, eggs, peanuts, tree nuts, fish, shellfish, soy, and wheat (foodallergy.com 2007).

In this approach, say the name of the allergen (to yourself) and tap for approximately twenty seconds on each of the treatment points listed below. This is different from other treatments that direct you to tap five to ten times. While you can use a watch, don't feel you need to tap for exactly twenty seconds, just focus on the substance. After several treatments, you should feel no stress when you think about the substance. Then, test the results, but first stay away from the substance for at least a week before reexposing yourself.

Treatment Sequence for Food Allergies

1. Focus your attention on the allergic substance (that is, think about it). Rate your level of distress on a scale of 0 to 10, with 10 representing the highest level of distress and 0 indicating no distress.

2. Treat for the possibility of reversal by tapping repeatedly on the Side of Hand (SH) or rubbing the Sore Spot (SS) while thinking or saying three times, "Even though I have this allergy, I deeply and completely accept myself." It also may be helpful to tap SH or rub the SS while thinking or saying three times, "I accept myself with all my problems and limitations."

3. Look at the diagram and the treatment sequence for food allergies under the diagram and tap for twenty seconds on each location in the following order: 1 → 2 → 3 → 4.

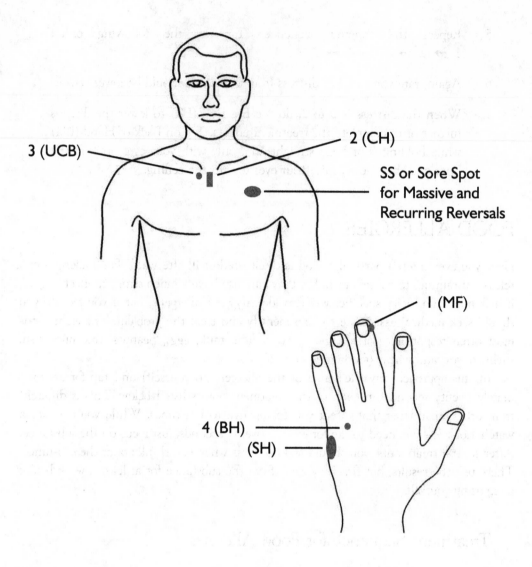

Diagram Thirty: Food Allergy

Treatment Sequence for Food Allergies

Meridian		Location
Middle Finger (MF)	1	Inside tip of fingernail on the side
Chest (CH)	2	Upper section of chest
Under Collarbone (UCB)	3	Under collarbone next to chest bone.
Back of Hand (BH)	4	Back of hand between little and ring fingers

4. Again, rate your distress on a 0 to 10 scale. If there is no decrease, go back to step 2 and cycle through the sequence again. If there is not a decrease after three attempts, this is probably not an appropriate sequence or there is another reversal that needs correction. Review the chapter on reversals for further instruction.

5. Next, do the Brain Balancer (BB) by tapping repeatedly at the Back of Hand (BH) point while rotating your eyes clockwise, rotating your eyes counterclockwise, then humming a tune, counting to five, and then humming again.

6. Repeat the tapping sequence as follows: 1 → 2 → 3 → 4.

7. Again, rate your level of distress from 0 to 10. It should be lower yet.

8. When the level of distress is 0 to 2, consider doing the Eye Roll (ER) to lower the distress further or to complete the treatment effects. To do this, tap on Back of Hand (BH), hold your head straight, and, moving only your eyes, look at the floor and then slowly raise your eyes toward the ceiling. Then rate your distress level again.

UNDERSTANDING YOUR IMMUNE SYSTEM

The human body is a fascinating and complex system. It has natural chemical messengers called neuropeptide transmitters, which are present on the cell walls of the brain and in the immune system. They carry neuronal messages throughout the body and can affect your emotions as well as your physiology. Given the communication pathways between the brain and the immune system, it is hardly surprising that immunological states can alter feelings and behaviors or that our emotions can influence immune functions. One measure of our immune system is heart rate variability (HRV), and it is used to explore the impact of negative emotions on the immune system.

Heart Rate Variability

Your immune system is very complex and many variables affect it, including normal aging, diet, and emotional stress. In recent years, it has become accepted that psychological stress can adversely affect the immune system (Graham et al. 2006). Research also indicates that chronic stress may speed the rate of normal immune dsyregulation (Kiecolt and Glaser 2001). This may permit disease and other age-related impairments to have a more powerful impact on your life.

One way to examine your immune system is by your *heart rate variability* (HRV). Heart rate variability is an analysis of the beat-to-beat variations of your heart rate. Let's say your heart beats sixty times in one minute. Although this is a good heart rate, if your heart beats once each second without change, that is not so good. This is called *low heart rate variability* and research is finding that it is associated with many health problems. It is actually healthier for your heart to beat in a slightly erratic manner, fast, then slow, then fast. This represents a balanced sympathetic-parasympathetic system (Appelhans and Luecken 2006).

Another view holds that your *sympathetic nervous system* gives you energy when you need it. This helps you to overcome difficult problems or work a long day, but it is also stimulated when you are angry and stuck in a traffic jam. The *parasympathetic nervous system* slows you down and helps to maintain your health. An example of its benefits can be felt after a midday nap. Problems arise when your emotions and behaviors chronically stimulate your sympathetic nervous system. This causes your neuroendocrine system to secrete many chemicals, which over time creates an imbalance in your body and weakens your immune functions.

Research has shown that after a heart attack, people with low HRV are five times more likely to suffer another heart attack (Carney et al. 2002). When you are sick or distressed, it is normal for your sympathetic nervous system to dominate temporarily; however, when chronic problems exist, the result is a weakened parasympathetic nervous system and a low HRV. Research has found that low HRV is associated with depression, anxiety, cardiovascular disease, poor sleep and autoimmune problems (Gorman and Sloan 2000; Hassett et al. 2007).

Hassett and colleagues (2007) are studying how to increase HRV using a strategy that involves breathing at a frequency that matches the heart rate. They found that they were able to increase HRV and also saw a decrease in depressive feelings and pain with fibromyalgia patients. Research has found that decreasing feelings of depression and stress or limiting behavioral problems such as smoking can also increase HRV (Carney et al. 2002).

YOUR IMMUNE SYSTEM

There is increasing evidence that negative changes in the immune system are related to psychosocial problems and chronic stress (Graham et al. 2006). In turn, this may increase the susceptibility to some diseases or even the susceptibility to their onset. A review of studies provides evidence that emotional responses to stressful life experiences are accompanied by autonomic and neuroendocrine changes that can decrease immune function (Beaton 2003).

On the other hand, behavioral interventions that reduce anxiety or distress decrease the intensity or duration of autonomic and neuroendocrine responses and can affect changes in immune function that promote wellness and/or recovery from disease (Raison, Capuron, and Miller 2006). For example, when you are chronically stressed, your body responds by releasing chemicals such as cortisol and adrenaline. One problem with the fight-or-flight response is that although the danger may be all in your mind, your body responds as if the threat is real. For example, if your thoughts trigger a fear or an attack response, your blood will thicken in anticipation of bleeding. If this fear or attack response become chronic, this can lead to being at risk for a stroke or pulmonary embolism (Carney et al. 2007).

Current and past traumas are also a concern, because they shock the body and may lead to emotional issues that can negatively affect your immune system. The diagnosis of an illness such as cancer is one such example. We know from our patients' feedback that they are often traumatized by this news from their physician. Such trauma is often over-looked as part of the treatment process and perhaps lessens the chances for successful recovery.

The treatment goal is to identify the stressors on your immune system and use energy psychology to help resolve them. In turn, this should help to improve your immune system. As we have pointed out throughout this book, issues involving chronic stress, depression, and traumatic events in your life are essential to resolve.

SUPERCHARGING YOUR IMMUNE SYSTEM

Your immune system includes your lymph nodes, spleen, tonsils, small intestine, liver, appendix, and other organs. It is at these locations that the various types of cells of your immune system (B-cells and T-cells) congregate to prepare to attack germs, viruses, allergens, or any other unwanted invaders. The thymus gland, located at the upper center of your chest, is the central gland in the development of immunity.

Your immune system can be strengthened through energy tapping and relaxation practices, aerobic exercise, adequate sleep, reducing alcohol and caffeine consumption, eating healthy organic foods, and taking certain vitamins, minerals, and herbs. Some of the supplements that enhance immunity include vitamins C and E, coenzyme Q10, proanthocyanidins, gamma-linolenic acid, and zinc. Some helpful herbs include astragalus, echinacea, and maitake mushroom. Deodorized garlic and elderberry extract are also known for their immunity-enhancing and antiviral properties.

Interestingly it appears that tapping in the location of the thymus gland at the upper center of your chest while affirming your health can be helpful in enhancing your immune system. This is probably the result of the calming benefits of tapping as well as stimulating the release of T-cells. One of the authors (Fred Gallo) has frequently interrupted the development of colds and flus by doing exactly that. As soon as the first symptoms appear, he taps on the thymus point (CH) while saying or thinking frequently throughout the day statements like, "I'm not becoming ill; I'm strong and healthy." Here's a treatment sequence that we recommend to help reduce stress and enhance immunity:

TREATMENT SEQUENCE FOR SUPERCHARGING YOUR IMMUNE SYSTEM

1. Focus your attention on any beginning symptoms of illness and rate the intensity on a scale of 0 to 10, with 10 representing the highest level of symptoms and 0 indicating no symptoms.

2. Treat for the possibility of reversal by tapping repeatedly on the Side of Hand (SH) or rubbing the Sore Spot (SS) while thinking or saying three times, "Even though I have these symptoms, I deeply and completely accept myself." It also may be helpful to tap the SH or rub the SS points while thinking or saying three times, "I accept myself with all my problems and limitations."

3. Steadily tap at the CH point (thymus point) while making a statement about your immune system being strong. Consider using this statement: "I'm not becoming ill; I am strong and healthy."

4. Again, rate the intensity of your symptoms, 0 to 10. If there is no decrease, go back to step 2 and cycle through the sequence again. If there is not a decrease after three attempts, possibly there is another reversal that needs correction. Review chapter 6 on reversals for further instruction.

5. Next, do the Brain Balancer (BB) by tapping repeatedly at the Back of Hand (BH) while rotating your eyes clockwise, rotating your eyes counterclockwise, humming a tune, counting to five, and then humming again.

6. Repeat tapping at the CH treatment point.

7. Again, rate the intensity of your symptoms from 0 to 10. It should be lower yet.

8. When your symptom rating is 0 to 2, do the Eye Roll (ER) to complete the treatment effects. To do this, tap on the Back of Hand (BH), hold your head straight and, moving only your eyes, look at the floor and then slowly raise your eyes toward the ceiling.

9. Repeat this treatment any time you notice a return of symptoms until the symptoms have been eliminated.

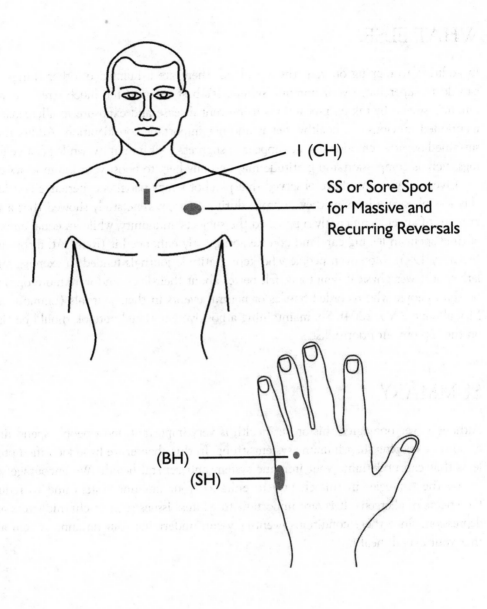

I (CH)

SS or Sore Spot
for Massive and
Recurring Reversals

(BH)
(SH)

Diagram Thirty-One: Supercharge the Immune System

Treatment for Supercharging the Immune System

Meridian		Location
CH	1	Chest

WHAT ELSE?

In addition to tapping on your thymus gland, there are a number of other things you can do to supercharge your immune system. It's best to avoid too much stress on your immune system by taking precautions to prevent disease and exposure to allergens. As mentioned previously, a healthy diet is another important consideration. Additionally, sustained negative emotional states appear to suppress your immunity, while positive feelings such as compassion and gratitude may actually help to boost your immune system.

Over the years, we have observed that psychotherapy patients experience considerably less physical illness as they improve during therapy. One study showed that a few minutes of anger significantly suppressed the subjects' immunity, while an equal amount of time spent in feeling care and compassion greatly enhanced it (Rein, Atkinson, and McCraty 1995). Moreover, people who kept gratitude journals tended to exercise regularly, had fewer physical symptoms, felt better about their lives, and were more optimistic than people who recorded hassles or neutral events in their journals (Emmons and McCullough 2003, 2004). So, maintaining a positive emotional outlook should be right on the top of your priority list.

SUMMARY

Although everyone agrees his or her health is very important, most people spend little or no time keeping their immune system strong. In this chapter we have identified problems that can undermine your immune system and general health. We encourage you to use the strategies in this chapter to enhance your immune system and to reduce the effects of allergens. It is also important to address issues such as chronic stress and depression, since these conditions eventually can undermine your immune system and thus your overall health.

Eating Disorders: Anorexia, Bulimia, and Binge Eating

"Contrariwise," continued Tweedledee, "if it was so, it might be: and if it were so, it would be; but as it isn't, it ain't."

—Lewis Carroll

Imagine a pencil-thin girl looking in the mirror and then claiming she is fat, which is exactly what pencil-thin girls with anorexia do. It would seem that confusion and denial are important parts of eating disorders. Anorexics are often hospitalized for life-threatening electrolyte imbalance, and yet they resume their self-destructive behaviors soon after they are released and are no longer supervised. They cannot control themselves, even though they know there are serious medical repercussions to their malnourished state. Their intellectual abilities appear to provide little guidance, as anyone knows who has been to an eating disorder clinic: The patients at such clinics often represent a who's who of the best schools and universities.

Eating disorders are *not* about being confused, needing to diet, or wanting to look like a model; they are complex psychological disorders in which the person's eating patterns become a strategy to cope with other problems. At the core of all eating disorders are the limiting core beliefs and psychological reversals that must be treated before other treatment strategies can be employed.

For those with eating disorders, dieting, bingeing, purging, and/or compulsive exercise may begin as a way to cope with and mask their painful emotions. These strategies provide them with a sense of power over their lives, but all too soon, the disorder takes control over their behaviors and life decisions.

Before we continue on this topic, it is important to stress that all mental health treatments for eating disorders need to be done in conjunction with ongoing medical advice and supervision, since some eating disorders can present a life-threatening situation. Ongoing medical advice is also important because being in a malnourished or serotonin-depleted condition will undermine any treatment strategy and lessen the chances for success.

According to the National Eating Disorders Association (2006), 10 million women and one million men in the United States starve themselves or engage in dangerous binge-purge cycles to control their weight, and another 25 million are struggling with binge-eating disorder. Hudson et al. (2007) reported the findings of a national survey that found up to 4.5 percent of all Americans experience an eating disorder at some point in their lifetime; although the researchers also say that this number may be underestimated due to the secretive nature of the problem. They also found that eating disorders coexist with other problems that often go undiagnosed and untreated.

One of the problems is that many people suffer from subclinical forms of the disorder. That is, although their eating and weight-control behaviors are not normal, they do not meet the clinical definition of having a particular eating disorder. The good news, according to the same study, is that eating disorders do not have to be lifetime problems (Hudson et al. 2007). The study suggests that for every severe case, there appear to be a number of milder cases. Nonetheless, eating problems may last for years and can create dire health consequences. More research is needed to understand why there are such differences in duration and severity among the three major eating disorders, anorexia nervosa, bulimia nervosa, and binge eating. These disorders are all discussed below.

ANOREXIA NERVOSA

According to the American Psychiatric Association (1994), anorexia nervosa is a serious, often chronic, and life-threatening eating disorder. Symptoms include a refusal to maintain minimal body weight within 15 percent of an individual's normal weight; an ongoing preoccupation with food and weight even when the individual is very thin; a distorted body image; and, in women, amenorrhea (the absence of at least three consecutive menstrual cycles). Individuals with anorexia have an intense fear of being fat, and being very thin does not reduce their anxiety about being fat and/or weight gain. They eat a very restricted diet, engage in self-induced vomiting, and misuse laxatives or diuretics to continue to lose and maintain their very low weight. These individuals may also focus on specific body parts as being too fat.

Types and Incidence of Anorexia

There are two subtypes of anorexia. People in the first subtype use dieting, fasting, and excessive exercise to achieve weight loss and to prevent weight gain. These activities may deceive others as they appear to serve a healthy goal. The second subtype engages in recurrent binge eating and purging episodes. These patterns of restrictive eating can lead to excessive weight loss, starvation, and serious medical complications that can result in death.

Anorexia nervosa tends to occur in pre- or post-puberty, but it can develop at any major life stage. Adolescent girls and young adult women comprise approximately 90 percent of the anorexic population, with young males and adult women completing the group (American Psychiatric Association 2000). However, Hudson and colleagues (2007) note that their survey found a higher percentage of anorexic males. In their survey, almost 25 percent of anorexics were male.

The presence of this illness may remain hidden for years, as those with an obsessive need to be thin may not be able to act out their desires in their home environments. It isn't surprising that going away to school often provides the opportunity to fully act out anorexic behavior patterns. Nevertheless, those who remain at home often manage to keep their anorexic activities secret.

Another concern is that such young women continue to receive social support for their behavior because being quite thin is widely considered a highly desirable state, especially for young women interested in careers like acting, dancing, or modeling. In any case, whether at school or at home, for anorexics—male or female—the end goal involves control; because people with anorexia nervosa ignore their hunger in order to control their desire to eat and to feel in control of their bodies and their lives.

The emotional satisfaction of their control over their body weight and food intake becomes very important to them, especially if the rest of their life is chaotic and emotionally painful (Sacker 2007; Liu 2007). Liu believes that anorexics view their ability to lose weight as a sign of great self-discipline, while weight gain is seen as a failure of will. She also notes that even when anorexics can acknowledge being thin, they will often deny the medical problems caused by being malnourished. These self-sabotaging beliefs are an important cause of their problems.

Anorexia and Other Disorders

Heffner and Eifert (2004) found several psychological disorders associated with anorexia. Their findings include obsessive-compulsive behaviors, such as perfectionism, the need for detailed rules, and an intense need to be in control. Most often, those with anorexia are likely to combine their disorder with rigid rules and compulsive behaviors. Other problems can include post-traumatic stress disorder (PTSD), which may include events like car accidents, crimes, natural disasters, and physical assaults, especially sexual assaults.

It would appear that the incidence of sexual assault is much higher in women with anorexia than it is in the total population (Danielson and Holmes 2004). There is also the concern that drug abuse leads to less treatment compliance and that the use of drugs helps to maintain their anorexic goals.

Causes of Anorexia

From a treatment prospective, Heffner and Eifert (2004) believe that many of the thoughts and beliefs that drive anorexic behaviors originate in the emotional centers of the brain; that is, the limbic system. In this part of the brain, basic emotions like sadness develop long before language, and many behaviors and desires appear to be instinctive.

Based on their belief that the disorder originates in the emotional parts of the brain, Heffner and Eifert think that learning from direct experiences will help anorexics to change their behavior faster than trying to help them revise their self-talk, because their problems originated before they were capable of rational thought. They also believe that the emotional parts of the brain do not respond as well to treatments utilizing only cognitive therapy.

NEGATIVE THOUGHTS

Peggy Claude-Pierre (1997) directs an eating disorder clinic and has written extensively about eating disorders. She believes that changing the internal beliefs that undermine self-esteem is a crucial part of the therapeutic process. Because eating disorders are symbolic of self-destructive behaviors, her work has identified specific thoughts that she believes originate in what she calls "the negative mind." These are degrading thoughts that undermine the self; they may include many different versions of the following type of self-denigrating self-talk:

- Everyone hates me

- There's nothing I do right

- Things will never work out for me

- I am fat and ugly

- I don't deserve to live

In addition, Claude-Pierre has identified more complex patterns of thinking that also revolve around the undermining self-worth. The essential components are eating and deserving; in effect, the anorexic person believes that she does not deserve to eat because she is a failure and is not worthy of food. In Claude-Pierre's experience, the negative mind is full of tricks leading to self-sabotage and to reasons why one cannot eat; often the use of guilt and blame are essential components.

Aimee Liu (2007) wrote a very insightful book, *Gaining: The Truth About Life After Eating Disorders*. It is a book we recommend to our clients to help them reach a better understanding of these complex issues. Both anorexia and bulimia appear to be different from binge eating and, as Liu notes, at 7 percent of the total population, the incidence of both disorders has remained constant since 1991. On the other hand, obesity, which includes binge eating, has soared to include almost one-third of the population. It has also become clear that the mind-body problems involved in anorexia and bulimia are not the same ones contributing to the current overeating epidemic, which has led to worldwide health problems.

Liu also believes that treating anorexia only with cognitive therapy is very difficult. This was demonstrated in her discussion of a popular book from the 1970s (*The Best Little Girl in the World*) that clearly portrayed the self-destructive lifestyle of an anorexic woman named Kessa. Liu remembers that a woman she knew and her friends were so fixated on losing weight that, far from being repulsed by Kessa's self-destructive ritual behaviors, they chose to imitate them. The fact that Kessa was having serious health problems and was well on her way to hospitalization was also lost on the readers of the book, since, for them too, weight loss was the only important outcome.

Liu's views about the world of self as experienced by anorexics and bulimics helps illuminate issues. In one chapter, Liu illustrates the language used to describe eating disorders: "Though filled with *self-loathing*, anorexics excel at *self-discipline* and *selfless acts* of generosity, which they often take to extremes of *self-denial* and *self-punishment*. Bulimics tend to be more *selfish* and *self-motivated*, but like anorexics, they are acutely *self-conscious* and riven with *self-doubt* and *self-contempt*" (Liu 2007, p. 39). Clearly, eating disorders create many *self*-sabotaging behaviors that need to be resolved.

REPRESSED MEMORIES

Sarno (2006) believes that many chronic problems, including eating disorders, exist in order to block repressed memories. Usually, these memories are of traumatic events that, if consciously articulated, would lead to feelings of rage; so the person's mind and body collaborate to focus on a suitable distraction. In this case, anorexia, a problem that controls and dominates the person's life serves as the distraction. Sarno believes that the mind-body interaction also creates a physical component, which leads to neuroendocrine-immune changes that help to perpetuate the anorexic's desires and behaviors. The treatment he recommends involves the identification and resolution of the repressed feelings. It is believed that this will change the person's thought processes and result in positive neuroendocrine-immune system changes for the better.

Here are the essential points to remember from these brief reviews about anorexia:

- Anorexia is not about not eating; not eating is just a symptom of the underlying problem. The issues about eating cannot be changed without resolving the underlying issues

- The sole use of cognitive therapy does not provide optimum treatment

- There are many self-sabotaging beliefs and behaviors that must be addressed before the eating disorder can be tackled

- There is a potential mind-body connection that alters the body's chemistry and helps to perpetuate the problem

AN ENERGETIC VIEW OF ANOREXIA

We hope that the information and books discussed above help you to identify some of the self-sabotaging beliefs that not only block treatment, but may make anorexic behaviors seem appropriate. It is difficult to overcome anorexia, because from inside, the self-sabotaging thoughts and beliefs don't seem like a problem. If you are an anorexic, because of your thoughts and beliefs, you feel that you are right. But you are not right. Just look around you, and observe how others eat. It is very important to overcome your self-sabotaging thoughts; that is why you should give this self-treatment a chance, while continuing to work with medical and mental health professionals who are knowledgeable about eating disorders.

Preliminary Treatment for Anorexia

We suggest doing the following steps before treating yourself with energy tapping for anorexia:

1. Make a list of all the beliefs and behaviors you think may help create your anorexic feelings and behaviors.

2. After making your list, reread chapter 6, and use the treatments to address each of the self-sabotaging reversals and beliefs you've identified. You should treat these beliefs and reversals before using the treatment sequence for anorexia below; otherwise, the treatment will be unlikely to be effective.

Note that repressed memories may also be an issue. These memories are not magically hidden: They come up when thought and attention are given to past events that you know have been problems for you in your life.

3. Do the treatment sequence that appears in the next section. Successful treatments with energy tapping can lead to changes in your autoimmune system and help correct the chemical imbalances that perpetuate the problem of anorexia.

We've also listed below some of the self-sabotaging beliefs and reversals that you may need to treat in step 2 of the treatment sequence; however, you can target any beliefs and reversals that you know are a problem for you. Note that the limiting beliefs and reversals are contained within self-acceptance statements.

LIMITING BELIEFS, REVERSALS, AND
SELF-ACCEPTANCE STATEMENTS

- Even though I am not ready to get well, I deeply and completely accept myself.

- Even though I deny the extent of my eating problem, I deeply and completely accept myself.

- Even though I feel my eating pattern gives me self-control, I deeply and completely accept myself.

- Even though I exercise compulsively, I deeply and completely accept myself.

- Even though my feelings of control are an illusion, and my eating disorder really controls me, I deeply and completely accept myself.

- Even though I use perfectionism to perpetuate my eating disorder, I deeply and completely accept myself.

- Even though perfectionism is a strategy I use to control anxiety, and it doesn't work, I deeply and completely accept myself.

- Even though I feel I don't deserve to feel valued or important, I deeply and completely accept myself.

- Even though I procrastinate and the result maintains my low self-image, I deeply and completely accept myself.

TREATMENT FOR ANOREXIA

The goal is to identify your individual, specific blocks to treatment, and the first step of treatment is for you to accept yourself. For example, if you believe that you are not quite ready to get well yet, you must first accept that belief in order to change it. Use the treatment below to help change your problem beliefs and behaviors.

Treatment Sequence for Anorexia

1. Think about a problem concerning a belief you want to change or a past life experience you want to resolve. For example, imagine a specific situation when you felt enraged or full of self-loathing. Then rate your distress on a 0 to 10 scale, with 0 representing no distress and 10 representing the highest level of distress.

2. Locate and rub the Sore Spot (SS) on the left side of your chest while saying to yourself three times, "I accept myself with all my problems and limitations." Then tap under the nose (UN) point three times, while saying, "Even though I believe that I don't deserve to be healthy or to value myself or my contributions to life, I deeply and completely accept myself." You can also add any specific sabotaging beliefs that you think are issues for you. For example, you may believe you cannot overcome your eating disorder using this approach. *If this happens, it is more likely that your sabotaging beliefs are blocking you and you need to use the treatments to deal with those issues.* Now focus on the problem you wish to address that may be a memory of a past event, a behavior you want to change, or a repressed memory that has just now come to the surface.

3. Look at diagram 32 and at the treatment sequence for eating disorder directly under the diagram. Now tap seven to ten times on the Eyebrow (EB), Under Eye (UE), Under Collarbone (UCB), Under Arm (UA), Little Finger (LF), Index Finger (IF), Under Nose (UN), and Under the Bottom Lip (UBL). The sequence is numbered, so just follow the sequence you'll see right under diagram: 1 → 2 → 3 → 4 → 5 → 6 → 7 → 8.

4. Again, rate your distress on a 0 to 10 scale (a number should just pop into your mind). If there is no decrease, go back to step 2 and cycle through the sequence again. If there is not a decrease after three attempts, this is probably not an appropriate sequence for this situation, or else there is another sabotaging belief (reversal) that needs correction.

5. Next, do the Brain Balancer (BB) by tapping repeatedly on the Back of Hand (BH) while rotating your eyes clockwise, rotating your eyes counterclockwise, then humming a tune, counting to five, and then humming again. (This step may not be needed if there is a reduction in distress.)

6. Now tap seven to ten times on the Eyebrow (EB), Under Eye (UE), Under Arm (UA), Little Finger (LF), Index Finger (IF), Under Nose (UN), and Under Bottom Lip (UBL) points. Just follow the treatment sequence under the diagram: 1 → 2 → 3 → 4 → 5 → 6 → 7 → 8.

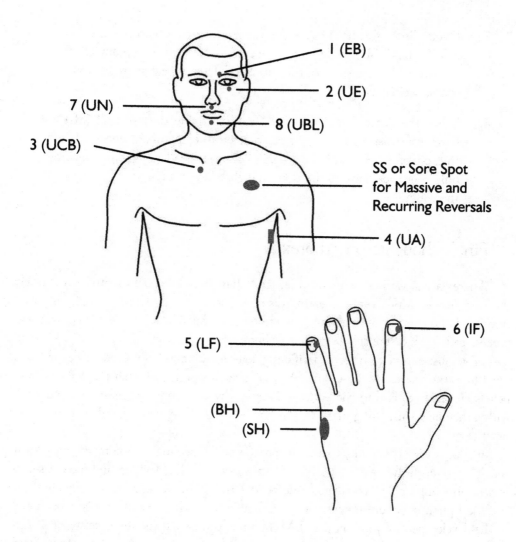

Diagram Thirty-Two: Eating Disorder

Treatment Sequence for Eating Disorder

Meridian		Location
Eyebrow (EB)	1	Beginning of eyebrow near bridge of nose
Under Eye (UE)	2	Under the center of the eye on tip of bone
Under Collarbone (UCB)	3	Under collarbone next to chest bone.
Under Arm (UA)	4	Six inches under armpit
Little Finger (LF)	5	Inside tip of little fingernail on the side
Index Finger (IF)	6	Inside tip of index fingernail on the side
Under Nose (UN)	7	Above upper lip and below the center of nose
Under Bottom Lip (UBL)	8	Below lower lip in cleft of chin

7. If your discomfort has not decreased even further, tap on the little finger Side of Hand (SH) while saying three times, "I deeply accept myself, even though I still have some of this problem." Then repeat steps 3 through 6 of this sequence.

8. When the distress level is 0 to 2, consider doing the Eye Roll (ER) to lower your distress further or to complete the treatment effects. To do this, tap on the Back of Hand (BH), hold your head straight and, moving only your eyes, look at the floor and then slowly raise your eyes toward the ceiling.

Final Thoughts on Anorexia

Anorexia is a very complex disorder, and changing one belief or situation is rarely the sole answer. Moreover, any eating disorder becomes a part of your daily life routines, and anorexia is no exception. You are reading this book and using this treatment process to take back control over your feelings, desires, and your life. This will not be easy. You must expect to treat a specific problem many times before you will experience relief from the distress it causes you. As you treat this problem, other problems or false beliefs are likely to rise to the surface. This is why we strongly suggest that you work with a therapist while using these treatments, especially one who is familiar with energy psychology.

We like to use the analogy that this process is like peeling an onion; you must treat one layer to reach the next and, as you do this, new troubling feelings and thoughts may appear and will have to be treated. We believe that early in your life you encountered specific troubling circumstances you were unable to resolve, and that this contributed to the development of your anorexia. At the time, you lacked the resources to deal with those circumstances, so your mind and body worked together to create a response—and that response was to become anorexic.

It is important to remember that, at that time, you were doing the best you possibly could, and there is no need for you to feel either guilt or blame. And as Liu put it: "Becoming self-aware and self-confident enough to avoid psychological traps such as eating disorders means more than controlling the contradictions within our own nature. It means, in a deep and honest way, appreciating them" (Liu 2007, p. 260). We believe that energy tapping will provide you with the tools you need to accept your past and to change the ways you respond to life situations today. Finally, we suggest that you should read the sections below on bulimia and binge eating. They contain additional strategies that may also apply to you.

BULIMIA NERVOSA

The diagnostic information about bulimia nervosa notes that, unlike anorexia, people with bulimia often have a normal body weight, which allows them to better keep their disorder a secret. Like anorexics, bulimics are also concerned with their body image and weight, but rather than not eating enough food, they regularly engage in binge-and-purge eating episodes: that is, they consume large amounts of food in a very short time followed by vomiting, fasting, or some other form of purging. Bulimics also may use compensatory behaviors including laxatives, overexercising, and other strategies to lose weight quickly to compensate for the excessive calories they consume when bingeing.

To qualify for a diagnosis of bulimia nervosa, the binge eating and compensatory behaviors must occur at least twice a week for a period of three months. Bulimia nervosa usually begins in late adolescence or early adulthood. Like binge eaters, bulimics experience the loss of self-control, so they will eat until they are uncomfortable or even painfully full. Then, at some point, they use inappropriate behaviors to prevent themselves from gaining weight.

Causes and Incidence of Bulimia

Hudson et al. (2007) found that females are three times more likely than males to exhibit bulimic behaviors. Hall and Cohn (1999) believe that people become addicted to substances—including food—to avoid feeling painful emotions. Some of the reasons for bulimic behaviors include low self-esteem and cultural pressures. The worst-case scenario occurs when bulimic people believe that they will never be fulfilled or happy or that their lives have no value. Although bulimics tend to lack a sense of self-worth, they also tend toward being overly judgmental of themselves and others. They are often uncomfortable in intimate relationships and food may become their ally and only friend.

BULIMIA AND OTHER DISORDERS

Bulimia is also a difficult problem because those who suffer with it, typically, are ashamed of their eating problem and try to keep it secret. It is also dangerous! There is a widespread misconception that bulimia doesn't create life-threatening situations, because there are no obvious extreme changes in bulimic bodies as there are with anorexics. Nevertheless, their recurring binge-and-purge cycles can have a devastating impact on the entire digestive system. Moreover, frequent purging can lead to potentially fatal electrolyte and chemical imbalances in the body that affect the heart and other major organs. Still other medical complications can include tooth decay, gastric rupture and inflammation, and rupture of the esophagus.

The *Diagnostic and Statistical Manual of Mental Disorders* (American Psychiatric Association 2000) states that associated mental disorders often accompany bulimia, as many people with the disorder also tend to suffer from depression and anxiety. Anxiety-related issues may lead to a fear of social situations, which, in turn, leads to feelings of loneliness that provide more opportunities for binge behaviors. In addition, about one-third of those with bulimia also have alcohol or substance abuse problems.

ENERGY TREATMENT FOR BULIMIA

The treatment sequence is the same as it is for anorexics. The differences, however, are the issues that must be resolved. Again, to resolve the root of the problem, it is not the behaviors of bingeing and purging that must be addressed, but the "reasons why." What is behind the loss of control that leads to such excessive eating that the eater becomes painfully full? As with anorexia, Sarno (2006) believes that repressed memories are at the basic core of bulimia. In this theory, the repressed memories create a mind-body interaction that uses the disorder so that the individual doesn't have to face the internal rage about past events that exists in his or her body and mind. As with anorexics, self-sabotaging reversals and beliefs are at the core of this eating disorder and must be treated before any other psychological strategies can be employed successfully.

We suggest that you should make a list of all the beliefs and behaviors you think are relevant to your bulimic behaviors. We also ask you to read this entire chapter, as it contains information relevant to the treatment process.

We offer the following list of self-sabotaging reversals and limiting beliefs because they may be useful to you when you make your own list. Note that each of these sabotaging beliefs and reversals is contained within a self-acceptance statement. If you can list your own sabotaging beliefs within such self-accepting statements, your list will have even greater value for you.

Limiting Beliefs, Reversals, and Self-Acceptance Statements

- Even though I use food to deal with anxiety, I deeply and completely accept myself.

- Even though I purge food and it is a habit that feels normal to me, I deeply and completely accept myself.

- Even though I am unable to control my eating when I am distressed, I deeply and completely accept myself.

- Even though I use my eating disorder to avoid intimacy, I deeply and completely accept myself.

- Even though I am ashamed of this problem, but still wish to keep it, I deeply and completely accept myself.

- Even though I believe that I will be unhappy in my whole life, I deeply and completely accept myself.

- Even though I believe that I will never be fulfilled and enjoy my life, I deeply and completely accept myself.

Once you have made your list of issues that must be addressed, return to the treatment sequence for anorexia earlier in this chapter, and use it to treat the issues on your list.

BINGE EATING

The *Family Medical Guide*, which is published by the AMA (2004), states that people who have a negative body image are more likely to be depressed, have low self-esteem, struggle with weight-related issues and with weight loss. Binge eating is not a listed mental disorder in the *Diagnostic and Statistical Manual of Mental Disorders* (APA 1994), as anorexia and bulimia are, but binge eaters comprise the largest group of people with an eating disorder.

Also, men have a much higher representation among binge eaters than they do among anorexics or bulimics. Almost 40 percent of binge eaters are men (Hudson et al. 2007). It is hard to get accurate numbers, but binge eating appears to be connected to the increase in obesity of the total population in the United States. Recent research has demonstrated that in the last two decades the prevalence of obesity has more than doubled, and includes almost one-third of the population; while two out of three people, although not clinically obese, are overweight (Ogden et al. 2006).

People with binge-eating disorder suffer from episodes of uncontrolled eating or bingeing followed by periods of guilt and depression. Binge eating is marked by the consumption of large amounts of food, sometimes accompanied by a pressured, "frenzied" feeling. There are certain warning signs that indicate when someone may be suffering from binge-eating disorder.

Common Warning Signs of Binge-Eating Disorder

An individual with binge-eating disorder may exhibit all or any combination of the following warning signs:

- Eats large amounts of food when not physically hungry

- Eats much more rapidly than normal

- Eats until uncomfortably full

- Eats alone because of shame or embarrassment

- After eating, feels depressed, disgusted, or guilty

- Has a history of extreme weight fluctuations

Hirschman and Munter (1998) say that compulsive eaters spend much of their lives thinking about food and controlling their desire to eat. They think of themselves as lacking willpower, behaving in a disgusting manner, and most importantly, believing they are fat, which to them means inadequate or bad. It is symbolic of their belief in an ideal body that they view themselves as socially unacceptable because of their overweight. They believe, too, that losing weight will make them more acceptable, even though they know they use food daily to help them cope with their emotional problems. Of course, ultimately, this behavior prevents them from achieving their goal of losing weight.

TREATMENT FOR BINGE EATERS

The self-sabotaging reversals and beliefs that accompany this disorder often involve boredom, loneliness, frustration, and stress. Binge eaters frequently view themselves as stuck in their lives with little chance for either growth or happiness. We suggest that you should begin your energy treatment by first making a list of all the beliefs and behaviors you think are relevant to your eating behaviors. Then read this entire chapter as it contains important information about the treatment process for all eating disorders.

We also recommend reviewing the personal problems that are frequently associated with weight issues in chapter 12. And we offer the following list of self-sabotaging reversals and beliefs because they may be useful to you when you make your own list. Note that each of these self-sabotaging beliefs and reversals is contained within a self-acceptance statement. If you can list your own sabotaging beliefs within such self-accepting statements, you will find your list will have much greater value for you.

Limiting Beliefs, Reversals, and Self-Acceptance Statements

- Even though I use food to deal with anxiety, I deeply and completely accept myself.

- Even though I am unable to control my eating when I am distressed, I deeply and completely accept myself.

- Even though I use this problem to cope with my loneliness, I deeply and completely accept myself.

- Even though I am unhappy when I overeat, I deeply and completely accept myself.

- Even though I have no control over my eating patterns, I deeply and completely accept myself.

- Even though I believe that I will never be fulfilled and enjoy my life, I deeply and completely accept myself.

Once you have made your list of issues to be addressed, return to the treatment sequence for anorexia earlier in this chapter and use it to treat the issues on your list.

EATING DISORDER TRIGGERS

Eating disorders often have many associated self-sabotaging behaviors that can trigger problematic episodes. We use the term *trigger* to mean any belief, behavior, or event that elicits the problem. For example, anorexics often have panic attacks that can later trigger their eating disorder in order to feel more in control of themselves. Problems such as these must be addressed, as well as using the treatment recipe offered in this chapter.

Specific situations such as loneliness can also create problems. This is quite complex because the problem that exists must be understood and resolved. For example, binge eaters may have mixed feelings about loneliness, because they want to be left alone to eat, without having to feel ashamed of their behavior. A large part of helping to resolve eating disorders is to change the situations that you know help to perpetuate the disorders. We suggest that you review the chapters related to any of these issues to better understand your specific triggers and to help you resolve your problems.

SUMMARY

Our goal in this chapter was to offer another "tool" that can be used to help people cope and hopefully resolve this very difficult problem. Eating disorders are the result of complex psychological issues that must be addressed before the eating disorder can be controlled. Given the nature of these problems, and the fact that they can be life-threatening, you are again encouraged to seek assistance both from medical and mental health professionals. Then you can use the energy tapping strategies represented here to help you resolve your difficult eating problems.

A Satisfying Relationship

*To effectively communicate, we must realize that we are all different
in the way we perceive the world and use this understanding as a
guide to our communication with others.*

—Anthony Robbins

Book titles about male-female relationships are very revealing as to how most Americans deal with the dynamics of their primary emotional connections. Consider these recent best-sellers: *Intimate Enemies, Men Who Hate Women and the Women Who Love Them, Men Are from Mars and Women Are from Venus, Perfect Husbands and Other Fairy Tales, Why You Can't or Won't Make Your Partner Happy,* and *How to Make Anyone Fall in Love with You.* Based on the messages of these titles, it would seem our relationships take place on a battlefield, where the people we love hate/love us and are from different planets. We fantasize about perfect partners, but we refuse to make the partners in our real-life relationships happy even though, in the end, we still want to be loved by them. If you are having problems in your primary relationship, these ideas may be familiar to you. Nonetheless, most of us still want to be in a successful relationship.

Many best-selling books about relationships actually do offer good ideas and strategies. In the end, however, it is your ability to rise above temporary negative emotions and self-sabotaging thoughts that is the primary key to your relationship success. This ability will help you choose the right person and will foster behaviors that will keep your relationship strong and growing in the right direction. Your relationship is not a "thing" that is separate from you. Instead, it is an ongoing activity in which you are responsible both for your actions and your responses to the actions of your partner.

> Relationships—good, bad, or nonexistent—are the most important and complex aspects of your life.

It is widely believed that families represent the foundation of our society and that the relationships within families are at the core of all relationships. Yet, in many ways, that foundation is falling apart. Each year more than a million couples get divorced, and their children are separated from at least one of their parents. To some degree, every divorce or breakup of a long-term relationship is a traumatic event. It is never an easy decision. The termination of a relationship is often decided over a long period of time and is commonly accompanied by anger, frustration, and the feeling of loss. Each person involved in the breakup must relinquish an important part of her or his life, and certainly raising children as a single parent is much harder and more emotionally draining than it is with a loving partner.

On the other side of the relationship coin are the growing numbers of people in their thirties and forties who haven't found their life partner yet. Most of them also struggle with their frustration and anxiety about why they aren't in a relationship. They worry whether they are doing something wrong or, worse, what is wrong with them. While they continue to seek and strive for relationships, they often behave in ways that sabotage themselves.

Although there are specific treatments for fixing bad relationships and creating good ones, this is not a simple task. It would take an entire book devoted exclusively to relationships to thoroughly cover this complex and important issue. The quality of your relationships is a reflection of how you feel about yourself and, from that, how you relate to those around you. For that reason, many of the treatments that will help to improve your relationships have already been provided in earlier chapters. In this chapter, however, common relationship issues are addressed and treatment sequences are provided that have proven especially useful for dealing with relationships.

When we think of "healthy relationships," words like tolerance, caring, pleasure, joy, laughter, love, forgiveness, compassion, and generosity come to mind. When relationships are not healthy, however, the words that come to mind are quite different; including, for example, misunderstanding, frustration, intolerance, conflict, anger, resentment, sadness, hatred, and vindictiveness. What happens?

One common situation occurs when long-term partnerships or marital relationships degenerate into an endless battle for control over what you and your partner must do in the relationship. The strategies and behaviors used to gain that control, even temporarily, will determine the success or failure of your relationships. As is true of all the issues discussed in this book, relationship problems can arise partly from a lack of knowledge. It might prove very useful for you and those you love if you were to read a few of the popular books about relationships. Unfortunately, all of the best-sellers written about relationships have not noticeably affected the divorce rate. Obviously, this indicates the presence of another problem.

As practitioners of energy psychology, we believe that energy imbalances and psychological reversals prevent people from behaving in ways that would benefit their relationships. Self-sabotaging thoughts and behaviors may temporarily reinforce poor judgment as well as allow people to behave in ways that anger their partner and create energy imbalances in that individual, which complicates the problem even further.

The topics examined in this chapter include (1) choosing the wrong person, (2) plunging too quickly into a relationship, (3) loneliness, (4) rage, (5) blaming, (6) relationship obsessions, and (7) abusive relationship dynamics. In addition, some common relationship emotions and behaviors are explored, including nagging, anger, frustration, rejection, and vindictiveness. Effective treatment sequences are provided for each.

DEVELOPING RELATIONSHIPS

Anyone can pick the wrong person with whom to be in a relationship, especially if that person has a quality you immediately find attractive. This is only a problem if, over a number of years, you continue choosing one wrong person after another. In effect, you keep choosing people who are not appropriate partners for you, while simultaneously rejecting the "right type" of people. In these situations, the right type of person may have a quality you don't find immediately attractive, or he or she lacks a trait that is especially appealing to you, so you push him or her away before you get to know the individual's other attractive qualities.

Although the problem of choosing the wrong person can be real for people in their twenties, it is usually more of an issue for those who are over thirty. In the end, you must decide what is the truth about you and your relationship behaviors. Note that your friends and family can be a source of valuable information about what it is that you actually do in this area in your life.

The problem may be seen in the form of an endless number of short-term relationships or in the fact that you become involved in long-term relationships you know from the beginning are not going to work. Of course, if you are psychologically reversed in this area, it can blind you to what is really going on in this part of your life. If you repeatedly fall in love and end up brokenhearted, it is likely that you are sabotaging the relationship aspects of your life.

The first step in treating relationship issues with energy psychology is to deal with any possible reversals and to complete the energy treatments for any other problem areas. To do this in a thorough manner, review chapters 5 and 6 to identify any problems you believe may be blocking your success or creating sabotaging beliefs. The next step is to identify the relationship situation that needs to change. To identify the relationship situation that needs to change, here are some examples of common issues that often interfere with the formation of a successful partnership:

- I rarely get involved in long-term relationships.

- I often seek relationships with men/women who use me.

- I tend to choose partners based on looks/money/power and not on how they make me feel.

- I find it very difficult to find anyone I could love.

- I get bored easily and give up on relationships.

- I am very picky and chase away many potentially good partners.

- I am often involved with men/women who make me feel that I'm not good enough.

The list could be endless. It is up to you to figure out, in your own words, what is happening to you in this area of your life. Once you select the situation, then you need to identify possible reversals (that is, underlying beliefs), such as the following:

- I don't deserve to be married or to have a mate.

- I don't deserve to be in a relationship with a man/woman who treats me right.

- I'll never be in a relationship that works.

- I won't do what it takes to be in a good relationship.

- It's impossible for me to find anyone whom I could love romantically.

- I feel I am not good enough to have a long-term relationship.

- It would be unsafe for me to have a secure relationship.

- I would feel deprived in other ways if I got married.

- It's not possible for me to commit to one person.

- I seek relationships with people who intimidate me.

- I become easily bored with people who don't intimidate me.

Psychological Reversals

There are four reversals or sabotaging situations that you should consider for treatment before you use the energy sequences to deal with a specific problem. If you have multiple problems and your relationship is only one of them, then use the treatment for a massive reversal. That is, briskly rub the Sore Spot (SS) on the left side of your chest while thinking or saying three times, "I deeply and profoundly accept myself with all my problems and limitations." If you have given up and believe that you will never find the right person, or that you will never resolve a specific relationship problem, then use the treatment for a deep-level reversal. You can apply this strategy to the relationship as a whole by repeatedly tapping on the Under Nose (UN) point and thinking or saying the following statement three times, "I deeply accept myself if I never have a successful, happy, loving relationship."

Another concern is that, at an unconscious level, you may have come to believe that you don't deserve to have a good relationship. For this, tap directly under your bottom lip (UBL) point while thinking or saying three times, "I deeply accept myself even if I don't deserve to have a successful, happy, loving relationship."

Most problems can be effectively treated by using the treatment sequence for a specific reversal (repeatedly tapping on the Side of the Hand (SH)). This type of reversal may be important in treating your relationship problem as a whole or any specific aspects of the problem, such as having a tendency to become angry with your partner or having a desire to cheat. Remember that reversal corrections are not necessarily permanent. Repeated corrections may be—and usually are—necessary. There are many problems that can negatively affect the vibrancy and longevity of relationships, including painful relationship memories, loneliness, rejection, and more.

Painful Relationship Memories

When you have a memory of a past relationship in which you were very badly hurt, you may unconsciously prevent yourself from being hurt again by sabotaging your current relationships. This can be the case even if you are no longer feeling the pain from your past, but still have an uncomfortable memory and, at times, wish your previous relationship had turned out differently. In these situations, you should refer to chapter 10, which addresses painful memories, and treat that problem.

Loneliness

Feeling lonely or feeling that you are unable to be alone and be comfortable with yourself can adversely affect potential relationships. To correct this, think about a situation that would distress you and treat yourself for specific reversal. First, tap on the Side of Hand (SH) while thinking or saying three times, "I deeply accept myself even though I am unable to be alone." Then, tap twenty to thirty times on the Back of Hand (BH) while thinking about being alone. Then, tap five times on the Under Collarbone (UCB) point. This may need to be followed by the Brain Balancer (BB). Repeat this process until you feel comfortable and secure with the idea of being alone. (See chapter 8 for more details.)

Rejection

If you feel unable to deal with any rejection and have given up even trying to get involved in a relationship, treat yourself for specific reversal. First, tap on the Side of Hand (SH) while thinking or saying three times, "I deeply accept myself even though I have this fear of rejection." Then, tap five times at each point in the following sequence: Eyebrow (EB), Under Eye (UE), Under Arm (UA), and Under Collarbone (UCB). This may need to be followed by the Brain Balancer (BB). Repeat this process until you feel comfortable that you can cope with rejection. (See chapter 8 for more details.)

Other Issues

There may be additional issues that indicate that you don't feel good enough about yourself to be in a successful relationship. In this situation, you must identify the exact problem, such as not feeling attractive or not feeling successful. Treat yourself for specific reversal. First, tap on the Side of Hand (SH) repeatedly while thinking or saying three times, "I deeply accept myself, even though I have this problem."

If you search through the previous chapters, you will find treatment sequences for most of the problems that may be blocking you from developing and maintaining a positive relationship. You are encouraged, however, to treat yourself daily for relevant reversals, as they often interfere with or block the development of healthy relationships.

CHOOSING THE WRONG PARTNER

In this section, we will present two case studies and appropriate treatment sequences. As previously noted, relationship treatments are much more complex than most other issues. The following scenarios provide many examples, but you can substitute other treatments if there are additional problems that need correction.

Tara: A Case Study

Tara was a bright, attractive, successful woman who had never married, liked to socialize, and periodically had short-term relationships. Tara was attracted to men in power positions. The problem was that her relationships with those men didn't work, and she continually made the same type of mistakes. The men she chose to be with misled or cheated on her. She also used a lot of her energy trying to make those relationships work. In the end, she always felt disappointed and hurt when the man stopped calling or broke off the relationship.

Although there could have been a number of reasons for this situation, in this case, Tara was choosing the wrong type of man for her. She was a very thoughtful woman who was interested in how people think and feel about the situations in their lives. Also, she needed a man who would give her the attention that she needed to feel happy. One problem was that when she met a man who showed a lot of interest in her, but wasn't the power type that she preferred, she would become bored and shut down. She often rejected men without getting to know them, because she assumed that they weren't exciting enough for her.

Interestingly, in her own life, Tara is very much like the average person. What she didn't do was to give men in less powerful positions a chance. Instead, by always seeking the wrong type of man for herself, she maintained a low self-image that reinforced her belief that only by being with someone very powerful or successful would she feel good about herself. The treatments for problems of this nature are complex, and people do not change instantly. Nonetheless, even though there are numerous steps, they can be done quickly. Once Tara began the treatments, she started having new thoughts about men and what kind of man she wanted.

Choosing the Wrong Person: Treatment Option 1

1. Define the problem in a sentence or two. It always is best to define it in your own words. Rate the problem on a scale of 0 to 10, with 10 being the worst situation and 0 meaning you feel clear about the type of person for you.

2. Treat for the specific reversals that interfere with your ability to develop a good relationship by tapping repeatedly on the Side of Hand (SH) or rubbing the Sore Spot (SS) while thinking about or saying aloud the problem three times. In Tara's case, for example, it was: "I deeply accept myself even though I need to be with men who I consider powerful and exciting." Another related reversal to correct might be, "I deeply accept myself even though I prefer men/women who don't love me and who lower my self-image." Although this may appear to be at odds with what you are trying to achieve, you must first accept your behavior before you can change it.

3. Next, balance your energy system to help you stop seeking or being attracted to the men/women who are not good for you. Think about a person whom you think was/is not good for you, but with whom you sought (or still seek) a relationship. Use the addiction treatments covered in chapter 13 to deal with this problem.

4. Again, rate your attraction to men/women who are not good for you on a 0 to 10 scale. If there is no decrease, go back to step 2 and cycle through this sequence again. If there is not a decrease after three attempts, then this is either not an appropriate treatment sequence for you, or else there is another sabotaging belief (reversal) that needs correction. (See step 8.)

5. Next, do the Brain Balancer (BB) by tapping repeatedly on the Back of Hand (BH) while rotating your eyes clockwise, rotating your eyes counterclockwise, then humming a tune, counting to five, and humming again.

6. Repeat step 3.

7. Again, rate your level of distress from 0 to 10. It should be lower yet. When the distress is within the 0 to 2 range, go to step 9. Sometimes, you'll need to repeat the treatment several times while you are imagining your concern—or even while you are in the actual situation—before you feel complete relief from this problem.

8. As long as there is a decrease in your level of distress, continue with the treatments until there is very little or no distress remaining. If the treatment stalls at any point, this indicates a mini-reversal. Treat this by tapping repeatedly on the Side of Hand (SH) while saying three times, "I deeply accept myself, even though I still have some of this problem."

9. When the distress is 0 to 2, consider doing the Eye Roll (ER) to lower the distress further and to complete the treatment effects. To do this, tap on the Back of Hand (BH), hold your head straight and, moving only your eyes, look at the floor and then slowly raise your eyes toward the ceiling.

10. This is a complex problem that requires additional treatments. The next step is to treat the "lack of interest" that you feel for men/women who would be best for you (unconsciously, you know who they are). In this case, think about a person whom you like, but for whom you don't feel an interest. Don't worry, you don't have to date that specific person, what you are doing is tuning in that feeling. To treat this problem, use the Midline Energy Treatment (MET) found in chapter 8.

11. Next, you should treat for a better sense of self or a positive belief about yourself. To do this, use the MET treatment while thinking or saying to yourself, "I am an attractive and intelligent person and I deserve to meet a man/woman who cares for me." This treatment should be repeated until you feel the validity of this statement. To determine this, rate from 0 to 5 the level of your belief about this statement, with five indicating that you absolutely believe it. Once you get to a five, you have completed this task. At times, it will be necessary to repeat this treatment so that the positive belief becomes an ongoing and active aspect of how you feel about yourself.

12. Lastly, you must develop more patience when you meet a new person who doesn't fit your exact criteria. Use the treatment for impatience in chapter 12, while thinking about how you feel about this new person.

The primary goal of this treatment is to stop wasting your energy on men/women who don't really care about you. These situations create reversals, lower your sense of self-esteem, and keep you stuck in negative, unproductive behaviors. Once you eliminate the problem, you will be more open to meeting the right type of person for you and, equally important, you will stop creating the emotional damage that takes place from continually chasing the wrong people.

Kyle: A Case Study

When Kyle came to see us, he was forty-two years old and had never been married. He had a good job and enjoyed many hobbies that kept him active and involved. He was afraid that if he were to get married, his wife would never be satisfied or that she would be an emotional drain. He imagined that he would spend all of his time catering to her needs and, in effect, lose his own lifestyle, which he really enjoyed. He had been involved with several women in the past who had exhibited such behavior, and that had caused him to end those relationships. In two of those relationships, he had really cared for the person, and he wanted to avoid going through the pain of separation again. Kyle was confused and, in part, he believed that the next woman would have the same problems. Perhaps unconsciously, Kyle behaved in such a manner that he attracted needy women, or perhaps he even sought them out to perpetuate his sabotaging beliefs.

Choosing the Wrong Person: Treatment Option 2

1. Identify the problem in a statement such as, "I was traumatized by two prior relationships that did not work out." You also believe that all men/women are only going to create problems in your life. Rate your level of distress from your past relationships on a scale of 0 to 10, with 10 being the worst situation and 0 meaning that trauma from past relationships does not currently cause problems in your life.

2. Treat for the possibility of the reversal that all men/women are the same by repeatedly tapping on the Side of Hand (SH) or rubbing the Sore Spot (SS) while thinking or saying three times to yourself, "I deeply accept myself even if I believe that all men/women will only create problems in my life." To treat the reversal that you can never attract emotionally healthy people, tap the Under Nose (UN) point three times while saying, "I deeply accept myself even if I can never attract men/women who are emotionally healthy."

3. Think about a situation in your past relationships that traumatized you. To treat this problem, use a treatment for trauma in chapter 10.

4. Again, rate your distress about past traumatic relationships on a 0 to 10 scale (a number should just pop into your mind). If there is no decrease, go back to step 2 and cycle through this sequence again. If there is not a decrease after three attempts, then this is either not an appropriate sequence for you, or else there is another sabotaging belief (reversal) that needs correction. (See step 8.)

5. Next, do the Brain Balancer (BB) by tapping repeatedly on the Back of Hand (BH) while rotating your eyes clockwise, rotating your eyes counterclockwise, then humming a tune, counting to five, and humming again.

6. Repeat step 3.

7. Again, rate your level of distress from 0 to 10. It should be lower yet. When the distress is within the 0 to 2 range, go to step 9. Sometimes, you'll need to repeat the treatment several times while you are imagining your concern—or even while you are in the actual situation—before you feel complete relief from this problem.

8. As long as there is a decrease in your level of distress, continue with the treatments until there is very little or no distress remaining. If the treatment stalls at any point, this indicates a mini-reversal. Treat this by tapping on the little finger Side of Hand (SH) while saying three times, "I deeply accept myself, even though I still have some of this problem."

9. When the distress level is 0 to 2, consider doing the Eye Roll (ER) to lower the distress further and to complete the treatment effects. To do this, tap on the Back of Hand (BH), hold your head straight and, moving only your eyes, look at the floor and then slowly raise your eyes toward the ceiling.

Kyle used these treatments to get over his trauma about bad relationships and his belief that all women are the same and will ruin his lifestyle. The first behavior change he noticed after treatment was that he no longer sought women who were needy and, when needy women did approach him, he was able to see the problem and not become involved. He also started to view women differently. Although he has not yet found his mate, he feels much clearer about who he wants to date and he now believes that he can become involved in a relationship again.

RELATIONSHIP OBSESSIONS

Relationships, or the lack thereof, always have the potential to create obsessive behaviors. Sometimes, people lose all rational perspective when they feel attracted to another person, even if the interest is not mutual. They feel compelled to continually phone the person and, in extreme cases, to stalk them. This loss of control blocks people from moving on with their lives and prevents them from being attracted to others. When it is extreme, obsession is a complex problem that requires professional therapeutic help. But energy psychology can address many obsessive behaviors that can undermine your ability to be in a satisfying relationship. Although the case study below deals with marital obsession, the same treatment could apply easily to those who are casually dating; for example, men who continually call women who have shown no reciprocal interest.

Kim: A Case Study

Kim is thirty-six years old and has never been married. Even when she isn't dating anyone, Kim's favorite conversation topic is her future wedding. She talked about all the ugly dresses she has been forced to wear as a bridesmaid and how she will do things differently at her wedding. The details she provided about this nonexistent event—her fantasized wedding—only revealed her obsession with getting married. Instead of simply enjoying dating, she was obsessively focused on finding the perfect husband. She also felt ashamed and embarrassed that she was not married yet, and this feeling worsened with every wedding invitation she received. All of these negative feelings made Kim extremely picky about whom she would date. If the man did not fit into her fantasy, she would think, "Why waste my time?"

Treatment for Obsession

1. Identify the obsessive behavior in a statement such as, "I must get married." Also, identify any beliefs, such as, "I should date only men/ women who clearly meet all my requirements for marriage." Think about a specific situation and rate your feelings of obsession on a scale of 0 to 10, with 10 being completely obsessed and 0 indicating that you have no obsessive thoughts at all.

2. Treat each sabotaging belief with the appropriate treatment. If there are multiple problems, treat yourself for a massive reversal. Otherwise, for example, tap on little finger Side of Hand (SH) or rub the Sore Spot (SS) while thinking or saying three times, "I deeply accept myself even though I am obsessed about getting married." The next reversal may involve finding the perfect husband (wife). To do this, tap the Side of Hand (SH) or rub the Sore Spot (SS) while thinking or saying three times, "I deeply accept myself even if I am looking for the perfect husband/wife."

3. Look at diagram 33 and the treatment sequence for obsession under the diagram to identify the locations for the meridian points for Under Eye (UE) and Under Collarbone (UCB). While thinking about the obsessive

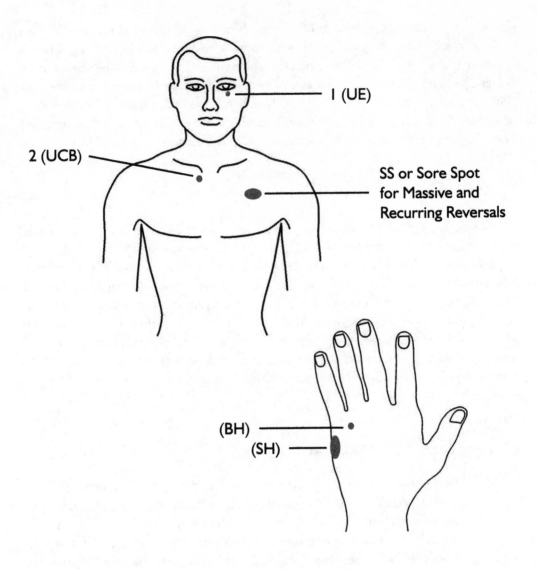

I (UE)

2 (UCB)

SS or Sore Spot
for Massive and
Recurring Reversals

(BH)
(SH)

Diagram Thirty-Three: Obsessive Behaviors

Treatment Sequence for Obsession

Meridian Point		Location
Under Eye (UE)	1	Under the center of the eye on tip of bone
Under Collarbone (UCB)	2	One inch under collarbone near throat

feeling, tap each of the meridian points five times. Tap them in the following order 1 → 2 → 1. **Note:** The UE is repeated twice in the sequence. Tap only hard enough to feel it. The tapping shouldn't cause any pain.

4. Again, rate your feelings of obsession on a 0 to 10 scale (a number should just pop into your mind). If there is no decrease, go back to step 2 and cycle through the sequence again. If there is not a decrease after three attempts, this is probably not an appropriate sequence for you, or else there is another sabotaging belief (reversal) that needs correction. (See step 8.)

5. Next, do the Brain Balancer (BB) by tapping repeatedly on the Back of Hand (BH) while rotating your eyes clockwise, rotating your eyes counter-clockwise, then humming a tune, counting to five, and humming again.

6. Repeat tapping sequence 1 → 2 → 1.

7. Again, rate your level of distress on a 0 to 10 scale. It should be lower yet. When the distress is in the 0 to 2 range, go to step 9. Sometimes, you'll need to repeat the treatment several times while you are imagining your concern—or even while you are in the actual situation—before you feel complete relief from this problem.

8. As long as there is a decrease in your level of obsession, continue with the sequence until there is very little or no obsession remaining. If the treatment stalls at any point, this indicates a mini-reversal. Treat this by tapping on the little finger Side of Hand (SH) while saying three times, "I deeply accept myself, even though I still have some of this problem."

9. When the distress level is 0 to 2, consider doing the Eye Roll (ER) to lower the distress further or to complete the treatment effects. To do this, tap on the Back of Hand (BH), hold your head straight and, moving only your eyes, look at the floor and then slowly raise your eyes toward the ceiling.

Because Kim was so obsessed with getting married, she was reversed; her behaviors and beliefs sabotaged her chances of ever finding the right person for herself. Kim used the treatments described above and eventually eliminated her obsession with marriage. She no longer feels any need to talk about her future wedding. She has not found her marriage partner yet, but she is having more fun on her dates. She believes she has started looking at men differently and has had fun dating men whom she previously would have seen as "less than perfect," and not acceptable to date.

IDENTIFYING SABOTAGING BELIEFS

The goal of this next exercise is for you to specifically identify any beliefs that may be blocking your ability to have a good relationship. All you have to do is use paper and pencil and start writing down your beliefs. They could be the list of traits you require your future partner to have or your beliefs about men or women in general. You are looking for the beliefs that block you from having the relationship that you desire, that is, one that will be truly successful. Here are a few examples of such general beliefs:

- Men always cheat.

- Women are only after money.

- Women are never satisfied.

- Men are only interested in a woman's looks.

- All men care about is sex.

- He/she will want to control me.

Next, identify the set of beliefs that are more specifically about yourself. Here are some examples:

- I will never settle for less than exactly what I want.

- I am not good enough to have a great relationship.

- I do not deserve to have a great relationship.

- I am too old to have a satisfying relationship.

- It is too hard to find a relationship that works.

- I'm afraid of commitments.

- I can't make a relationship work.

Although there are many beliefs that can interfere with having a positive relationship, the essential goal is to identify them, target them, and then alleviate them by using the energy treatments. It may not be sufficient simply to try to talk yourself out of the belief with rational disputing and positive thinking. For example, if you think you're too old to get married, knowing that more than 10 percent of all marriages in the United States involve people over the age of forty probably will not affect your beliefs. You can treat the self-sabotaging belief that you are too old to have a successful, loving relationship by addressing the following reversals:

1. Tapping on the Side of Hand (SH) while thinking or saying three times, "I deeply accept myself, even though I believe I'm too old to have a successful, loving relationship."

2. Tapping Under Nose (UN) while thinking or saying three times, "I deeply accept myself, even though I believe I'm too old to ever have a successful, loving relationship."

3. Tapping on Under Bottom Lip (UBL) while thinking or saying three times, "I deeply accept myself, even though I believe I'm too old to deserve to have a successful, loving relationship."

Sometimes these beliefs work in combination with each other. Some people who are unable to find a suitable partner often believe (unconsciously) that they are not deserving of a good relationship, that it's impossible for them to have a successful relationship, and that all relationships are unsafe. These underlying beliefs and concerns sabotage their relationships.

Often people who would like to find a partner will meet someone who treats them well and has interests and many characteristics that please them, yet they don't follow through in developing a relationship with that person. Their surface rationale or excuse might be that the person doesn't look good enough, doesn't make enough money, or isn't exciting enough. Deep inside themselves, however, they move away from the person because they believe that they do not deserve to be treated that well.

What often happens is that these people spend their time and energy seeking partners who have looks, money, and are exciting, along with a knack for making them feel second-best. They do this because being made to feel second-best matches their internal feelings and the belief they hold within themselves, an unconscious belief that drives them to fail.

To correct the beliefs and reversals that are blocking you, you must identify them in a sentence. Don't worry about being precise—you know what you feel and believe. Once you treat these reversals—and you may have to do this on a daily basis for a while—it will free up your thinking and your feelings, and you will spend less time chasing the wrong people.

THE RELATIONSHIP PLUNGE

Another type of relationship problem might be referred to as the *relationship plunge*, which is the tendency to rush into a relationship before you really get to know the person. In this case, you immediately are attracted to the person for various reasons such as his or her looks, style, mannerisms, achievements, or interests. You fall deeply in love right away, and then you later come to realize that you and this person are simply not compatible. At this point, some people leave their relationship, only to repeat the same mistake with someone else. Others make the error of sticking it out, living in a state of boredom or unhappiness.

If you have an obvious desire to take the relationship plunge, you may scare away the other person. Such behavior comes across as needy, and the reason you wish to spend a lot of time with your potential partner is not clear. The following treatment sequence will address your tendency to plunge into relationships too quickly.

Treatment for the Relationship Plunge

1. Identify the problem in a statement such as this: "I try to make relationships happen too quickly" or "I always chase men/women away." Think about an appropriate situation and rate your feelings of your need to rush into things about that specific situation on a scale of 0 to 10, with 10 indicating the strongest impulse to take the plunge and 0 indicating no impulsive feelings at all.

2. Treat for the possibility of reversal by tapping on the Side of Hand (SH) or rubbing the Sore Spot (SS) while thinking or saying three times, "I deeply accept myself, even though I rush into relationships." You can be more specific and use your own words. It also may be helpful to tap the SH or rub the SS while saying, "I deeply accept myself with all my problems and limitations."

3. Look at diagram 34 and the treatment sequence under the diagram to identify the locations for the points for Forehead (F), Under Nose (UN), Under Bottom Lip (UBL), and Chest (CH). While thinking or saying aloud to yourself, "I rush into relationships," tap five times on each of these points. Tap them in the following order: 1 → 2 → 3 → 4. Tap only hard enough to feel it. The tapping shouldn't cause any pain.

4. Again, rate your feeling about the situation on a 0 to 10 scale (a number should just pop into your mind). If there is no decrease, go back to step 2 and cycle through the sequence again. If there is not a decrease after three attempts, this is probably not an appropriate sequence for you, or else there is another sabotaging belief (reversal) that needs correction. (See step 8.)

5. Next, do the Brain Balancer (BB) by tapping repeatedly on the Back of Hand (BH) while rotating your eyes clockwise, rotating your eyes counterclockwise, then humming a tune, counting to five, and humming again.

6. Repeat the tapping sequence 1 → 2 → 3 → 4.

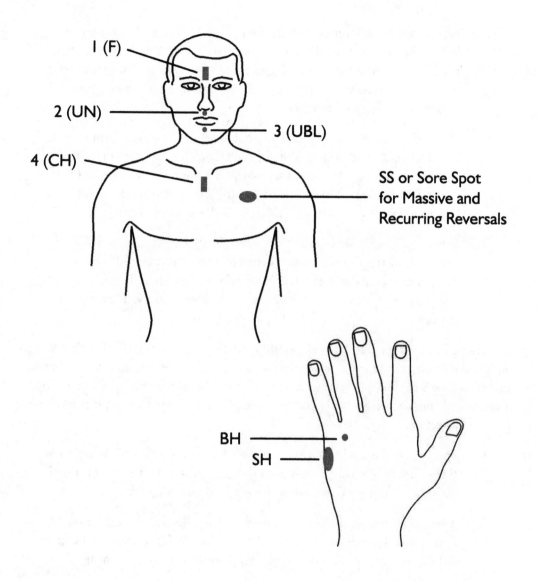

Diagram Thirty-Four: Relationship Plunge

Treatment Sequence for Relationship Plunge

Meridian Point		Location
Forehead (F)	1	One inch above and between eyebrows
Under Nose (UN)	2	Above upper lip and below center of nose
Under Bottom Lip (UBL)	3	In depression between your lip and chin
Chest (CH)	4	Two inches below and between collarbones

7. Again, rate your level of distress from 0 to 10. It should be lower yet. When the distress is in the 0 to 2 range, go to step 9. Sometimes, you'll need to repeat the treatment several times while you are imagining your concern—or even while you are in the actual situation—before you feel complete relief from this problem.

8. As long as there is a decrease in your level of distress, continue with the treatments until there is very little or no distress remaining. If the treatment stalls at any point, this indicates a mini-reversal. Treat this by tapping on the little finger Side of Hand (SH) while saying three times, "I deeply accept myself, even though I still have some of this problem."

9. When the distress level is 0 to 2, consider doing the Eye Roll (ER) to lower the distress further and to complete the treatment effects. To do this, tap on the Back of Hand (BH), hold your head straight and, moving only your eyes, look at the floor and then slowly raise your eyes toward the ceiling.

The tendency to plunge into relationships often comes from the belief that you are not good enough or that you'll never find someone to love. A sense of desperation can strongly influence your approach to relating. When this is the case, the inner sense of urgency and the low sense of self-worth should also be targeted by using the following reversal correction:

1. Tapping on the Under Bottom Lip (UBL) while thinking or saying three times, "I deeply accept myself even though I believe that time is running out and I'm not good enough to have a loving relationship."

2. Then again tap the points five times that are illustrated on diagram 34: Forehead (F), Under Nose (UN), Under Bottom Lip (UBL), and Chest (CH), while saying aloud or to yourself, "Rushing into relationships."

Besides using this treatment before you even begin a relationship, you should also use it whenever you find yourself beginning to take the plunge. By doing this, you can help yourself to remain secure while getting to know the person. You need to accumulate enough experience with the other person before falling "hopelessly in love." In this way, love truly becomes a choice.

UNDERSTANDING AND ACCEPTING DIFFERENCES

In 1992, John Gray wrote the best-seller *Men Are from Mars, Women Are from Venus.* In his book, Gray attempts to help men and women understand their differences and to better communicate with one another. Gray offers insightful advice about how men and women typically respond to situations and how each can learn to react differently to improve their relations. Although he provides readers with numerous scenarios, the two recurring themes throughout the book are as follows:

1.   Women should stop blaming or acting in a disapproving manner when their mates make mistakes or are in difficult situations. Supporting your partner in these situations can eliminate many problems.

2.   Men need to be more attentive by means of affectionate gestures, such as giving flowers, loving touches, and tender hugs. Moreover, they must show more interest in their mate's daily life. Showing your partner that you care also can eliminate many problems.

Although we do not wish to oversimplify Gray's book, these two simple behaviors are difficult to maintain on a regular basis, and may be the cause of many problems in relationships. We encourage you to read books of this nature to increase your knowledge and to further stimulate your thinking about relationships. We also recommend *Divorce Is Not the Answer: A Change of Heart Will Save Your Marriage* by George Pransky (1992) and *Why Marriages Succeed or Fail: And How You Can Make Yours Last* by John Gottman (1995). These books offer commonsense and research-based information about various sources of relationship problems and how to correct them.

To create the relationship you desire, however, you must invest your time in the self-examination that is required to determine what beliefs or behaviors are creating problems and blocking you from achieving success. Once you have done this, you can use the energy treatments in this book to eliminate or minimize these tendencies. Simply stated, insight and knowledge are often not enough to create healthy relationships. You need to target unwanted thoughts, feelings, and behaviors and then balance your energy around these issues with the treatment sequences in this book.

Relationship Issues

The following section deals primarily with the negative emotions and behaviors that may be hurting or ruining your relationships. Although we have selected a few examples here, no doubt you know which feelings and behaviors are having the greatest affect on your relationships. Be sure to review previous chapters to treat those problems.

Accepting Your Partner and Eliminating the Urge to Nag

One reason you nag your mate is because he or she behaves in a manner you refuse to accept. For example, consider this scene: In the waiting room in a doctor's office an elderly man walked toward the exit door, pulled a cigar from his coat pocket, put the cigar in his mouth, and pulled out his lighter. His wife, who was following closely behind him, exclaimed to everyone sitting nearby, "Look at him! Look at him! He hasn't even left the doctor's office and he's already trying to smoke that stinking cigar!" To which the man replied, "I'm ninety-two years old. Sixty years she has nagged me about this cigar, sixty years." As the man proceeded out the door trying to light his cigar, his wife followed him, shaking her head.

In almost every marriage or long-term relationship, there is some behavior or belief that one partner has that drives the other partner crazy. These behaviors, sometimes are referred to as *pet peeves*, often lead to one of the most common complaints in relationships—a nagging partner. Naggers believe that by continual nagging and frequent scolding of their mate, they will change (control) their mate's behavior. What usually happens, however, is that the person being nagged withdraws emotionally from the nagging partner. This doesn't mean that the nagging mate doesn't have a legitimate concern; it's just that the strategy of excessive nagging rarely works to produce the desired result. Nagging is a combination of anger and frustration. If it is incessant and ineffective, you can be sure that a psychological reversal lies at the heart of it.

1. Think about a situation where you nag or do not accept a behavior of your partner. Try to be as specific as possible. Rate your level of frustration and/or anger on a scale of 0 to 10, with 10 representing the most distress and 0 indicating no distress.

2. Treat for the possibility of reversal by tapping repeatedly on the Side of Hand (SH) or rubbing the Sore Spot (SS) while thinking or saying three times, "I deeply accept myself even though I nag my partner when (name the situation)." It also may be helpful to tap the SH or rub the SS while saying, "I deeply accept myself with all my problems and limitations."

3. Look at diagram 35 and the treatment sequence for nagging under the diagram to identify the locations for the meridian points for Eyebrow (EB), Under Eye (UE), Under Arm (UA), Under Collarbone (UCB), and Little Finger (LF). While thinking about the situation (don't get into it so much that you experience any major discomfort during the process), tap five times at each of these meridian points. Tap them in the following order: 1 → 2 → 3 → 4 → 5. Tap only hard enough to feel it. The tapping shouldn't cause any pain.

4. Again, rate your feeling about this situation on a 0 to 10 scale (a number should just pop into your mind). If there is no decrease, go back to step 2 and cycle through the sequence again. If there is not a decrease after three attempts, this is probably not an appropriate treatment sequence for this event, or else there is another sabotaging belief (reversal) that needs correction. (See step 8.)

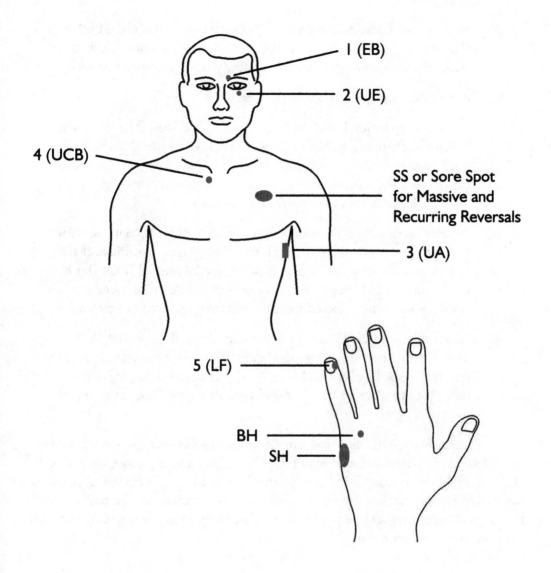

Diagram Thirty-Five: Nagging

Treatment Sequence for Accepting Your Partner and Eliminating the Urge to Nag

Meridian		Location
Eyebrow (EB)	1	Beginning of eyebrow near bridge of nose
Under Eye (UE)	2	Under the center of the eye on tip of bone
Under Arm (UA)	3	Six inches below and under the armpit
Under Collarbone (UCB)	4	One inch under collarbone near throat
Little Finger (LF)	5	Inside tip of little fingernail on the side

5. Next, do the Brain Balancer (BB) by tapping repeatedly on the Back of Hand (BH) while rotating your eyes clockwise, rotating your eyes counter-clockwise, then humming a tune, counting to five, and humming again.

6. Repeat the tapping sequence 1 → 2 → 3 → 4 → 5.

7. Again, rate your level of distress from 0 to 10. It should be lower yet. When the distress is within the 0 to 2 range, go to step 9. Sometimes, you'll need to repeat the sequence several times while you are imagining the distress—or even while you are in the actual situation—before you feel complete relief from the distressful situation.

8. As long as there is a decrease in your level of distress, continue with the treatments until there is very little or no distress remaining. If the treatment stalls at any point, this indicates a mini-reversal. Treat this by tapping on the little finger Side of Hand (SH) while saying three times, "I deeply accept myself, even though I still have some of this problem."

9. When the distress level is 0 to 2, consider doing the Eye Roll (ER) to lower the distress further and to complete the treatment effects. To do this, tap on the Back of Hand (BH), hold your head straight and, moving only your eyes, look at the floor and then slowly raise your eyes toward the ceiling.

In addition to nagging, there are a number of behaviors that can stem from anger or frustration. These can include low or no sexual desire for your partner, cruel remarks, and a general lack of caring about your partner. You need to treat any associated negative beliefs and reversals, and then treat your feelings of anger and frustration. To do this, refer to the various chapters in this book that provide treatment sequences for the emotions you are experiencing.

Vindictive Behavior

When you are feeling vindictive, your behavior is blinded by anger, resentment, and an unwillingness or inability to forgive and forget. If you have children, vindictive behavior can be very destructive because your negative emotions often may lead you to use your child as a vehicle to hurt your partner. Everyone loses in a vindictive situation. If you are reversed on this issue, however, you will not see yourself as vindictive.

To treat vindictive behavior, you need to identify, examine, and address any painful memories that are causing it (see chapter 10 on trauma and painful memories). Next, determine and treat the emotions that are driving your feelings (see chapter 8). Do you need to eliminate your feelings of anger? Do you need to forgive your partner? If you feel stuck in your vindictive behavior, reversals are often at the source, as you are no longer thinking rationally about your partner when you are wishing to hurt him or her (see chapter 6 on reversals and self-sabotage).

Battered Partners, Rage, and Blame

We would be remiss if we did not mention how energy psychology can affect the complex and dangerous issues of abusive relationships. On the surface, these types of relationships are a mystery. Why would anyone stay in a relationship with someone who continually blames her or his partner for their problems and takes out her or his rage by beating the partner? For both, the person who is battered as well as the one who batters, massive reversals are generally the driving force. Our hope is that if either partner repeatedly treats his or her massive reversal (see chapter 6), the problem will be seen for what it is and the partner can use the other treatments in this book to treat the painful memories, rage, and addictions that are so often at the core of abuse issues. However, because abusive relationships are dangerous, in most instances, professional therapeutic help is a necessity.

TREATMENT FOR THE BATTERED

If you are involved with a partner who has hit you or who abuses you verbally, the following treatment sequence may be helpful. These treatments need to be repeated regularly.

1. Think about a situation when you were abused and rub the Sore Spot (SS) on the left side of your chest while thinking or saying three times, "I deeply and unconditionally accept myself with all my problems and limitations." Then tap on the Side of Hand (SH) while saying three times, "I deeply and unconditionally accept myself even though I allow myself to be in this unfulfilling and abusive relationship, and even if I unconsciously believe that I deserve to be abused."

2. Now define your problem in a statement and use the treatment for trauma provided in chapter 10.

3. If you have any related problems, such as a drinking problem or fear of being alone, these issues must also be treated.

Although these treatments can prove to be helpful, an abusive relationship is a significant problem, we strongly recommend that you seek the assistance of a qualified therapist.

TREATMENT FOR THE BATTERER

If you find that you are unable to control your insecurity and anger, resulting in you hitting or being cruel and abusive toward your partner or other people, regularly use the following treatment:

1. Think about a time when you were abusive to your partner and rub the Sore Spot (SS) on the left side of your chest while thinking or saying three times, "I deeply and unconditionally accept myself with all my problems and limitations." Then tap on the Side of Hand (SH) while saying three times, "I deeply and unconditionally accept myself, even though I'm abusive."

2. Now define your problem in a statement such as, "When I am drunk, I let my anger get out of control, I beat my partner, and I blame him or her for my problems." Now use the treatments for anger and rage provided in chapter 8.

3. If you have any related problems, such as heavy drinking, shame, jealousy, or dealing with rejection, they must also be treated.

We strongly recommend that you seek the assistance of a qualified therapist to help you resolve this damaging behavior as safely and expediently as possible. It is important that both the batterer and the battered partner recognize that serious problems exist in their relationship. One way to do this is to treat any sabotaging beliefs and related problems, such as alcoholism. The more clarity you attain on this issue, the more likely you will seek the outside assistance that is needed. Clarity may also help the battered individual to recognize that her or his safety is at risk and to take the proper steps to deal with this problem.

SUMMARY

It is impossible in one chapter to do justice to the complex issue of relationships. The issues that exist in relationships are endless. You cannot change your partner. He or she will change only if he or she is willing to participate in self-examination and apply treatment applications. Therefore, you must focus on how you can help *yourself* to cope with these problems, and to develop strategies to resolve them. You can also examine how your behaviors create or maintain problems in your relationship.

Emotionally charged issues, such as infidelity, may require multiple treatments, but you must first treat any reversals that are blocking your ability to deal with the problem. Your self-sabotaging behaviors may be helping to maintain the problem and/or may be preventing you from finding a strategy to stop it. Always treat any related emotional feelings, such as anger or jealousy (even when you believe they are justified), and painful memories or trauma. For some people, the problems in their relationships are chronic, meaning that they experience them in most or all of their relationships.

Our advice is this: Don't give up, even if repeated and ongoing energy treatments are required. Relationship problems often have a long history attached to them and, generally, no one can push your buttons better than a family member, especially your mate. Consider whether your mate or the person with whom you are in a relationship is energetically imbalanced or if his or her behavior sabotages your relationship. If your treatments are effective, then you should be able to feel or recognize your relationship issue and be able to respond in an appropriate manner. This certainly doesn't mean that every situation will work out in an ideal way, but it may allow you to spend less of your time upset about your relationships.

In closing, relationships are ongoing activities. You are responsible for your actions and your response to the actions of your partner. If your relationships are not working well, then there is some behavior or belief that is helping to sabotage them. Relationships are far too complex an issue to present specific case studies that cover all relationship issues. If you use the personal profile in chapter 5, however, and list all of your problems and treat them, you will eliminate the underlying issues and should have less difficulty using energy psychology to treat the specific issues in your relationships.

18

Sustaining Passion and Romance

Nothing great in the world has ever been accomplished without passion.

—Christian Friedrich Hebbel

In the beginning of a couple's relationship, passion and romance flourish. You're excited, fascinated, enthralled, obsessed, and charmed out of your minds! In short, you're romantically in love. However, as time passes, too often the passion and romance fade and die. Although some couples part after romantic love is gone, others remain together because they really do love each other. Still other couples remain together for various reasons: the "status" and security of being married, their children, finances, religion, and fear—fear of failure, fear of being alone, fear of the unknown, and fear of not being able to find true love.

On the basis of our experience with many Americans and Europeans there seems to be a general belief that, if a couple has true love for each other, the romantic love inevitably transforms into a deeper love. Move to the back of the stage *Eros*, take center stage *Agape*, the Greek word for love described as unconditional, spiritual, nonsexual, and nonphysical. But why should this be? Not that the spiritual side of love isn't a good thing; it would be foolish to denigrate the Spirit and Platonic love. But why not have both? You know, have your cake and eat it too!

There's really no reason why Eros can't survive just as long as the spiritual side of love can. Surely, Eros adds spice to life and to that deeper love. Oh yes, passionate love is both physical and psychical with all the wonderful emotions that give lovers' lives meaning and significance and make them want to contribute to the happiness of the beloved. Romantic love is healing. That sounds pretty good to us, even quite spiritual. After all, aren't meaning, significance, contributing to, and connecting with another person also spiritual?

So what's been happening to Eros? Why all the bad press? We're convinced that it is the result of a far-reaching limiting belief about romance and passion. Furthermore, this belief comes in many guises, as demonstrated by the many common sayings about romantic love. Here are some of those everyday sayings:

- Romantic love doesn't last.

- Romantic love inevitably fades.

- Romance is not true love.

- Romance is self-absorption.

- Romance is a sign of weakness.

- Romance is silly.

In short, this limiting belief maintains that passion and romance cannot be sustained—and some might even say that it shouldn't be sustained, since it detracts from the more important things of life. You know—cooking, knitting, miniature golf, taking out the garbage, and such.

RETHINKING PASSION AND ROMANCE

Let's look at the word "sustain." To *sustain* means to uphold, support, and "to supply with sustenance." Related words include food, fuel, nutrition, and nourishment. If passion and romance die, then surely they didn't get enough nourishment, resulting in frailty and eventual starvation. They've been starved for affection, attention, meaning, and significance. So, to carry the metaphor to its logical conclusion, isn't the solution to feed and nurture passion and romance so that they will regain strength and vitality?

Of course, if your passion and romance are truly dead, it might take a monumental effort to resurrect the poor souls. Yet the effort is certainly worthwhile, unless you have reached the proverbial point of no return and perhaps you are even repelled by the idea of reviving passion with the person you're with. Let's assume that you haven't reached that point yet; or, at the very least, that you intend for a future relationship to flourish with passion and romance. If that is the case, please read on.

THE SAGA OF JOHN AND MARY

John and Mary started dating in college and one year after graduating they decided to tie the knot. They got married on a beach in South Carolina, with only close relatives and dear friends invited. They liked the experience of a small, personal wedding, rather than a massive, extravagant one. At the time, John had an entry-level job with an accounting firm and Mary was working as a substitute elementary school teacher. They enjoyed each other and their work. In the early days of their marriage they spent a lot of time together and enjoyed dancing, sports, and going to parties and planning outings with friends.

Then, after two years of marriage, Mary became pregnant and their focus became their baby girl Anna. Almost immediately they stopped going out except to infrequently dine at a restaurant with their infant. At times, they tried to use a babysitter, but their families lived great distances away and they didn't feel comfortable leaving Anna for a long stretch of time with anyone else than family. Generally, their outings together were only for an hour or two to get some groceries, lunch, or to go for a run. The responsibilities of building a family were upon them.

Before long, John and Mary were paying less and less romantic attention to each other. In five years, their relationship had become dedicated to the business of raising a child, working, and managing a household. Although they still loved each other, sadly their passion and romance were gone. A sense of emptiness marred their relationship, and they were longing for something more. They needed a relationship fix. Fortunately, John and Mary were able to successfully use the following techniques to give their relationship the boost it needed.

REVIVING PASSION AND ROMANCE

Romance fades when lovers are neglectful or do hurtful things to each other. John and Mary neglected to pay romantic attention to each other, and it's no exaggeration to say that their failure to act to correct this was damaging their marriage. If your partnership is undergoing similar stress, that is, if you have been neglecting each other's romantic needs, you are endangering your relationship.

To reverse this pattern, here are some important questions to consider. Take out a pencil and paper and write down your answers to the following questions:

1. On a scale of 0 to 10, how do you rate your Subjective Units of Relationship Quality (SURQ), with 10 indicating the highest degree possible for passion and romance, and 0 indicating, well, a big fat zero. The SURQ is your estimate of how much passion and romance exist between you and your lover. This number must take into account the various behaviors between you and your lover, as well as how romantically you think and feel about each other. If your SURQ is 8 to 10, then we suppose you are hopelessly in love, and you need read no further. Scores below this range indicate that your relationship can benefit from some additional attention.

2. If your relationship had not experienced a loss or significant reduction of passion and romance, what specifically would be different? Go into as much detail as is possible.

3. If something were to magically transform your relationship into a superbly passionate and romantic one, how would you know that this had occurred? How would your behavior be different than it has been as of late? Guessing is absolutely allowed.

4. What would a friend who knows you really well observe and feel about your new behavior? What would your friend notice? What would he or she see, hear, and even wonder about? If you're perplexed about what your friends would notice, you might like to ask them.

5. Recall some moments and events when you and your lover felt really passionate and romantic about each other. How would you rate the SURQ during those moments and events, on a scale of 0 to 10? Describe those moments or events in detail.

Contrast your memories with what you've been doing, thinking, saying, and feeling about your relationship lately. Again, think back to when your passion was alive and thriving. Recall those times in detail and write down your answers to the following questions:

- What were you doing then?

- What persistent thoughts did you have about your lover?

- What was different about the way you talked to each other?

- How did you play with each other?

- How much fun were you having?

- What was different about the way you touched and kissed?

- How did you hug and hold each other?

- What was it like to look into each other's eyes?

- Was your tone of voice and choice of words different then?

- What about the way you moved and smiled?

- How did you feel about the way your lover smelled and tasted?

- Do you remember the gestures and facial expressions of your lover that were so endearing?

- What was different about your behavior then?

Remember when you were enthralled with learning everything you could about your lover? There's always more to learn, and now is the time to resume the adventure of discovery.

Thoughts, Feelings, and Behaviors Are Linked

It's important to understand that thoughts, feelings, and behaviors are all intimately connected to each other. If you have negative thoughts about someone, it is understandable that your feelings will be congruently negative. Resentful thoughts elicit resentful feelings; angry thoughts result in angry feelings; hopeful and loving thoughts produce hopeful and loving feelings; and so on.

Try this experiment. Vividly imagine a lemon. Look at it up close. If it's not already sliced, in your mind slice it and look at the insides. See the rind, all the sections, the seeds, the little packets of lemon juice. Can you smell the lemon fragrance? Now bite into your imaginary lemon and notice the sensation in your mouth. What happens? Most people experience their mouths watering, along with a sour and bitter sensation. So what accounts for this? Where is the real lemon?

Obviously, there is no real lemon, just an imaginary one. This lemon is merely a thought in your mind. However, the thought of a lemon can send energetic messages throughout your body, like electricity through a wire, and you then experience specific sensations. Your mind and body are intricately joined together. You get to experience your thoughts as though they were palpable, touchable, that is, real. However, essentially, thoughts are not real; except as real electrochemical impulses.

Okay, so you've thought about how it used to be, you've imagined, remembered, got in touch with what it was like when passion and romance were thriving in your life. Excellent. Yet that's not enough; now you need to do something with those thoughts and feelings. We all know that words pale in comparison to vivid images. There is truth to the saying, "a picture is worth a thousand words." Well, there is something even more powerful than a picture, and that's action. A picture may be worth a thousand words but action is worth even more!

If you consciously practice loving behaviors for two to four weeks, you'll find that they will become increasingly easy and natural to do; your feelings and thoughts will also change. It won't be long before you realize that this is truly the way you really think and feel about your lover, deep within the very core of your being. Your consciously chosen behaviors will start becoming automatic, even unconscious in many ways. But it's important to stay conscious, too!

This is just the beginning. Persistence pays big dividends. You can't just wish or hope for something to become better; you've got to really want it, and you've got to give your want reality by persistently and consistently putting it into action. In this way, you elevate your want to an even higher level; it becomes a must—an imperative need to act in a loving way. Moreover, if both you and your lover act from an imperative need to be loving, the benefit you both will reap will increase exponentially.

Shifting Out of Reverse

Now that all sounds easy enough, doesn't it? Well, at least it does here, on the pages of this book. However, consider this analogy: If your car or truck is stuck in reverse, it doesn't matter how much you intend to drive forward; it isn't going to happen. It doesn't matter how hard you step on the accelerator. If you're driving in reverse, you won't get to your intended destination any faster.

Obviously, if you are going to move forward, you have to shift out of reverse and into the forward gears. The same holds true with actualizing passion and romance in your relationship. Even if you know what to do to create the love that you want, if your actions are incongruent with your expressed intention, it isn't going to happen. And, if your actions are incongruent with your expressed intention, something is interfering with the imperative. What could it be?

UNDERSTANDING PSYCHOLOGICAL REVERSAL

In energy psychology and energy tapping, we make use of the concept of psychological reversal or, simply, *reversal*. This is a self-sabotaging tendency to treat what's healthy as if it were unhealthy, and what's unhealthy as if it were healthy—thus the term "reversed." We can also say that *psychological reversal* is the tendency to treat what's good, as though it's bad; and what's bad, as though it's good; what's useful, as though it's not, and what's not useful, as though it were, and so forth. *Psychological reversal* is a misalignment of intention and action, such that the actions tied to the intention prevent the fulfillment of the intention.

In other words, when you are reversed, you behave incongruently. Your intention and actions are not on the same page and you repeatedly shoot yourself in the foot. What you intend and what you do don't match. For more details on this process, please refer to chapter 6, Understanding Psychological Reversals and Self-Sabotage.

What Causes Psychological Reversal?

What causes this state of affairs? Well, actually, we all become reversed at times. It's part of the human condition, spoken of in many spiritual traditions. Paul, of the New Testament, speaks of this in his letter to the Romans, chapter 7, verses 12 to 16:

> I cannot understand my own behavior. I fail to carry out the things I want
> to do, and I find myself doing the very things I hate. When I act against my
> own will, that means I have a self that acknowledges that the Law is good,
> and so the thing behaving in that way is not myself but sin living in me.

Psychological reversal does not necessarily involve sin, but it does involve going against your stated values and intentions. When you are psychologically reversed, your actions go against your goals. The causes take place at many levels. Psychological reversal can be seen as a conflict between your conscious and unconscious mind, between the right and left hemispheres of your brain, or between the higher cortical areas of the brain and the areas of the more primitive limbic system, which is constantly scouting the environment for danger.

Reversal may also be a disruption of energy flow through the acupuncture meridians and the nervous system. (The acupuncture points are discussed in the introduction.) At one level you want one thing, and at another level you want something else—or you feel that, if you follow your conscious intention, you'll lose something. In this sense, there is a conflict of intentions. And guess which intention is winning the battle when you are reversed? For an easy example, think about what happens when some people want to lose weight, but eating certain foods gives them immediate comfort and joy. They don't want to lose those benefits along with the weight. The comfort and joy of eating certain foods outweigh their intention to weigh less.

In situations involving romantic love, the reversal might include feelings of resentment, vulnerability, or some other negative fear. Then passion and romance are to be avoided, since they are associated with fear. It is also possible that the reversal of energy is fundamental, while the cognitive considerations (the thoughts in your mind) are really secondary or even tertiary. That is, perhaps you behave as though you don't want passion in your life simply because your energy is reversed; not because you really don't want the passion. As Paul said, "I fail to carry out the things I want to do, and find myself doing the very things I hate."

CORRECTING PSYCHOLOGICAL REVERSAL ABOUT ROMANTIC LOVE

The causes of reversal are many and, sometimes, there may be underlying considerations. Furthermore, although it can be useful to understand the underlying motives, psychological reversal is often a fairly simple matter to correct. Physically tapping at specific acupuncture meridian locations on your body while stating an affirmation can help to disengage reversal and help you realign with your intentions of creating passion and romance in your relationship. Here's one way to accomplish this:

1. Think about the lack of passion and romance in your life.

2. Tap on the little finger Side of your Hand (SH).

3. While tapping, think or say several times, "Even though I have this passion and romance problem, I deeply love and accept myself."

4. Do this several times a day and then observe the ways that passion and romance will have been jump-started in your relationship.

Correcting reversal is a function of two factors: (1) Alleviating energetic blocks, and (2) fully accepting yourself with the problem that you are experiencing at the time. The best way to change is not through self-rejection, but through self-acceptance. An affirmation, when combined with tapping on the side of your hand (SH), which corresponds to the third acupoint on your small intestine meridian, balances energy and consciousness in the direction of good health and your highest good.

Of course, you will still have to take other actions to activate the passion and romance in your life again. This method simply helps to disengage the reversal that prevents you from doing what you know how to do. Other types of reversal are covered in chapter 6, and we recommend that you review that chapter in detail.

RESENTMENTS AND OTHER NEGATIVE EMOTIONS

At times practically every couple experiences anger toward each other during the course of their relationship. The problem is not the anger. The problem is that when you *hold on to* anger, resentment, and hurt feelings, these emotions must be resolved before the relationship can move in a positive direction. It is difficult, if not impossible, to get to passion when negativity is blocking the pathway. And although there is a lot to be said for a change of heart—making a decision to let go of the past and move on—a simple energy tapping technique can often facilitate and speed up the process.

Let's say that your lover did something that hurt you deeply or that you had an argument and terrible, hurtful words were exchanged. These actions or words have a way of replaying in your mind along with the hurt and scared feelings. In a broad sense of the term, this is a trauma. Maybe at the time you also made a decision to quit feeling so deeply about him or her. You may have backed away from your previous feelings so that you wouldn't get hurt again, and maybe you gave your lover a bitter taste of his or her own medicine. Maybe you concluded that the two of you are incompatible, that your "lover" isn't good enough, or maybe you now believe that you are unlovable. Regardless of your reasons for doing so, you may have given the axe to your love, and now the passion and romance have been greatly diminished or even disappeared.

When you're stuck with a trauma and its associated belief, there are several energy tapping techniques that can help to rapidly resolve the trauma so that you can move on in a more positive way. We recommend that you review chapter 10, Resolving Trauma and Painful Memories Rapidly, for more details on this subject. However, for your convenience, one of the treatments is covered here.

TREATMENT PLAN FOR A PAINFUL RELATIONSHIP

1. Think about the painful event. It should be a single, specific event. Rate your level of distress on a scale of 0 to 10, with 10 representing the highest level of distress and 0 indicating none.

2. Treat for the possibility of reversal by tapping repeatedly on the Side of your Hand (SH) or rubbing the Sore Spot (SS) while thinking or saying three times, "Even though I am still upset about what happened, I deeply love and accept myself." You can be specific about the event. It also may be helpful to tap the SH or rub the SS while saying, "I accept myself with all my problems and limitations."

3. Look at diagram 36 and the treatment sequence for a painful relationship event directly under the diagram to identify the location of the meridian points for Eyebrow (EB), Under Eye (UE), Under Arm (UA), Under Collarbone (UCB), Little Finger (LF), and Index Finger (IF). While thinking about the event, don't get into it so much that you experience any major discomfort during the process. Tap five times at each of these meridian points. Tap them in the following order: $1 \rightarrow 2 \rightarrow 3 \rightarrow 4 \rightarrow 5 \rightarrow 4 \rightarrow 6 \rightarrow 4$. **Note:** The UCB appears three times in the sequence. Tap only hard enough to feel it. The tapping shouldn't cause any pain.

4. Again, rate your distress on a 0 to 10 scale (a number should just pop into your mind). If there is no decrease, go back to step 2 and cycle through the sequence again. If there is not a decrease after three attempts, this is probably not an appropriate sequence for this event, or else there is another self-sabotaging reversal that needs correction. Also, there may be an earlier trauma that needs to be addressed.

5. Next, do the Brain Balancer (BB) by tapping repeatedly on the Back of Hand (BH) while rotating your eyes clockwise, rotating your eyes counterclockwise, then humming a tune, counting to five, and humming again.

6. Repeat the tapping sequence $1 \rightarrow 2 \rightarrow 3 \rightarrow 4 \rightarrow 5 \rightarrow 4 \rightarrow 6 \rightarrow 4$.

7. Again, rate your level of distress from 0 to 10. When the distress is within the 0 to 2 range, go to step 9. Sometimes, you'll need to repeat the treatment several times while thinking about the event before you feel complete relief about the distressing situation.

8. As long as there is a decrease in the level of distress, continue with the sequence until there is very little or no stress remaining. If the treatment

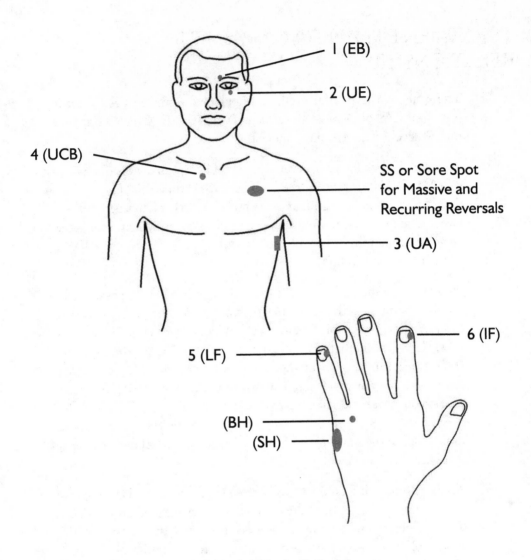

Diagram Thirty-Six: Painful Relationships

Treatment Sequence for a Painful Relationship Event

Meridian		Location
Eyebrow (EB)	1	Beginning of eyebrow near bridge of nose
Under Eye (UE)	2	Under the center of the eye on tip of bone
Under Arm (UA)	3	Six inches under armpit
Under Collarbone (UCB)	4	One inch under collarbone near throat
Little Finger (LF)	5	Inside tip of little fingernail on the side
Index Finger (IF)	6	Inside tip of index fingernail on the outside

stalls at any point, this indicates a mini-reversal. Treat this by tapping on the little finger Side of your Hand (SH) while saying or thinking three times, "I deeply accept myself, even though I'm still upset."

9. When the distress level is 0 to 2, do the Eye Roll (ER) to lower the distress further or to complete the treatment effects. To do this, tap on the Back of your Hand (BH), hold your head straight and, moving only your eyes, look at the floor and then slowly raise your eyes toward the ceiling. Relax.

In most cases, once a trauma has successfully been treated with this sequence, the distress will not return. However, if distress should return at a later time, repeat these treatments. In time, the distress will become less and less frequent.

Reinforcing the Shift

Once you are no longer experiencing distress about the event, reevaluate what happened then. Was your lover feeling insecure at the time of the event? When we are in low moods, we often say or do things that we would not do otherwise. Was your lover psychologically reversed at the time? Are you able to let it go now? Is it appropriate to let it go now? Are you now able to reaffirm your love? Or are there other events that need to be neutralized first? Often, treating one event elicits others that also need attention. If so, use the process described here (or other treatments discussed in chapter 10, Resolving Trauma and Painful Memories Rapidly) to resolve any and all issues that are getting in the way of you having the love that you want and deserve.

Most people report that, once a painful memory has been relieved in this way, their thoughts about the event change significantly. The event seems more distant and they feel more tranquil, serene, and peaceful. If they felt damaged and wounded before doing the energy tapping technique, after doing it, they experience themselves in a healthier, more vigorous way. If you notice a shift of this sort, you can strengthen and reinforce it by doing the following:

1. Rate the level of the positive belief and emotion you are feeling on a scale of 0 to 10, with 10 now representing the positive end of the continuum. This is referred to as the Positive Belief Score (PBS).

2. Now tap on the Back of your Hand (BH) while attuning to your current more positive belief and feeling. Your intention is to increase the strength of this new understanding by visualizing or thinking about it in other ways, while tapping.

3. Pay attention as your PBS increases. As a goal, the strength of the emotion and belief should be within the 8 to 10 point range. Usually, this treatment will result in a significant shift within a few minutes, at most.

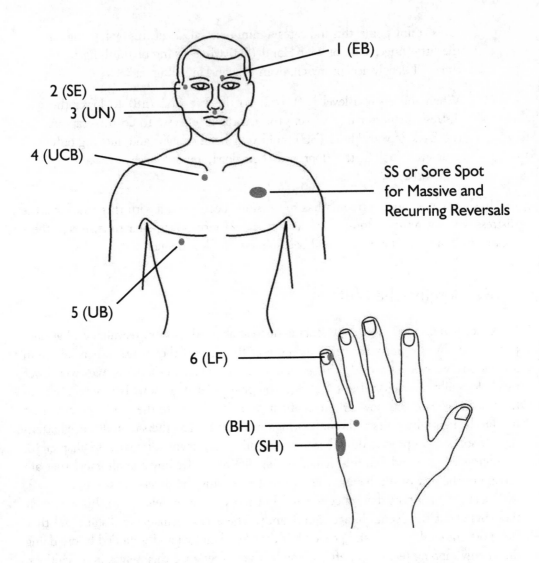

Diagram Thirty-Seven: Negative Relationship Triggers

Treatment Sequence for Negative Relationship Triggers

Meridian		Location
Eyebrow (EB)	1	Beginning of eyebrow near bridge of nose
Side of Eye (SE)	2	Under the center of the eye on tip of bone
Under Nose (UN)	3	Above upper lip and below the center of nose
Under Collarbone (UCB)	4	One inch under collarbone near throat
Under Breast (UB)	5	Under breast close to where rib cage ends
Little Finger (LF)	6	Inside tip of little fingernail on the side

4.   If the progress stalls at any point, treat for psychological reversal in this way: While tapping under your nose (UN), think or say three times, "Even if my positive feelings and beliefs don't get any stronger, I deeply love and accept myself."

5.   Then resume tapping at the Back of your Hand (BH) until the strength of this new understanding is within the 8 to 10 point range.

NEUTRALIZING TRIGGERS

Relationship meltdowns are often activated by subtle behaviors from you and your partner. The technical term for this is *stimuli*, but we'll call them *triggers*. There are all kinds of positive and negative triggers in your environment. Some songs and melodies can transport you back to the time when you went to dances or attended football games in high school. On a sadder note, another song or other memorabilia might take you back to the memory of how you felt after a breakup.

Regarding your lover, your triggers could be specific words, a tone of voice, the volume of voice, gestures, facial expressions, rolling of the eyes, wet towels left on the bathroom floor, the proverbial cap left off the tube of toothpaste, and more. Triggers can be either positive or negative and they affect you accordingly, although we're more concerned with negative triggers in this chapter. Sometimes, a trigger can be an absence of behavior, such as your lover not remembering to take out the garbage or not noticing something that you did for him or her. You know what we mean.

When the trigger occurs, it's just like a switch being turned on; you instantly react and lose your bearings. However, even though you may feel justified, your reaction is not necessarily the best way to go about enhancing your relationship or getting what you want. If you can truly maintain your composure when one of your triggers has gone off, if you can actually not be activated in a negative way, then you'll be able to increase your level of rapport with your lover because you will be able to communicate more effectively.

In truth, change usually comes about more certainly through positive rather than negative means. You know the old saying, "You can catch more flies with honey than with vinegar." There are several energy tapping techniques that can help you to neutralize your triggers rapidly so that not only can you maintain your cool, but you can also create and maintain warmer feelings in your relationship. Here's how you do it:

1. Think about a trigger that sends you into a tailspin. It should be a single, specific trigger. Rate your level of distress on a scale of 0 to 10, with 0 being no emotional upset and 10 being "going through the roof."

2. Treat for the possibility of reversal by tapping repeatedly on the Side of your Hand (SH) or rubbing the Sore Spot (SS) while thinking or saying three times, "I deeply accept myself even though I become upset when (fill in the trigger). You should be specific about the trigger. It also may be helpful to tap the Side of the Hand (SH) or rub the Sore Spot (SS) while saying, "I accept myself with all my problems and limitations."

3. Look at diagram 37 and the treatment sequence for negative relationship triggers under the diagram to identify the locations for the meridian points for Eyebrow (EB), Side of Eye (SE), Under Nose (UN), Under Collarbone (UCB), Under Breast (UB), and Little Finger (LF). While thinking about the trigger, tap five times at each of these meridian points. Tap them in the following order: 1 → 2 → 3 → 4 → 5 → 6. Tap only hard enough to feel it. The tapping shouldn't cause any pain.

4. Again, rate your distress on a 0 to 10 scale (a number should just pop into your mind representing the way you feel). If there is no decrease, go back to step 2 and cycle through the sequence again. If there is not a decrease after three attempts, perhaps the trigger is not specific enough or there is a reversal that needs correction. Also there may be a trauma related to the trigger that needs to be addressed.

5. Next, do the Brain Balancer (BB) by tapping repeatedly at the Back of Hand (BH) while rotating your eyes clockwise, rotating your eyes counterclockwise, then humming a tune, counting to five, and humming again.

6. Repeat the tapping sequence 1 → 2 → 3 → 4 → 5 → 6.

7. Again, rate your level of distress from 0 to 10. It should be lower yet. When the distress is within the 0 to 2 range, go to step 9. Sometimes, you'll need to repeat the treatment several times while thinking about the trigger before you feel complete relief.

8. As long as there is decrease in the level of distress, continue with the sequence until there is very little or no stress remaining. If the treatment stalls at any point, this indicates a mini-reversal. Treat this by tapping on the little finger Side of Hand (SH) while thinking or saying three times, "I deeply accept myself, even though I'm still upset."

9. When the distress level is 0 to 2, do the Eye Roll (ER) to lower the distress further or to complete the treatment effects. To do this, tap on the

Back of Hand (BH), hold your head straight and, moving only your eyes, look at the floor and then slowly raise your eyes toward the ceiling.

In most cases, once a trigger has successfully been treated with this sequence, the trigger will no longer cause distress. However, if distress should return at a later time, repeat these treatments. In time, the trigger will become less and less likely to activate negative feelings, and you will be able to maintain your composure more easily.

A WORD OF CAUTION: ABUSIVE VERSUS HEALTHY RELATIONSHIPS

We're assuming that any altercations between you and your lover were not physical abuse, or any other highly destructive or violent behavior. Resolving a trauma and neutralizing negative triggers are excellent things to do, since they are in your best interests; but what you choose to do afterward is another issue. The treatments described here are not intended to enable you to remain in a destructive, unhealthy relationship. The purpose of these exercises is to help you to reclaim passion and romance in an otherwise healthy relationship.

SUMMARY

On the subject of sustaining passion and romance, there is much more to consider than what has been covered here. There are degrees of being in love, and degrees of wanting to rekindle romance. The more intensely you want to have a romantic relationship, the better, in terms of being able to make it happen. No technique, no matter how elegant or powerful, can ever replace the power of your intention and your willingness to make something happen. The material we've covered in this chapter is merely to assist you; the true power for creating and sustaining passion and romance lies within you.

19

Tools for a Lifetime

Be the change you want to see in the world.

—Mahatma Gandhi

This second edition of *Energy Tapping* has reintroduced a new approach to overcome psychological and emotional problems, based on harnessing the powers of your body's own energy system. Many people who have worked with energy psychology consider it to be a far-reaching approach for self-help. In this book, we've provided a number of therapeutic sequences that can be used to rapidly eliminate or significantly reduce a variety of problems, including traumas and painful memories, depression and low moods, anxiety and phobias, eating disorders, chronic pain, and self-limiting beliefs.

Properly used, energy psychology makes it possible for you to efficiently enhance your golf swing or batting average, and realize improvement in many other areas of your life. And it's simple. All that's required is for you to identify the problem by thinking about it, and then tap in sequence on specific meridian points combined with certain positive affirmations to treat the problem.

Although we find this approach to be highly effective, in reality nothing works all the time, at least not in our practice. There is always room for improvement, as there should be. Any claims that an approach works one-hundred percent of the time, or nearly as much, must be based on limited experience with the method or downright deception. However, of all the methods we've had the opportunity to study and practice so far, energy psychology is far above the rest. We believe that it is the therapy of the new millennium. You are going to see and hear a lot more about it in the years to come. As a self-help approach, it offers you wonderfully effective tools for a lifetime. It's the psychological equivalent of the Heimlich maneuver or CPR.

In this final chapter, we would like to explore some ideas about the current and future practice of energy psychology. We hope that this will spur interest and innovation in the application of this approach to areas we haven't yet considered.

INTO THE MAINSTREAM

As increasing numbers of therapists are trained in the application of energy psychology, they are applying this efficient method to assist their patients and clients in resolving many long-standing problems, such as those described in *Energy Tapping*. This approach is applicable to many other areas, some of which we've added to this second edition. These include eating disorders, allergies, enhancing your immune system, hypertension, enhancing and sustaining your romantic life, and many other physical and psychological conditions. Although it would take a multitude of volumes to address all of the problems that you might be interested in, we encourage you to try some of these sequences, especially the Midline Energy Treatment (MET; see chapter 8), to treat and resolve any issue you'd like. Feel free to try it on anything.

Energy psychology is entering the mainstream not only because of its efficiency, but also due to the great need that exists throughout society. Most traditional therapies do not yield quick results and, for some issues, they aren't effective at all. Although using energy psychology to treat particular problems sometimes requires a longer period of time, there are many problems that can and should be resolved rapidly. The sooner a psychological problem is resolved, the less likely it is that it will become a chronic, debilitating problem.

We believe that sometimes it is the form of therapy itself that causes certain conditions to become chronic. For example, if you experience a severe trauma and the therapy you choose involves extensive reviewing of the trauma, perhaps even dredging up all varieties of forgotten traumas, then the therapy may not only prove to be emotionally upsetting, it can also cause the traumas to become more deeply ingrained. This process, called *retraumatization*, is very unlikely to happen with effective use of energy psychology techniques. See chapter 10, Resolving Trauma and Painful Memories Rapidly, for more detailed coverage and effective techniques for trauma and post-traumatic stress disorder (PTSD).

There are many debilitating conditions that people tolerate because they believe that therapy is invariably a long-term, arduous process. However, because this is generally not the case with energy psychology, people are more inclined to pursue the brief, highly effective therapy that this approach affords. The same consideration applies to a wide array of problems that people seek to resolve in therapy. We believe that the healthier your energy system, the healthier you will be overall—physically, emotionally, and psychologically.

ENERGY PSYCHOLOGY AND THE FUTURE

Energy psychology is so efficient and effective that in time it will be applied extensively in the fields of therapy, medicine, education, vocational guidance, business, sports training, various performance areas, and so forth. This is already happening. The applications appear to be limitless.

In the area of education, we believe that energy psychology is readily applicable to the needs of inner-city children who suffer many barriers to success, such as violence in their neighborhoods and schools. Energy psychology provides opportunities for students to challenge and alleviate obstacles to motivation, overcome test anxiety, and surmount learning blocks. Equipping school psychologists and counselors with these methods will lead to improvement in these and related areas for students. These methods may also help to reduce the incidence of adolescent problems in the larger community.

Energy psychology also complements traditional medical approaches. The impact of stress on physical health, for example, is well documented. Excessive and continual stress can limit the healing process, slow down recovery from surgery, and lead to many other illnesses and problems, such as heart disease and hypertension. Energy psychology provides a tool that you can use to gain more personal control over your health.

Using energy work to enhance sports performance is a relatively new area. This easily applied technique can help athletes to reduce anxiety and alleviate self-sabotaging beliefs that produce many mental errors. It provides a means of regaining focus in crucial situations and helps athletes to separate their natural ability from their mental mistakes.

In the areas of business and vocational pursuits, energy psychology offers an efficient means of coping with job stress, enhancing creativity, repairing relationship problems, improving morale, and so forth. Managers who are trained in these methods can help to establish an organization-wide energy balance that will result in a positive trickle-down effect to benefit the entire organization.

INSIGHT

Maybe you believe that simply treating a psychological problem by tapping is not enough. You may also want to gain some insight into the cause of your problem, which might lead you to seek talk therapy. Many discussion-focused therapists have begun using energy psychology techniques with their clients. These techniques are applied at strategic points during the session to quickly resolve areas in which the client feels stuck. This still leaves plenty of room for insight work to proceed.

Gaining greater insight into your issues may be important to you even if you aren't working with a professional therapist. If this is the case, after you treat your specific issue—trauma, depression, anger, relationships, whatever—take some time to think about the problem that you used to have. Frequently, relevant insights will emerge. As a rule, you will find that you think quite differently about your problem once the emotional charge has disappeared. Insightful thoughts can go a long way toward preventing the original problem from returning and can produce an even greater sense of satisfaction in your newfound understanding of yourself and others.

BEYOND TAPPING

Once your energy system has become balanced through energy tapping, you can identify the instant connections between your thoughts and feelings more easily. Observe that after treating a problem with energy psychology, your thoughts about the problem will no longer have a negative emotional charge. You will feel calm and centered about the issue. It will take only a few experiences of this kind to teach you to truly understand that your thoughts cannot have a negative effect on you unless you allow them to. You are now in a position of choosing how you will feel about specific issues. You will no longer need to react in specific ways to old triggers that used to bring you nothing but trouble.

These are important lessons to take with you throughout life. In the future, each time you balance your energy around an emotionally charged issue, it will be easier to simply dismiss negative thoughts, even without having to tap on meridian points. Essentially, you are training your brain and your energy system to remain centered in balance more consistently.

FEELINGS

Our lives are filled with the wonderfully diverse positive emotions of curiosity, anticipation, surprise, joy, gratitude, love, respect, appreciation, and so on. We cherish these feelings, but we also have the capacity for the negative emotions, such as fear, irritation, anger, rage, jealousy, guilt, sorrow, grief, and shame. Here, the term *negative* should not be interpreted as meaning *bad*. In reality, there is no such thing as a bad emotion. All emotions are essentially a part of you. To a large extent they are hardwired.

Emotions are forms of information and communication. For example, fear or anxiety alerts us to danger; anger tells us that we strongly disapprove of something; guilt lets us know that we ourselves have violated a value or a moral; with jealousy we see someone trying to "rob" us of something that is ours; and the list goes on and on. Just as we benefit from the emotions of joy and love, the so-called negative emotions listed here also serve an admirable purpose.

Energy Tapping is about getting to the point where we can experience the full spectrum of our emotions, even the negative ones, without having them dominate our entire existence. In the words of the Sufi poet Rumi, "Welcome and entertain them all! Because each has been sent as a guide from beyond." Negative feelings become a problem only when we habitually reside in their landscape; that is, when we spend most of our time living there.

However, we never want to get to the point where we lose the capacity to make the differentiation that our negative emotional responses afford us. Negative and positive emotions are essential to our internal communication system, informing us of the meaning and quality of our thoughts. It's not about creating a Stepford society, but about properly utilizing this approach to eliminate emotional responses that have become problems in our lives.

In closing, we would like to express our gratitude to you for taking the time to explore and apply these effective tools in your life. We believe that energy has a resonating effect, both positive and negative. As more and more people apply energy tapping to enhance their energy and positively improve their lives, the lives of others will also benefit and, in time, possibly the whole of society will be better for it. Changing yourself is truly the place to begin if you wish to help others. As Mahatma Gandhi wisely advised: "Be the change you want to see in the world."

APPENDIX

Research in Energy Psychology

The first reported research in energy psychology (EP) was a case report from 1980. Since that time the number of case reports has grown steadily. Many additional case examples are presented in this book.

A PIONEERING CASE REPORT

The first report from Dr. Roger J. Callahan was about Mary, who presented with a severe water phobia from early childhood (Gallo 2005). Mary had difficulty taking a bath, could not go out of her house when it was raining, felt fear when looking at a body of water, whether it was a swimming pool or the ocean, and had weekly nightmares about water engulfing and drowning her. This phobia appeared to be hereditary, since she had had it all her life and there was no evidence of a traumatic event.

Mary was in treatment for about eighteen months with Dr. Callahan and experienced little progress even after a variety of therapeutic techniques were tried with her. Dr. Callahan tried cognitive therapy, hypnosis, behavioral therapy, systematic desensitization, placebo techniques. Eventually, Mary was able to sit near the shallow end of a swimming pool and dangle her feet in the water. She could not, however, look at the water and would get a severe headache after each session.

Because so little progress had taken place, Dr. Callahan decided to try a new approach with her, one based on applied kinesiology (AK) and acupressure. He asked Mary to think about water while he gently tapped on the bony orbits under her eyes with his fingertips. Within a minute or so, Mary said that she no longer got a sick feeling in her stomach while thinking about water. Then she went outside to the swimming pool, looked at the water, and with delight she vigorously splashed some water on her face! Mary's fear of water remained permanently cured after only a few minutes of energy tapping.

CLINICAL RESEARCH

Although case studies are interesting and informative, they are not considered to be scientific proof for the effectiveness of a therapeutic approach. It is possible that the success with Mary and other cases treated with energy psychology was due to factors other than the tapping. For example, because reports of individual cases do not include information from a placebo control group, the placebo effect may be a possible explanation for the clinical success. The *placebo effect* implies that the reason patients get better in a controlled test is due to their belief that the treatment will help them. But, if that was the case here, why didn't Mary believe in the other approaches that were tried—to no avail? In Mary's case, and for many other clients treated by the authors, other techniques were unsuccessfully tried. Isn't it likely that the placebo effect would have occurred earlier? You would think so!

Another plausible explanation might be that the therapists' enthusiasm was the key factor in the client's recovery. And that enthusiasm might have been caused by the accumulative effect of all the different kinds of therapies done with this client. But why would therapists use methods they didn't feel positive about in the first place?

We find these and other explanations difficult to swallow. Instead, we firmly believe that the tapping and repeating self-loving affirmations while tuning in to the trauma or other psychological problem made it possible for these people to get better quickly.

Nevertheless, from the standpoint of the rules of science, more evidence is needed before any approach can be considered to be widely effective. Several studies have supported the effectiveness of EP for the treatment of phobias and anxiety disorders, including fear of heights (acrophobia), blood-injection-injury phobia, public-speaking anxiety, and post-traumatic stress disorder (PTSD), in addition to a variety of other psychological problems.

In 1987, an informal study showed significant decrease in the subjective units of discomfort (SUD) of call-in subjects treated with thought field therapy (TFT) on radio talk shows (Callahan 1987). This study was later replicated by Dr. Glen Leonoff, who obtained essentially equivalent results (Leonoff 1996). However, these were not rigorous scientific studies, since they could not include control groups, placebo treatments, follow-up evaluations, or any other quantitative measures that are typically included in scientific studies.

Although many researchers might dismiss these studies, since they showed only a decrease in SUD, the same criticism is not raised when a study shows that a tranquilizer relieves anxiety or an antidepressant relieves depression. Most follow-up studies would not support the effectiveness of the tranquilizer or antidepressant in relieving emotional distress after the medication is discontinued. Nevertheless, the ability of a treatment to give temporary relief is considered acceptable by the medical community and by the patient.

These studies by Callahan and Leonoff each had sixty-eight subjects with various phobias and anxiety problems. All told, 132 of the 136 subjects were successfully treated. This translates into a 97 percent success rate, which is really remarkable and unheard of in the area of psychological treatment. The average pre-treatment SUD rating (on a 10-point scale) was over 8; after treatment, the ratings ranged from 1.50 to 2.10. Furthermore, the treatment times ranged from four to six minutes, which is again exceptionally unusual with psychological treatment.

In 1995, researchers at Florida State University conducted a systematic clinical demonstration project that evaluated the effectiveness of an EP approach (TFT) and three other brief treatments for trauma and PTSD (Carbonell and Figley 1999). This was a more sophisticated and detailed research study that included evaluations of the subjects throughout the course of the study. Follow-up evaluations within four to six months showed that all of the approaches were effective in reducing SUD levels, although the EP treatment was the fastest and showed the greatest overall decrease in SUD.

Earlier experimental research looked at the TFT phobia treatment and its effects on self-concept (Wade 1990). Two self-concept questionnaires were used to evaluate subjects with various phobias. Sixteen of the subjects treated with TFT had a drop in SUD ratings of four or more points, while only four of the no-treatment controls showed a decrease in SUD ratings of two or more points. Two months after treatment, statistical tests revealed significant improvements in the TFT-treated subjects' self-acceptance and self-esteem. Results support the effectiveness of TFT for the treatment of phobias and for improving self-concept.

Another experiment evaluated the effectiveness of TFT in the treatment of height phobia, or acrophobia (Carbonell 1997). Forty-nine college students were initially screened from a total of 156 students with the use of an acrophobia questionnaire. All of the students completed a behavioral task, which involved approaching and possibly climbing a four-foot ladder. The four-foot path leading to the ladder was also calibrated in one-foot segments. As the students approached and climbed the ladder, SUD ratings were taken at each floor segment and rung of the ladder. The students were permitted to discontinue the task at any time if they became too fearful.

After these measures were obtained, each student met with an experimenter in a separate room and a SUD rating was taken while the student thought about the anxiety-provoking situation related to height. The students were then randomly assigned to one of two groups: TFT phobia treatment or placebo "treatment." All of the students were treated for psychological reversal (discussed earlier in this book), whether they had it or not. The placebo group tapped at body areas other than the meridian points used in TFT.

After the TFT treatment was done, SUD measures were taken again. If the student did not get a rating of zero, the procedure (treatment or placebo) was administered once again. Although both treatment and control groups showed improvement (maybe because of the treatment of reversal and because body stimulation itself has some therapeutic effects), the TFT students showed significantly greater improvement, especially when actually approaching and climbing the ladder.

Another phobia study involved TFT treatment of twenty students with blood-injection-injury phobia (Darby 2001). The measures included SUD ratings and a fear inventory. Treatment time was limited to one hour with the energy diagnostic approach used in TFT. Although this study contains many methodological flaws, one-month follow-up measures revealed statistically significant treatment effects. That is, the students showed significant reductions in phobic symptoms.

A trauma case study used the TFT diagnostic approach combined with a measure of brain waves, or electroencephalograph (EEG) to assess physiological changes after treatment (Diepold and Goldstein 2000). Statistically abnormal brain-wave patterns were recorded when the patient thought about a trauma compared to a neutral (baseline) event. Reassessment of the brain-wave patterns associated with the traumatic memory immediately after TFT revealed no statistical abnormalities. Eighteen months later, a reevaluation showed that the patient continued to be free of emotional upset regarding the treated trauma, and the patient's brain-wave pattern remained normal. This study strongly suggests that the EP treatment does not merely suppress traumatic stress, but actually eliminates its physiological traces.

During five separate two-week trips in the year 2000, therapists reported on treatment of trauma victims in Kosovo with TFT (Johnson et al. 2001). No control group was used. Treatments were given to 105 Albanian patients with 249 separate violent traumatic events in their past histories. The traumas included rape, torture, and witnessing the massacre of loved ones. Total relief from the traumas was reported by 103 of the patients, and for 247 of the 249 separate traumas treated. Follow-up data averaging five months revealed no relapses. Although this data is based on treatments administered without control groups, the absence of relapse garnered considerable attention, because a 98 percent spontaneous remission of PTSD had never happened previously.

To provide another measure of the scope of EP, another study demonstrated the clinical and statistical significance of the treatments that were used with 714 patients who suffered from a variety of psychological problems. The patients' conditions included anxiety, adjustment disorder with anxiety and depression, anxiety due to medical conditions, anger, acute stress, bereavement, chronic pain, cravings, panic, PTSD, trichotillomania (hair pulling), and more (Sakai et al. 2001).

Another study involved thirty-nine cases (without a control group), that were treated for a variety of clinical problems with EP, observing that in most cases improvement in SUD ratings coincided with improvement in heart rate variability (HRV). The HRV is a measure of the health of the heart. It is not easily affected by conscious choice and tends to be stable and free of placebo effect (that is, an improvement in health not attributable to an actual treatment) (Pignotti and Steinberg 2001).

Several EP approaches have been subjected to experimental tests. A recent trial compared diaphragmatic breathing with an EP approach, which involves tapping on several meridian acupoints, for the treatment of specific phobias of small animals (Wells et al. 2003). Subjects were randomly assigned and treated individually for thirty minutes with either EP (eighteen subjects) or diaphragmatic breathing (seventeen subjects). Statistical analysis revealed that both treatments produced significant improvement in phobic reactions, although tapping on meridian acupressure points produced significantly greater improvement behaviorally and on three self-report measures. The greater improvement for the EP was maintained at six to nine months follow-up on avoidance behavior.

These results were achieved in a single thirty-minute treatment without inducing the anxiety typical of traditional exposure therapies and with only imaginary exposure to the animals during the treatment phases.

Since similar levels of imaginary exposure, experimental demand, and cognitive processing were present in the two treatment conditions, this suggests that additional factors contributed to the results achieved by the EP treatment. The researchers suggested that intervening in the body's energy system through the meridian acupoints may have been the deciding factor. These results are certainly encouraging for the effectiveness of meridian-based therapies with specific phobias.

Another EP study focused on subjects who had been involved in motor vehicle accidents and who experienced post-traumatic stress associated with the accident (Swingle, Pulos, and Swingle 2005). All subjects received two treatment sessions and all reported improvement immediately following treatment. Brain-wave assessments before and after treatment indicated that subjects who maintained the benefit of the treatments demonstrated unique brain-wave patterns. This study also indicated that the treatment effects of EP involve positive neurological changes.

A rather perplexing study examined an EP approach that involves tapping on many meridian points for phobias and other fears with a sample of 119 nonclinical university students who were treated in group settings (Waite and Holder 2003). The four conditions that were treated included EP, placebo-control (tapping fake points on the arms), modeling (tapping the EP points on a doll), and a no-treatment control group.. A statistically significant decrease in SUD ratings occurred with all three treatment groups. Interestingly, tapping at locations other than the EP points as well as tapping at EP acupoints on the doll had the greatest improvement! Although this was not a patient population, the study suggests that some treatment effects can be achieved by simply stimulating your body and by vicariously observing tapping taking place on another body—even a doll body.

Yet another EP study involved 102 participants who were rated on a symptom checklist one month before and at the beginning of an educational workshop (Rowe 2005). The subjects were also treated at the conclusion of the workshop in addition to two follow-ups at one month and six months. There was a statistically significant decrease in all measures of psychological distress during all follow-up assessments.

A doctoral dissertation experimental study of the EP technique Be Set Free Fast (BSFF) that involves a four-point tapping routine combined with affirmations, suggests that this approach is effective in the treatment of insect phobia (Christoff 2003). This research involved four single case studies. Two of the subjects were phobic of crickets, one of ants, and one of caterpillars and worms.

For each subject, extensive pre- and post-testing was done during six twice-weekly sessions to establish baselines, followed by six treatment sessions and evaluation. Continued monitoring with psychological instruments was conducted at the six treatment sessions. Also SUD and heart-rate measures were obtained throughout the entire study. The major portion of phobic reduction occurred during the first treatment session, with some additional improvement in the next two sessions. All subjects experienced significant drops in their phobic symptoms and no longer had anxiety in the presence of the phobic object.

A pilot study examined the effect of EP on claustrophobia with four claustrophobic subjects and four normal subjects (Lambrou, Pratt, and Chevalier 2005). All subjects were evaluated with pencil-and-paper tests, biofeedback measures, SUD ratings, and behavioral measures before and after treatment and at an approximately two-week follow-up. A unique feature of this study was that the electrical properties in the acupuncture meridian system were measured. Statistical analysis revealed significant differences before and after treatment between the control group and the claustrophobic group. The researchers noted, too, that the measures of autonomic functions included in the study are less susceptible to placebo or positive expectancy effects.

The most extensive preliminary study on the effectiveness of EP was conducted in South America over fourteen years with 31,400 patients (Andrade and Feinstein 2004). A substudy of this group took place over five and a half years with 5,000 patients diagnosed with PTSD and a variety of other psychological conditions including phobias, addictive urges, panic disorder, generalized anxiety, depression, and so forth. Included in the substudy were only those conditions in which EP and a standard of care control group (cognitive behavioral therapy [CBT] plus medication when indicated) could be used.

At the end of treatment and at follow-up periods of one month, three months, six months, and twelve months the patients were interviewed by telephone by interviewers who had not been involved in the patients' treatment. These follow-up interviews revealed that with CBT plus medication, 63 percent of the patients reported some improvement and 51 percent had complete elimination of symptoms. However, with EP alone, 90 percent of the patients reported some improvement and 76 percent had a complete elimination of symptoms. These results are exceptionally significant, suggesting that EP was superior to CBT and medication for a wide range of psychological disorders. Furthermore, the average number of sessions in the CBT and medication group was fifteen, while the average number of sessions in the EP group was only three.

In a study sponsored by the National Institutes of Health, Elder et al. (2007) found that an EP approach—the Tapas Acupressure Technique—was significantly more effective at helping people maintain their weight loss after dieting compared with qi gong and a self-directed support group. The researchers concluded that EP offered an easy-to-use approach that was not time-consuming, while qi gong, another approach for balancing energy might have been more difficult to do and was more time-consuming. This is an important study, because there has been little research on EP in the United States sponsored at this level. In addition, a synopsis of patient interview data found that EP is a helpful tool for curbing food cravings and controlling overeating. It was also perceived to be a helpful stress-management technique.

There are a number of EP studies that were not completed or published at the time of this review. Within the next few years, many more studies will appear in journals and other publications. It is highly probable that an increasing number of studies will support the effectiveness of EP approaches and decipher the most essential elements in this new and exciting therapeutic approach.

References

American Medical Association (AMA). *Family Medical Guide* (4th ed.). 2004. New York: John Wiley and Son.

American Psychiatric Association (AMA). 1994. *Diagnostic and Statistical Manual of Mental Disorders* (4th ed.). Washington, DC: American Psychiatric Association.

Andrade, J., and D. Feinstein. 2004. Energy psychology: Theory, indications, evidence. In *Energy Psychology Interactive*. Edited by D. Feinstein. [CD]. Ashland, OR: Innersource.

Appelhans, B. M., and L. J. Leucken. 2006. Heart rate variability as an index of emotional responding. *Review of General Psychology* 10:229-240.

Azar, B. 2001. A new take on psychoneuroimmunology. *Monitor on Psychology* 32:11 (December).

Beaton, D. B. 2003. Effects of stress and psychological disorders on the immune system. www.personalityresearch.org/papers/beaton.html

Beck, A. T., and G. Emery. 1985. *Anxiety Disorders and Phobias*. New York: Basic Books.

Becker, R. O. 1990. *Cross Currents*. New York: G. Putnam and Sons.

Becker, R.O., and G. Selden. 1985. *The Body Electric*. New York: Morrow.

Bleil, M. E., J. M. McCaffery, M. F. Muldoon, K. Sutton-Tyrrell, and S. B. Manuck. 2004. Anger-related personality traits and carotid artery atherosclerosis in untreated hypertensive men. *Psychosomatic Medicine* 66: 633-639.

Bohm, D. 1980. *Wholeness and the Implicate Order*. Boston: Routledge and Kegan Paul.

Burr, H. S. 1972. *Blueprint for Immortality: The Electric Patterns of Life*. Essex, England: Saffron Walden.

Burton Goldberg Group. 1993. *Alternative Medicine: The Definitive Guide*. Puyallup, WA: Future Medicine Publishing.

Callahan, R. J. 1987. Successful psychotherapy by radio and telephone. *International College of Applied Kinesiology* (Winter).

Callahan, R. J., and J. Callahan. 1996. *Thought Field Therapy and Trauma: Treatment and Theory*. Indian Wells, CA: The Callahan Techniques.

Carbonell, J. L. 1999. Promising PTSD treatment approaches. *Traumatology* 5(1):32-48.

Carbonell, J. L., and C. R. Figley. 1999. A systematic clinical demonstration project of promising PTSD treatment approaches. *TRAUMATOLOGY* 5(1):article 4. Available from www.fsu.edu/trauma/promising.html

Carney, R. M., K. E. Freedland, G. E. Miller, and A. S. Jaffe. 2002. Depression as a risk factor for cardiac mortality and morbidity. A review of potential mechanisms. *Journal of Psychosomatic Research* 53:897-902.

Carney, R. M., K. E. Freedland, P. K. Stein, G. E. Miller, M. W. Rich, and S. P. Duntley. 2007. Heart rate variability and markers of inflammation and coagulation in depressed patients with coronary heart disease. *Journal of Psychosomatic Research* 62:463-467.

Chobanian, A. 2006. Prehypertension revisited. *Hypertension* 48(5):812-814 (November).

Chobanian, A., G. Bakris, H. R. Black, W. C. Cushman, A. L. Izzo, J. L. Jones, et al. 2003. The seventh report of the Joint National Committee on prevention, detection, evaluation, and treatment of high blood pressure. The JNC 7 Report. *Journal of the American Medical Association* 289(19):2560-2572.

Chopra, D. 1993. *Ageless Mind Timeless Body: The Quantum Alternative to Growing Old*. New York: Three Rivers Press.

Christoff, K. M. 2003. Treating specific phobias with BE SET FREE FAST. A meridian-based sensory intervention. Unpublished doctoral dissertation. Anaheim, CA: Trinity College of Graduate Studies.

Claude-Pierre, P. 1997. *The Secret Language of Eating Disorders*. NewYork: Vintage Books.

Craig, G., and A. Fowlie. 1995. *Emotional Freedom Techniques: The Manual*. The Sea Ranch, CA: Self-published.

Curtis B. M., and J. O'Keefe. 2002. Autonomic tone as a cardiovascular risk factor: the dangers of chronic fight or flight. *Mayo Clinical Proceedings* 77(1):45-54.

Danielson, C. K., and M. M. Holmes. 2004. Adolescent sexual assault: An update of the literature. *Current Opinion in Obstetric Gynecology* 16(5):383-388 (October).

Darby, D. 2001. The efficiency of thought field therapy as a treatment modality for individuals diagnosed with blood-injection-injury phobia. Unpublished doctoral dissertation. Minneapolis, MN: Walden University.

de Shazier, S. 1988. *Clues: Investigating Solutions in Brief Therapy.* New York: Norton & Co.

Diamond, J. 1985. *Life Energy.* New York: Dodd, Meade and Co.

Diepold, J. 1999. Touch and Breathe. Paper presented at the Energy Psychology Conference: Exploring the Creative Edge, 16 October, in Toronto, Canada.

Diepold, J. H., and D. Goldstein 2000. Thought field therapy and QEEG changes in the treatment of trauma: A case study. Moorestown, NJ: Energy Psychology.

Elder C., C. Rittenbaugh, S. Mist, M. Aickin, J. Schneider, H. Zwickey, et al. 2007. Randomized trial of two mind-body interventions for weight-loss maintenance. *Journal of Alternative and Complementary Medicine* 13:67-78.

Ellis, A. 1995. *Better, Deeper, and More Enduring Brief Therapy: The Rational Emotive Behavior Therapy Approach.* New York: Bruner/Mazel.

Emmons, R. A., and M. E. McCullough. 2004. *The Psychology of Gratitude.* New York: Columbia University Press.

———. 2003. Counting your blessings versus burdens: Experimental studies of gratitude and subjective well-being in daily life. *Journal of Personality and Social Psychology* 84:377-389.

Esler, M., and D. Kaye. 2000. Sympathetic nervous system activation in essential hypertension, cardiac failure and psychosomatic heart disease. *Journal of Cardiovascular Pharmacology* 35 (Supp 4) 7:S1-S7.

Fields L., L. Vicki, J. Burt; J. A. Cutler, J. Hughes, E. J. Roccella, et al. 2004. The burden of adult hypertension in the United States 1999 to 2000: A rising tide. *Hypertension* 44:398.

Figley, C. R., and J. Carbonell. 1995. The "Active Ingredient Project: The Systematic Clinical Demonstration of the Most Efficient Treatments of PTSD, a Research Plan." Tallahassee: Florida State University Psychosocial Stress Research and Clinical Laboratory.

Foodallergy.com http://www.aboutus.org/FoodAllergy.com. 2007.

Gallo, F. P. 2005. *Energy Psychology: Explorations at the Interface of Energy, Cognition, Behavior, and Health,* 2nd ed. Boca Raton, FL: CRC Press.

———. 1998. *Energy Psychology: Explorations at the Interface of Energy, Cognition, Behavior, and Health.* Boca Raton, FL: CRC Press.

Gallo, F. P., and H. Vincenzi. 2000. *Energy Tapping: How to Rapidly Eliminate Anxiety, Depression, Cravings, and More Using Energy Psychology.* Oakland, CA: New Harbinger Publications.

Gangwisch, J. E, S. B. Heymsfield, B. Boden-Albala, R. M. Buijs, F. Kreier, T. G. Pickering et al. 2006. Short sleep duration as a risk factor for hypertension: Analysis for the First National Health and Nutrition Examination Survey. *Hypertension* 47(5):833-839 (May).

Gerber, R. 1988. *Vibrational Medicine.* Santa Fe, NM: Bear and Company.

Gorman, J. M., and R. P. Sloan. 2000. Heart rate variability in depressive and anxiety disorders. *American Heart Journal* 140:S77-S83.

Gottman, J. 1995. *Why Marriages Succeed or Fail: And How You Can Make Yours Last.* Great Falls, MT: Fireside Books.

Graham, J. E., L. M. Christian, J. K. Kiecolt, and R. Glaser. 2006. Stress, age and immune function: Toward a lifespan approach. *Journal of Behavioral Medicine* 29(4) 389-400.

Gray, J. 1992. *Men Are from Mars, Women Are from Venus.* New York: HarperCollins.

Greene, B., and O. Winfrey. 1999. *Making the Connection: Ten Steps to a Better Body and a Better Life.* New York: Hyperion.

Hajjar I., and T. A. Kotchen. 2003. Trends in prevalence, awareness, treatment, and control of hypertension in the United States, 1988-2000. *Journal of the American Medical Association* 290(22):2940-2946.

Hall, L., and L. Cohn. 1999. *Bulimia: A Guide to Recovery,* 5th ed. Carlsbad, CA: Gurze Books.

Hassett, A. L., D. C. Radvanski, E. G. Vaschillo, B. Vaschillo, L. H. Sigal, M. K. Karavidas et al. 2007. A pilot study of the efficacy of heart rate variability (HRV) biofeedback in patients with fibromyalgia. *Applied Psychophysiological Biofeedback* 32(1):1-10 (March).

Hawkins, D. 1985. *Power versus Force: The Hidden Determinants.* Sedonia, AZ: Veritas Press.

Heffner, M., and G. H. Eifert. 2004. *The Anorexic Workbook: How to Accept Yourself, Heal Your Suffering and Reclaim Your Life.* Oakland, CA: New Harbinger Publications.

Hirschman, J. R., and C. H. Munter. 1998. *Overcoming Overeating.* NY: Ballantine Books.

Hsia J., K. Margolis, C. B. Eaton, N. K. Wenger, M. Allison, L. Wu et al. 2007. Prehypertension and cardiovascular disease risk in the Women's Health Initiative. *Circulation* 115(7):855-860.

Hudson, J. I., E. Hiripi, G. P. Harrison, and R. C. Kessler. 2007. The prevalence and correlates of eating disorders in the national comorbidity survey replication. *Biological Psychiatry* 348-358.

Hypertension Week. 2004. Pre-hypertension an accurate predictor of high blood pressure. vol. 4(5) (May). http://www.hypertensionweek.org

Inter-Asia. 2003. Cardiovascular risk factor levels in urban and rural Thailand. The International Collaborative Study of Cardiovascular Disease in Asia. *European Journal of Cardiovascular Disease Prevention and Rehabilitation* 10:249-257.

Jeffers, S. 1987. *Feel the Fear and Do It Anyway*. New York: Ballantine Books.

Jibrin, J. 1998. *The Unofficial Guide to Dieting Safely*. New York: Macmillan.

Johnson, C., M. Shala, X. Sejdijaj, R. Odell, and K. Dabshevei. 2001. Thought field therapy—soothing the bad moments of Kosovo. *Journal of Clinical Psychology* 57(10):1237-1240.

Johnson, E. H. 1990. *The Deadly Emotions: The Role of Anger, Hostility, and Aggression in Health and Emotional Well-Being*. New York: Praeger Publishers.

Kendler, K. S., E. E. Walters, K. R. Truitt, A. C. Heath, M. C. Neale, N. G. Martin et al. 1994. Sources of individual differences in depressive symptoms: Analysis of two samples of twins and their families. *American Journal of Psychiatry* 151:1605-1614.

Kiecolt, J. K., and R. Glaser. 2001. Stress and immunity: Age enhances the risks. *Psychological Science* 10:18-21.

Koestler, A. 1967. *The Ghost in the Machine*. London: Hutchinson & Company.

Kottke T. E., R. J. Strobel, and R. S. Hoffman. 2004. JNC-7. It's more than high blood pressure (editorial). *Journal of the American Medical Association* 289(19):2573-2574.

Lambrou, P., G. Pratt, and G. Chevalier. 2005. Physiological and psychological effects of a mind/body therapy on claustrophobia. *Journal of Subtle Energies and Energy Medicine* 14(3):239-251.

Langevin, H., M. Jason, and A. Yandow. 2002. Relationship of acupuncture points and meridians to connective tissue planes. *The Anatomical Record.* 269:257-265. http://www.med.uvm.edu/neurology/downloads/Relationshipofacupuncturepointsand meridianstoconnectivetissueplanes.pdf

Langman, L. 1972. The implications of the electrometric test in cancer of the female genital tract. In *Blueprint for Immortality: The Electric Patterns of Life*, edited by H. S. Burr. Essex, England: Saffron Walden: 137-154.

Leonoff, G. 1996. The successful treatment of phobias and anxiety by telephone and radio: A replication of Callahan's 1987 study. *TFT Newsletter* 1(2).

Linde, K., and G. Ramirez. 1996. St. John's Wort for depression—an overview and meta-analysis of randomized clinical trials. *British Medical Journal* 313:253-258.

Liu, A. 2007. *Gaining: The Truth About Life After Eating Disorders*. New York: Warner Books.

Lloyd-Jones, D. M., J. C. Evans, M. G. Larson, and D. Levy. 2002. Treatment and control of hypertension in the community: A prospective analysis. *Hypertension* 40: 640-646.

Lockie, A., and N. Geddes. 1995. *The Complete Guide to Homeopathy*. New York: Dorothy Kindersley.

Marano, H. E. 2004. The blues can break your heart. *Psychology Today Online* April. www.psychologytoday.com.

McDougall, W. 1938. Fourth report on a Lamarkian experiment. *British Journal of Psychology* 28:321-345.

Myss, C. 1997. *Why People Don't Heal and How They Can*. New York: Three Rivers Press.

National Eating Disorders Association. 2006. www.nationaleatingdisorders.org/p.asp

National Health and Nutrition Examination Survey (NHANES). 2005. Prevalence of Overweight and Obesity Among Adults: United States, 2003-2004. http://www.cdc. gov/nchs/products/pubs/pubd/hestats/overweight/overwght_adult_03.htm. Latest final mortality rates. 47:No. 19. Washington, D.C.: National Center for Health Statistics.

Ogden, C. L., M. D. Carroll, L. R. Curtin, M. A. McDowell, C. J. Tabak, and K. M. Flegal. 2006. Prevalence of overweight and obesity in the United States, 1999-2004. *Journal of the American Medical Association* 295:1549-1555.

Ogden, C. L., M. D. Carroll, M. A. McDowell, and K. M. Flegal. 2007. *Obesity Among Adults in the United States—No Change Since 2003-2004*. Division of Health and Nutrition Examination Surveys, NHCS Data Brief #1, Hyattsville, MD: National Center for Health Statistics. (November) www.cdc.gov

Olds, J., R. Schwartz, and H. Webster. 1996. *Overcoming Loneliness in Everyday Life*. Secaucus, NJ: Birch Lane Press.

Peale, N. V. 1996. (Reissued edition.) *The Power of Positive Thinking*. New York: Ballantine.

Pignotti, M., and M. Steinberg. 2001. Heart rate variability as an outcome measure for thought field therapy in clinical practice. *Journal of Clinical Psychology* 57 (10):1193-1206.

Pransky, G. S. 1992. *Divorce Is Not the Answer: A Change of Heart Will Save Your Marriage*. (Also published as *The Relationship Handbook*.) Blue Ridge Summit, PA: HIS and TAB Books.

Pulos. L. 1999. Personal communication.

Raison, C. L., L. Capuron, and A. H. Miller. 2006. Cytokines sing the blues: Inflammation and the pathogenesis of depression. *Trends in Immunology* 27:24-31.

Rakel, D. P., and N. Faass. 2005. *Complementary Medicine in Clinical Practice*. Boston: Jones Bartlett Publishing.

Rapp, D. 1991. *Is This Your Child? Discovering and Treating Unrecognized Allergies in Children and Adults*. New York: William Morrow.

Rein, G., M. Atkinson, and R. McCraty. 1995. The physiological and psychological effects of compassion and anger. *Journal of Advancement in Medicine* 8 (2):87-105.

Rowe, J. E. 2005. The effects of EFT on long-term psychological symptoms. *Counseling & Clinical Psychology Journal* 2(3):104-111.

Rozanski, A., J. A. Blumenthal, K. W. Davidson, P. G. Saab, and L. Kubzansky. 2005. The epidemiology, pathophysiology and management of psychosocial risk factors in cardiac practice: The emerging field of behavioral cardiology. *Journal of the American College of Cardiology* 45(5):637-650.

Rumsfield, J. S., and P. M. Ho. 2005. Depression and cardiovascular disease: A call for recognition (editorial). *Circulation* 111(3):250-253.

Sacker, I. M. 2007. *Regaining Your Self: Breaking Free From the Eating Disorder Identity*. New York: Hyperion.

Sakai, C., D. Paperny, M. Mathews, G. Tanida, G. Boyd, A. Simons et al. 2001. Thought field therapy clinical application: Utilization in an HMO in behavioral medicine and behavioral health services. *Journal of Clinical Psychology* 57:1215-1227.

Sarno, J. E. 2006. *The Divided Mind: The Epidemic of Mindbody Disorders*. New York: HarperCollins Publishers.

Sheldrake, R. 1988. *The Presence of the Past*. New York: Times Books.

Steward, H. B., S. Morrison, S. Andrews, and L. Balart. 2003. *The New Sugar Busters: Cut Sugar to Trim Fat*. New York: Ballantine Books.

Swingle, P. G., L. Pulos, and M. K. Swingle. 2005. Neurophysiological indicators of EFT treatment of posttraumatic stress. *Subtle Energies and Energy Medicine* 15(1):75-86.

Unestahl, L-E. 1988. Evolution of Psychology Conference. Ericksonian Approaches to Hypnosis and Psychotherapy Conference in 1986.

Wade, J. F. 1990. *The effects of the Callahan phobia treatment techniques on self-concept*. San Diego, CA: The Professional School of Psychological Studies.

Waite, W. L., and M. D. Holder. 2003. Assessment of the emotional freedom technique: An alternative treatment for fear. *The Scientific Review of Mental Health Practice* 2(1):20-26 Spring/Summer.

Wall Street Journal. 1999. Nearly half of all employees are a little angry at work. 7 September. Section C, p. 31.

WebMD.com 2007.

Weil, A. 1995. *Health and Healing.* Boston: Houghton-Mifflin.

Wells, S., K. Polglase, H. Andrews, P. Carrington, and A. H. Baker. 2003. Evaluation of a meridian-based intervention, emotional freedom techniques (EFT), for reducing specific phobias of small animals. *Journal of Clinical Psychology* 59(9): 934-966.

Wolpe, J. 1958. *Spontaneous Healing.* Boston: Houghton Mifflin.

Wright, C. E., P. C. Strike, L. Brydon, and A. Steptoe. 2005. Acute inflammation and negative mood: Meditation by cytokine activation. *Brain, Behavior and Immunity* 19(4):345-350.

Yang, H. Q., S. S. Xie, X. L. Xu, L. Chen, and H. Li. 2007. Appearance of human meridian-like structure and acupoints and its time correlation by infrared thermal imaging. *American Journal of Chinese Medicine* 35(2):231-240.

Fred P. Gallo, Ph.D., founded Gallo and Associates Psychological Services, a private clinical psychology practice that offers services tailored to the individual needs of clients in Hermitage, PA. He is a licensed psychologist, a nationally recognized leader in the field of energy psychology, and author of several books, including *Energy Tapping for Trauma* and the clinical book *Energy Psychology*. He is also a leading trainer for professionals in Advanced Energy Psychology™.

Harry Vincenzi, Ed.D., is a licensed psychologist who travels worldwide lecturing on energy psychology He conducts professional development seminars and individual coaching sessions and specializes in sports psychology. He is an expert in energy psychology and is author of *Changes*, a self-help book for adolescents. Further information on his work with energy tapping can be found at energytapping.org.